St. Louis Community College

Library

5801 Wilson Avenue
St. Louis, Missouri 63110

The Fiery Trail

ATLANTA !

OUR GALLANT ARMY have TAKEN POSSESSION OF THIS STRONGHOLD OF THE REBELLION !

All patriotic and Union-loving Citizens of CAMBRIDGE, are invited to meet at the

CITY HALL,

THIS EVENING,

to congratulate each other on this glorious event.

☞ Let the hearts of our brave soldiers be encouraged, that they may achieve still greater and more glorious victories !

"And the star-spangled banner in triumph shall wave
O'er the land of the free and the home of the brave."

CAMBRIDGE. SEPT. 3, 1864.

The Fiery Trail

A Union Officer's Account of Sherman's Last Campaigns

EDITED, WITH AN INTRODUCTION,
BY RICHARD HARWELL AND PHILIP N. RACINE,
AND WITH A FOREWORD
BY WILLIAM S. MCFEELY

THE UNIVERSITY OF TENNESSEE PRESS / KNOXVILLE

Endpapers: Sherman and His Generals at Savannah. Print. From the
original picture by Brt. Lt. Col. Otto Botticher. New York, published
by John C. Buttre, No. 48 Franklin Str. Special Collections Department, University of Georgia Libraries, Athens.

Frontispiece: Atlanta! Cambridge, Mass., Broadside, September 1864.
Collection of Richard Harwell.

The paper used in this book meets the minimum requirements of the
American National Standard for Permanence of Paper for Printed
Library Materials, Z39.48-1984. Binding materials have been chosen
for durability.

Library of Congress Cataloging in Publication Data

Osborn, Thomas Ward, 1896-1898.
   The fiery trail.

   Includes index.
   1. Sherman's March to the Sea—Personal narratives. 2. Sherman's
March through the Carolinas—Personal narratives. 3. Osborn, Thomas
Ward, 1836-1898—Diaries. 4. Osborn, Thomas Ward, 1836-1898—
Correspondence. 5. Soldiers—New York (State)—Correspondence.
6. Soldiers—New York (State)—Diaries. I. Harwell, Richard Barksdale.
II. Racine, Philip Noel. III. Title.
E476.69.083 1986   973.7'378   85-27620
ISBN 0-87049-500-3

*For Ali and Russell Racine
and for John Paul Rozier*

There is many a boy here to-day who looks on war as all glory, but, boys, it is all hell.

—Gen. William T. Sherman,
Ohio State Journal, Columbus, August 12, 1880.

Foreword

Thomas Osborn had a job to do—a nasty job. His assignment was to serve as an artillery officer with Gen. William T. Sherman in the conquest of Georgia and the Carolinas, in the demoralization of the Confederacy, and in the restoration of the Union. Osborn wrote when his work was nearly done:

> When, and even before, the war had fairly begun the South frankly said they would be independent or exterminated. The country took them at their word, and slowly and surely the work of extermination has been going on. . . . The people of the North can form no conception of the barrenness of the South in able bodied men; they have all been absorbed.

As he rode with his commanders, Gen. O. O. Howard and Sherman, at Atlanta, on the March to the Sea, and, then, in the triumphant trek north to Raleigh, Osborn, in letters to his brothers and in a journal, wrote one of the most clear-sighted descriptions of the Civil War that exists.

Osborn's account joins a famous subgenre of the literature of the Civil War that focused on Georgia in 1864. Sherman told of his relentless sweep across the state in his *Memoirs* in 1875; in our century, Margaret Mitchell, in the most famous novel about the war, *Gone With the Wind,* told of those who stood in Sherman's terrible path. Thomas Osborn's was a quieter, almost businesslike voice and a steady and sharply observant eye. His story enriches our knowledge of the greatest of Sherman's Civil War campaigns.

Osborn's chronicle is now presented to us in an edition prepared splendidly by two able scholars of the Civil War. And, if what is recounted so coolly by Osborn is a tale, finally, of great animosity, then its retelling in this volume is an act of friendship worthy of the wartime friendships that enriched the lives of men like Osborn, even as they were engaged in the business of killing.

Richard Harwell, distinguished both as a historian of the Confederacy and as a librarian, conducted an excellent seminar on the Civil War at Bowdoin College in the 1960s. He sent his students into that school's remarkable manuscript collections to meet civil warriors in their own letters and journals. Philip Racine was one of the students lucky enough to be sent on one of those quests.

One of the most valuable of those manuscripts was that of Thomas Osborn, which is here published for the first time—and not without some delay. Before the teacher and the student could get around to the editing of the soldier's work, Racine had fallen victim to the contagious attractions of the whole of American history, which he pursued in graduate work at Emory University and which he teaches presently at Wofford College. Their separate paths took them South—to the University of Georgia for Harwell—but now the two good friends have done the job they have long wanted to do, and done it well. With *The Fiery Trail,* they invite all of us to travel with Thomas Osborn until, finally, at Raleigh, he could write, "We are through with our work."

—William S. McFeely,
South Hadley, Massachusetts

Contents

Illustrations and Maps

ILLUSTRATIONS

MAPS

Introduction

Gen. William Tecumseh Sherman ceased his fruitless chase of Gen. John B. Hood through northern Georgia and Alabama in late October, 1864. The Confederate general headed north toward Tennessee and the wreck of his army in the battles of Franklin and Nashville. At Gaylesville, Ala. the Federal general rested his troops, did some hard thinking and important planning, and on October 29 turned his men back toward Georgia and new campaigns.

"One thing is certain," wrote Maj. J. A. Connolly, "there is no use of this Army of 70,000 'gallivanting' up and down through Georgia after Hood and his 40,000 any longer, for its like an elephant chasing a mouse; he won't let us catch him, and unless we can catch him so as to whip him soundly his 40,000 are worth more to the rebels than our 70,000 are to us, for it takes less to clothe, feed and pay them. So I believe we *are* going to do *something* but I hardly guess what, yet."[1]

This was a turning point in the course of the Civil War—no battle, no conference between opposing forces, but a momentarily quiet change of events. "It surely was a strange event," recorded Gen. Sherman, "—two hostile armies marching in opposite directions, each in the full belief that it was achieving a final and conclusive result in a great war; and I was strongly inspired with the feeling that the movement on our part was a direct attack upon the rebel army and the rebel capital at Richmond, though a full thousand miles of hostile country intervened, and that for better or worse, it would end the war."[2]

The Federal troops marched back to Atlanta as a gathering point for the March to the Sea. They moved through Rome and on to Kingston. At Cartersville the telegraph wires were cut and communications with the North ended with a message to Gen. George Thomas at Nashville November 12 saying "All is right."[3]

Maj. George Ward Nichols of Sherman's staff wrote the next day: "Behind us we leave a track of smoke and flame."[4] The fiery trail that eventually swept across Georgia and the Carolinas began November 13 at Acworth. "Our soldiers," declared Connolly, "burned the village of Acworth *without orders.*" He wrote his wife: "I tried to prevent the burning, but while I watched one house to keep it from being fired, another some where else would take fire; so I concluded to give it up. . . . It is evident that our soldiers are determined to burn, plunder and destroy everything in their way on this march."[5]

On November 15 the torch was applied to everything in Atlanta still of potential value to the Confederacy. "The heaven," says Nichols' *The Story of the Great March,* "is one expanse of lurid fire; the air is filled with flying, burning cinders; buildings covering two hundred acres are in ruins or in flames; every instant there is a sharp detonation or the smothered booming sound of exploding shells and powder concealed in the buildings, and then the sparks and flames shoot away up into the black and red roof, scattering cinders far and wide."[6]

Sherman remarked, according to Maj. Henry Hitchcock, one of his most trusted aids: "This city has done and contributed probably more to carry on and sustain the war than any other, save perhaps Richmond. We have been fighting *Atlanta* all the time, in the past; have been capturing guns, wagons, etc., etc., marked *'Atlanta'* and made here, all the time; and now since they have been doing so much to destroy us and our Government we have to destroy them, at least enough to prevent any more of that."[7]

Troops started marching out of Atlanta on November 15, and Sherman and his staff left early the next day. Riding ahead of Gen. Sherman with Gen. Oliver Otis Howard's staff was Maj. Thomas Osborn, chief of artillery of the department and Army of the Tennessee.

This is Tom Osborn's story.

Osborn wrote his own introduction to the story of his army career from August 1, 1864, to the end of May 1865 when he wrote a covering letter for the journal of the march through the Carolinas and sent it to his brother Abraham C. Osborn from Goldsboro, N.C., April 4, 1865:

> In writing this detailed account ordinary of the campaign from
> Savannah to Goldsboro, it has been my intention, so far as pos-

sible, to give you an idea of the campaign as it looked to me during the operations.

I made it a practice each evening before retiring, to minute down the incidents of the day, what information we had received, the substance of our speculations, the enemy's doings, and what his movements indicated. In fact I attempted to transfer the items of the head-quarters to paper, without at any time intimating what we intended to do in the future, for the notes might, by some mishap, fall into the enemy's hands. In transcribing them I have endeavored to adhere closely to the notes, and only when it was necessary to modify the phraseology, have I departed from them. There will be quite a number of miscalculations noticed, of the enemy's intentions and his whereabouts; yet I have transcribed them, that you may judge how accurately we calculated on all of Beauregard's and Johnston's movements.

As well as in this long document, Osborn's story is told in his letters to his brothers, A. C. and S. C., both preachers in St. Louis, including two other extended accounts—the first a record of the chase after Hood and the second a diary of the campaign from Atlanta to Savannah.

Osborn was born at Westfield, N. J., March 9, 1836, the ninth child of eleven children, born to his parents. In 1842 the family moved to Wilna, Jefferson County, N. Y. After a meager education in district schools he studied, beginning in the fall of 1854, for two years at the Wesleyan Seminary in St. Lawrence County. He next entered Madison (now Colgate) University at Hamilton and was graduated with, in his words, "a very moderate record in 1860." After graduation, he worked and studied in the law offices of Starbuck and Sawyer in Watertown until the news of the Federal defeat at the first battle of Bull Run determined him to go at once into the service. He enlisted August 10, 1861. In a brief sketch written for Charles Lanman on July 4, 1868 Osborn said:

I did all the labor of raising a company of Light Artillery and was mustered into the service on the 28th of August 1861 as Company D. of the 1st New York Light Artillery, Colonel Guilford Bailey com[man]ding the regiment. I was mustered in as first Lieutenant on the 3d of October. I returned to Syracuse New York, was examined and admitted to the bar as an attorney. The same month I was promoted to the captaincy of my company. After remaining in the Artillery school of instruction on East Capitol Hill till the first of March I joined General Hooker's command near Port Tobacco, Md. and with his command joined McClellan's Army on the peninsula.

The Battery took an active part in the battles of Williamsburg, Fair Oaks, was actually engaged six days during the seven days fighting at the retreat to Harrison's Landing. I was afterward in all the battles in which the 3d Corps was engaged. At Chancellorsville I was Chief of Artill[er]y of the 2nd, Berry's Division, of the 3d Corps and was in immediate command of most of the Artillery fighting with the 3d Corps in that battle.

On the 3d of June 1863 I was assigned as Chief of Artillery of the 11th Corp, having been promoted to the rank of Major. At Gettysburg I commanded all the Artillery on Cemetery Hill during the engagement. In September I went with Genl. Hooker's comd, i.e. the 11th and 12th Corps to Bridgeport Alabama & from that time was with the 11th Corps until the consolidation of the 11th & 12th when I was assigned to the command of the Artillery of the 4th Corps, where I remained until the 28th of July 1864, excepting a portion of the time when I was under the Surgeon's care having had an ankle crushed by a train of cars being thrown from the track. On the 28th of July I was assigned to duty as Chief of Artillery of the Army and Department of the Tennessee where I served until the final surrender, having served since June 3d, 1863 as Chief of Artillery t[o] Genl. Howard. During the entire war I was on duty in the field excepting about four months when I was injured [in] the R. R. accident at Stevenson, Ala. I was in all the battles that the Army I was with was engaged in. Was wounded three times in battle.

Osborn's letters and journal take his story from here to the Grand Review in Washington May 23 and 24, 1865. The sketch he wrote for Lanman is a modest account to have been written by a United States senator only thirty-two years old. Allan Nevins comments in a note for his editing of Colonel Charles S. Wainwright's *A Diary of Battle:* "Thomas W. Osborn, of the First New York Regiment of Light Artillery, soon rose to be a division artillery chief with the rank of major. He became in fact one of the most noteworthy artillery officers of the war, and particularly distinguished himself at Gettysburg as chief of artillery of the Eleventh Corps."[9] In the battle at Williamsburg, Col. Wainwright's regular army troops failed him. The colonel "then went back to Captain Osborn's four-gun battery, which had come up, and called for volunteers in manning these pieces. Every cannoneer at once sprang to the front, and headed by their officers, opened fire."[10] The battery performed well and Brg. Gen. S. P. Heintzelman remarked in his report: "Captain Osborn and his lieutenants in their first engagement gave promise of making brave and efficient officers."[11]

Osborn's first report of his own work was of the action at Savage Station, Va., June 29, 1862. Making a small success in a generally indecisive fray, one in which the Confederate attack was repelled as much by approaching darkness and a thunderstorm as by the Federal soldiers, Osborn wrote with a youngster's enthusiasm, and Gen. Joe Hooker called the attention of his superiors to the artilleryman's report. "Fifteen or twenty minutes before sunset," Osborn recorded, "the infantry of the two armies became engaged, and the roar of musketry was incessant and terrific till after dark, when the enemy was routed, and fled before our forces at least half a mile. Our infantry made charge after charge upon the enemy's front, and the determined shouts and huzzas rang distinctly above the roar of the musketry. I consider the whole affair a splended and magnificent one. The enemy's troops fought bravely, but our own surpassed them in every particular."[12]

Osborn was promoted to major in March 1863. With Hooker as its leader, new confidence permeated the beleaguered Army of the Potomac. In April the Union soldiers set off on another "On to Richmond" campaign. As they advanced toward Chancellorsville the Confederate forces seemed to be retreating, a reasonable move for an army in which 60,000 were opposing over 130,000. Gen. Robert E. Lee, however, split his forces and made a daring offensive move. As the Federals entrenched, Gen. Howard's right flank was left "in the air." Gen. T. J. ("Stonewall") Jackson led his men around it and attacked. When Howard's troops began to give way, Osborn was ordered to the front as part of a force of fifty guns under Gen. Dan Sickles. Osborn wrote of what he saw:

As we passed General Hooker's headquarters, a scene burst upon us which, God grant, may never again be seen in the Federal Army of the United States. The Eleventh Corps had been routed, and were fleeing to the river like scared sheep. The men and artillery filled the roads, its sides, and the skirts of the field and it appeared that no two of one company could be found together. Aghast and terror stricken, heads bare and panting for breath, they pleaded like infants at the mother's breast that we would let them pass to the rear unhindered. The troops in the old division, unwavering, and the artillery, reckless of life and limb, passed through this disorganized mass of men.[13]

The fifty guns brought up by Sickles stayed the Confederate advance, but far from a great victory on Hooker's part, Chancellors-

Sherman's army destroying the Macon railroad between Rough and Ready and Jonesboro. *Harper's Pictorial History of the Civil War,* vol. II (New York: 1868).

ville proved to be Lee's finest battle. But it was a Pyrrhic victory, for it was here that the Confederates lost Gen. Jackson and their aggregate losses, though less in total, comprised a larger percentage of their troops engaged than did Federal losses of their troops engaged.

Gettysburg was the sequel of Chancellorsville. Although it was only in a delayed reaction that the Federal and Confederate commanders realized the importance of the long battle at Gettysburg, it was there that the Confederates reached their high tide of war—and of courage—and the Federals showed their determination and stamina.

At Gettysburg, Osborn, chief of artillery of Howard's Eleventh Corps, stationed his guns on Cemetery Hill, overlooking a broad plain. On July 3, 1863, the third day of the battle, Gen. Lee determined to knock out the Union batteries with a heavy connonade and then to charge the lines on Cemetery Ridge. The artillery duel was fierce. The Union guns would not be silenced. Sensing Lee's desire to attack over a difficult field, the Federal officers were apprehensive that they might lose a potential advantage by discouraging the Confederates from launching their charge. Maj. Osborn suggested: "Why not let them out while we are in good condition? I would cease fire at once, and the enemy could reach but one conclusion, that of our being driven from the hill."[14]

The batteries quit their fire at staggered intervals, thus reinforcing the impression that they were being knocked out by Gen. Porter Alexander's Confederate artillery. The cessation of fire was followed by eerie silence, and then, as Osborn described it, came Pickett's Charge:

> A few moments later the infantry of the enemy broke over the crest from where their artillery had been playing, and made their grand charge across the plain ·upon our lines. The left of the charging column rested on a line perpendicular to our front, then stretching away to the right beyond our view, thus offering an excellent front for our artillery fire. We used, according to distance, all descriptions of projectiles. The whole force of our artillery was brought to bear upon this column, and the havoc produced among their ranks was truly surprising.
>
> The enemy's advance was most splendid, and for a considerable distance the only hinderance offered it was by the artillery, which broke their lines fearfully, as every moment showed that their advance under this concentrated fire was most difficult; and though

they made desperate efforts to advance in good order, were unable to do so, and I am convinced that the fire from the hill was one of the main auxiliaries in breaking the force of this grand charge. But while the enemy was advancing, and after having been repulsed I insisted that the artillery fire be turned intensely upon the infantry, and no notice whatever was to be taken of their artillery.[15]

Osborn's work at Gettysburg did much to help remove the stain that Howard's failure at Chancellorsville had left on the general's reputation. Of Osborn's performance at Cemetery Hill, Howard said: "No officer could work harder or do better than he did during the battle." The two officers served together throughout the rest of the war.

At the close of the Savannah campaign Howard wrote:

Major Osborn always ably assisted me in using the artillery on the field, and I always found him and his officers able and hearty cooperators, frequently giving me material aid not connected with that special department. Whenever an opportunity has afforded, our batteries have been located, intrenched, and handled in the most skillful manner. Quite brisk artillery duels transpired after our investmant of Savannah, where my attention was more particularly called to the artillery of the command, and when I have had occasion to admire the skill and bravery of its officers and men.[17]

William S. McFeely remarks in *Yankee Stepfather,* the finest and most recent book about Howard: "[His] relationships with his staff members were intimate. Men such as Thomas Osborn and Eliphalet Whittlesey were not merely trusted subordinates; they were close friends."[18] Of the journal Osborn kept during the march through the Carolinas, McFeely says: "His diary . . . reveals much about Howard's personality."[19]

It is an exceptional account of the campaigns in Georgia and the Carolinas from the time Osborn rejoined the army in late July 1864 to the end of the war. It is a much more reliable account than the books written by G. S. Bradley, S. H. M. Byers, David P. Conyngham, F. Y. Hedley, George Ward Nichols, George W. Pepper, and James Pike. It does not, of course, rival General Sherman's *Memoirs* as a source of history or as excellent writing. It was a primary source for Gen. Howard's *Autobiography.* It is not as intimately written as James A. Connolly's *Three Years in the Army of*

Atlanta in ruins. G. W. Nichols, *The Story of the Great March* (New York, 1865).

the Cumberland or as Henry Hitchcock's wonderful book, *Marching with Sherman,* but it ranks just below them and with, or above, Thaddeus C. S. Brown's *Behind the Guns,* John W. Rowell's *Yankee Artileryman,* and Theodore F. Upson's *With Sherman to the Sea.* It is particularly good in its descriptions of the march through the Carolinas and the last days of the war. Osborn wrote more freely as the campaigns progressed, as he became more practiced as a writer, and, especially, as the chances of capture of his letters or journal became less likely. His figures are sometimes exaggerated, but any soldier is entitled to a little exaggeration, and even a little boasting.

"I think," declared Osborn, on December 31, 1864, "this campaign just closed will be one of the really historical campaigns of the war, much more so than some where vastly more fighting was done. It was brilliant in conception and well executed." Just before the Federals left the coast for the interior of South Carolina he said: "This is a great game that is being played and great men are playing it."[20] And after Sherman's armies reached Goldsboro, N.C., he wrote on March 24: "I heard General Sherman remark today that the march of this Army from Savannah to this place, the consequent capture of Charleston, without going within a hundred miles of it, and the junction of this Army with a column moving from Kinston, and another from Wilmington, would be considered by able military men as one of the most perfect military movements in history."

The Fiery Trail is Osborn's story, but it is also Sherman's story. Sherman conducted a brilliant campaign in moving from Dalton to Atlanta, flanking Johnston's army, again and again, and attacking only when necessary. At the first of September he was able to cut the railroads southward from Atlanta. Early on September 3, 1864, he reported to Maj. Gen. H. W. Halleck in Washington: "Hood, at Atlanta, finding me on his road, the only one that could supply him, and between him and a considerable part of his army, blew up his magazines in Atlanta and left in the night-time, when the twentieth corps, General Slocum, took possession of the place. So Atlanta is ours, and fairly won."[21]

In a long, "private" letter to Halleck he wrote September 4: I hope. . .that you will keep up my army to its standard 100,000 men. . .and I pledge to you to take Macon and Savannah before spring, or leave my bones. My army is now in the very condition

to be supplied with recruits. We have good corporals and ser-
geants, and some good lieutenants and captains, and those are far
more important than good generals. They all seem to have implicit
confidence in me. They observe success at points remote, as in this
case of Atlanta, and they naturally say that the old man knows
what he is about. They think I know where every road and by-
path is in Georgia, and one soldier swore that I was born on Kenesaw Mountain.[22]

Sherman had seen much of the area over which the Atlanta campaign was fought in 1844. In the revised editions of his *Memoirs,*
he added a chapter concerning the years before the first edition
takes up his story. In it Sherman tells in some detail of his months
in Georgia. "We remained in Marietta about six weeks, during
which time I repeatedly rode to *Kenesaw Mountain,* and over the
very ground where afterward, in 1864, we had some hard battles."
He proceeded from Marietta to Bellefonte, Ala. On his way he observed the topography of Allatoona Pass, Rome, Raccoon Ridge,
among others. "Thus by a mere accident," he wrote, "I was en-
abled to traverse on horseback the very ground where in after-
years I had to conduct vast armies and fight great battles. That the
knowledge thus acquired was of infinite use to me, and consequently to the Government, I have always felt and stated."[23] Later
in the same year he began a stay of several months at the Augusta
Arsenal.

In that same letter to Halleck he made some judicious comments on his generals:

> George Thomas, you know, is slow, but as true as steel; Schofield
> is also slow and leaves too much to others; Howard is a Christian,
> elegant gentleman, and conscientious soldier. In him I made no
> mistake. Hooker [who resigned because Howard was appointed
> over him] was a fool. Had he staid a couple of weeks he could
> have marched into Atlanta and claimed all the honors. I therefore
> think I have an army on which you may safely build.

Then he added:

> Grant has the perseverance of a Scotch terrier. Let him alone, and
> he will overcome Lee by untiring and unceasing efforts. The Mo-
> bile column is the one that needs a head, and no time should be
> wasted on that city. The river, Montgomery, and Columbus, Ga.,
> are the strategic points . . . . It will not be safe to push this line far-

The "bummer." G. W. Nichols, *The Story of the Great March*.

ther until that [move toward Mobile] is done, but stores may be accumulated here, and the country behind the Chattahoochee purged a little more.[24]

～ At the end of September, Gen. Hood went scurrying off to the north. Sherman followed him, knowing Hood was attempting to draw him from his principal goal but using the march for further "purging" the country. He sent Thomas to Nashville and chased Hood as far as Gaylesville.

Before he left Atlanta, Gen. Sherman had noted in a dispatch to Halleck on September 15: "Governor Brown has disbanded his militia, to gather the corn and sorghum of the State. I have reason to believe that he and Stephens want to visit me, and I have sent them a hearty invitation."[25] No such invitation to the obstreporous governor of Georgia and the vice president of the Confederacy, who despised President Davis at least as much as he did the Yankees, appears in the *Official Records*. It was probably an oral message, relayed by mutual friends. Sherman believed that he had broken the back of Confederate opposition in the capture of Atlanta and wanted to make the most of it, not only in securing Lincoln's reelection but in the quick and forthright end of the war.

The answer to Sherman's message to Washington came not from Halleck but from President Lincoln himself: "I feel great interest in the subjects of your dispatch mentioning corn and sorghum and contemplated visit to you."[26] Lincoln's telegram was sent at 10:00 a.m. September 17 and later that day the general replied:

A. Lincoln, *PRESIDENT OF THE UNITED STATES:*
    I will keep the Department fully advised of all developments as connected with the subject in which you feel so interested. A Mr. Augustus R. Wright, former member of Congress, from Rome, Ga., and a Mr. Barrington King, of Marietta, are now going between Governor Brown and myself. I have said that some of the people of Georgia are now engaged in rebellion, begun in error and perpetuated in pride, but that Georgia can now save herself from the devastation of war preparing for her only by withdrawing her quota out of the Confederate army and aiding me to repel Hood from the borders of the State, in which event, instead of desolating the land as we progress, I will keep our men to the high roads and commons and pay for the corn and meat we need and take. I am fully conscious of the delicate nature of such assertions, but it would be a magnificent stroke of policy if I could, without surrendering a foot of ground or of principle, arouse the latent enmity to Jeff. Davis of Georgia. The people do not hesitate to say

that Mr. Stephens was, and is, a Union man at heart, and they feel that Jeff. Davis will not trust him, or let him have a share in his government.[27]

◄ The efforts toward negotiation failed. The nearest that Sherman came to meeting either Vice President Stephens or Georgia Governor Brown in 1864 was when he occupied the Governor's Mansion in Milledgeville the day after Brown fled from it. This failure had an effect on the vigor with which Sherman pursued his policy of living off the country. It had also a large effect on the situation evolving from his first efforts to make terms with Gen. Johnston in April 1865 by giving him a precedent in treating civil affairs.

◄ Sherman had Grant's approval of a plan for a great raid to the south. Grant, however, appeared to favor a move toward Mobile, while Sherman more and more felt that a march to the ocean to meet a Federal fleet somewhere between Brunswick, Ga., and Charleston was a more desirable move. Grant hastened Sherman's decision by sending Maj.-Gen. James H. Wilson to him at Gaylesville. Sherman knew his higher-ups were impatient—for a victory over Hood or a move to the coast. In Wilson they had sent him a man who might become a formidable rival, if the chance were offered him. With Grant's somewhat reluctant approval of Sherman's choice of direction, Sherman divided his cavalry and sent Wilson to raid through Alabama.

Nichols reconstructed the situation which might have happened, but probably never occurred exactly as he wrote it, in late October 1864:

> Let us for a moment look at General Sherman as he appeared at Gaylesville, seated upon a camp-stool in front of his tent, with a map of the United States spread upon his knees. General Easton and Colonel Beckwith, his chief quartermaster and commissary, are standing near. By his side are Generals Howard and Slocum, the future commanders of the right and left wings. General Sherman's finger runs swiftly down the map until it reaches Atlanta; then, with unerring accuracy, it follows the general direction to be taken by the right and left wings, until a halt is made at Milledgeville. "From here," the general says, "we have several alternatives; I am sure we can go to Savannah, or open communications with the sea somewhere in that direction." After studying the map a while, tracing upon the tangled maze of streams and towns a line from Savannah north and east, at Columbia, South Carolina, General Sherman looks up at General Howard with the

remark, "Howard, I believe we can go there without any serious difficulty. If we can cross the Salkahatchie, we can capture Columbia. From Columbia"—passing his finger quickly over rivers, swamps and cities to Goldsboro, North Carolina—"that point is a few days' march through a rich country. When we reach that important railroad junction—when I once plant this army at Goldsboro—Lee must leave Virginia, or he will be defeated beyond hope of recovery. We can make this march, for General Grant assured me that Lee can not get away from Richmond without his knowledge, nor without serious loss to his army."[28]

Nichols doubtless put these words into Sherman's mouth in retrospect, but they are basically true. Then on November 12 the last lines north were cut; the army was committed to a destination the soldiers knew not.

Sherman had that *sine qua non* of great generals, the ability to inspire for himself the complete confidence of his men. "They would follow him anywhere," said Osborn. Nichols wrote: "Sherman says 'Come,' and that is the entire vocabulary to them."[29] The general himself wrote his brother, Sen. John Sherman, from Savannah on December 31: "I hear the soldiers talk as I ride by, 'There goes the old man. All's right.' Not a waver, doubt, or hesitation when I order, and men march to certain death without a murmur if I call on them, because they know I value their lives as much as my own."[30]

Sherman had as great confidence in his men as they in him. He became the man that Southerners—particularly Georgians and South Carolinians—have for generations loved to hate, not so much for any defeats they suffered by his troops as for the destructiveness of his armies and the bitterness left behind him. A swath from forty to sixty miles wide was devastated across more than five hundred miles. "The State of South Carolina," said Osborn," . . . has been the greatest sufferer, and is ruined for a quarter of a century to come."[31]

Sherman's foragers—the "Bummers"—learned how to perfect this havoc in their operations in Georgia, and such officers as Hitchcock and Howard were appalled even then. The Bummers put what they had learned into full operation in South Carolina. Lloyd Lewis, Sherman's biographer, says:

> Sherman had become so attached to his men that he could not bear to punish them. Again and again he threatened to send the

Eighth Missouri to the rear only to see them behave so coura-
geously in battle that "I would have pardoned them for anything
short of treason." He finally rationalized it thus:

"Fighting is the least and easiest part of war, but no general ever
was or will be successful who quarrels with his men, who takes
the part of citizens against the petty irregularities or who pun-
ishes them unduly for gathering firewood, using wells and springs
of water, and even taking sheep, chickens and food when their
regular supplies are insufficient."

Furthermore, he believed that his hobo soldiers, ranging far
afield, saved the army much bloodshed; exploring sometimes
twenty miles in advance, they often menaced Southern intrenchments so confidently that defenders retired in the belief that Sherman's whole force was at hand.[32]

/The Bummers were definitely a powerful force. So was the im-
age of cruelty that Sherman projected among Southerners, an im-
age that he valued as a potent psychological weapon. Undeniably
the Bummers capitalized both on the fear of Sherman and on his
permissiveness. Gen. Howard on February 20, 1865, wrote separately the same letter to Gens. Frank P. Blair, Jr. and John A. Logan,
commanders of the Seventeenth and Fifteenth Army Corps:

> *GENERAL:* I desire to call your attention to the fact that some of
> our soldiers have been committing the most outrageous robberies
> of watches, jewelry, &c. A case has come to my notice where a
> watch and several articles of jewelry were stolen by a foraging
> party under the eye of the commissioned officer in charge. An-
> other, where a brute had violently assaulted a lady by striking her,
> and had then robbed her of a valuable gold watch. In one instance
> money was stolen to the amount of $150, and another, where an
> officer with a foraging party had allowed his men to take rings off
> the fingers of ladies in his presence. To–day a soldier was found
> plundering, arrested, placed under the guard of one of General
> Corse's orderlies, and was liberated by some of his comrades who
> had arms in their hands, and who threatened the life of the guard.
> These outrages must be stopped at all hazards, and the thieves and
> robbers who commit them be dealt with severely and summarily
> . . . . I call upon you and upon all the officers and soldiers under
> you, who have one spark of honor or respect for the profession
> which they follow, to help me put down these infamous proceed-
> ings and to arrest the perpetrators.[33]

This is the flaw in Sherman's greatness as a general. When Confederate Gen. Richard Taylor wrote of Sherman's sending civilians
out of Atlanta, he quoted Sherman's letter to Halleck of September

Soldiers voting for Lincoln. *Harper's Pictorial History of the Civil War,* II.

4 that ends with the words, "If the people raise a howl against my barbarity and cruelty, I will answer that war is war, and not popularity-seeking. If they want peace, they and their relations must stop the war." Taylor reviewed the request of Atlanta's mayor and councilmen to revoke the order, at least in regard to women and children in poverty and distress, and noted Sherman's reply: "I have read [your petition] carefully, and give full credit to your statements of the distress that will be occasioned, and yet shall not revoke my orders, because *they were not intended to meet the humanities of the case.*" Taylor quoted a telegram from Sherman to Grant (October 9, 1864) saying: "Until we can repopulate Georgia, it is useless to occupy it; but the utter destruction of its roads, houses, and people will cripple their military resources. I can make this march, and make Georgia howl." Taylor put the word to it in concluding: "It could hardly be expected that troops trained by this commander would respect *the humanities.*"[34]

Sherman's fame may be flawed. Nevertheless, Basil Henry Liddell Hart, the greatest of British military historians of this century, save Churchill, took a view different from Taylor's. When he wrote of him in the late 1920s, Liddell Hart considered Sherman "the genius of the Civil War." More than thirty years later he reiterated in an introduction to the Folio Society's edition of Sherman's own account (edited as *From Atlanta to the Sea*): "William Tecumseh Sherman was the most original and versatile of the many remarkable commanders produced by the American Civil War. Besides the great part he played in the decisive stages of that war, his concepts, and later ones developed from study of his operations, had a far-reaching influence on the future course of warfare."[36] Liddell Hart examined the effects of Sherman's strategy and tactics through campaigns as late as those of World War II.

He summarized:

Sherman was outstanding as a commander, as an innovator, and in personality. He showed both the qualities and characteristics of genius. While frequently described as "extraordinary," he was no less frequently called a "typical" American. He was tall, lean, angular, and loose-jointed. Often careless and unkempt in dress, he had a restlessness of manner that was emphasized by his endless chain-smoking of "segars" and the way he scattered the ash. He had an insatiable curiosity of mind, and instinctive rebelliousness against custom and authority, a raciness of language, and a fondness for picturesque phrases. Such features made him seem typical. But there were other features that made him extraordinary, especially in the way he blended contrasting qualities. His quickness of mind was combined with minute exactness of observation. His dynamic energy went along with philosophical reflectiveness. He had faith in his own vision but a doubt of his own abilities that could only be dispelled gradually by the facts of actual achievement. He combined democratic tastes and manners with a deep and sardonic distrust of democracy. His rebelliousness was accompanied by a profound respect for law and order. His logical ruthlessness was coupled with compassionateness.

In generalship, he was brilliant both as a tactician and strategist. But what made him outstanding was the way he came to perceive and exploit the changing conditions of warfare produced by mechanical and scientific developments....

The havoc that his march produced in the opponent's back areas left a legacy of bitterness in later years—more than in immediate postwar years. That has recoiled on Sherman's historical reputation. But it is questionable whether that bitterness or the impoverishment of the South would have been as prolonged, or grave, if the peace settlement had not been dominated by the vindictiveness of the Northern extremists who gained the upper hand after Lincoln's assassination. For Sherman himself bore in mind the need of moderation in making peace. That was shown in the generous terms of the agreement he drafted for the surrender of Johnston's army—an offer for which he was violently denounced by the Government in Washington. Moreover he persistently pressed the importance, for the future of the forcibly reunited nation, of reconciling the conquered section by good treatment and helping its recovery. His vision extended beyond the horizon of war to the peace that would follow.[37]

Sherman marched to fame and infamy through Georgia and the Carolinas. It was indeed a fiery trail: Acworth, Marietta, Atlanta, Planters' Factory, Millen, McBride's Plantation, Orangeburg, the pitch forests, Columbia, Winnsboro, Cheraw—all burned; fortifications destroyed along the way; the arsenal at Fayetteville broken to bits. Columbia was the worst. There both men and wind got out of control. It is difficult for a sane man to believe that Sherman ordered the burning of Columbia. It is almost as difficult to believe, with the near perfect discipline of his soldiers, that he could not have prevented its rapid spread. He had threatened to turn his men loose on Savannah; they turned themselves loose on Columbia.

The Charleston railroad depot was fired by the Confederates the day before Federal troops entered Columbia. There is an abundance of contradictory testimony as to how the cotton in the city's

main street caught fire. Having once caught, a fire in cotton can be
thought out but smolder for a long time. In 1873 Gen. Howard's
deposition before "The Mixed Commission on British and American Claims," growing out of damages during the war, was published. His testimony is certainly as good as any and better than
most. Under oath he told how he had entered the city in company
with Sherman, "riding side by side, before any other troops from
this leading brigade had passed" Howard continued:

> As my troops alone were to have charge of the city, I observed
> very carefully the disposition of the guards of the leading brigade,
> Colonel Stone's; sentinels were located in front of buildings of any
> considerable importance, and on the main street the principal
> portion of the brigade was in rest, waiting for orders; there was
> only that one brigade; we were ahead of all the rest; near the bri-
> gade was an immense pile of cotton; bales were broken open in
> the middle of the streets, and were on fire; an engine was playing
> upon the fire, and soldiers and citizens were engaged apparently
> in extinguishing it; General Sherman was met with much enthusi-
> asm by a company of soldiers; observing them closely I saw that
> some of them were under the influence of drink. . . . I ordered
> those that were drunk under guard immediately, and made every
> disposition necessary for the protection of property; we rode to-
> gether past the market down to the railroad depot, called the
> Charleston depot, I think, on the road going from Charleston to
> Columbia; that depot was smouldering, having been burned by
> the rebel troops on evacuating Columbia. . . .
> We rode to a foundry where guns had been cast, and observed
> that, and went afterwards through several streets together, when I
> separated from General Sherman, selected my headquarters, and
> gave the necessary orders for the thorough care of the troops and
> of the city for the night. After this disposition I lay down to take a
> little rest, and was awaked first about dark by one of my aids, who
> said the city was on fire; I sent the aid, Captain Gilbreth, immedi-
> ately to ascertain where the fire was and to call upon General Cha-
> rles R. Woods, the division commander, who had the immediate
> command of the city, to prevent the extension of the fire; I then at
> once dressed myself and went to the scene; there I met General
> John A. Logan, who was my next in rank and who commanded
> the corps; we consulted together, and took every precautionary
> measure we could think of to prevent the extension of the flames,
> sometimes ordering the tearing down of sheds and small build-
> ings, protecting the citizens, assisting them in the care of their
> property, and guarding it; much of the property was thrown into
> the streets; personally I set a great many soldiers during the night
> to extinguishing the flames from the houses, and they went to the

Sherman's army entering Columbia, South Carolina. *Harper's Pictorial History of the Civil War,* II.

top of the houses where water was passed up to them; nearly everything in my immediate vicinity was saved; a perfect gale from
the northwest had commenced about the time we crossed the
bridge, or before that, and continued all night, or until, I should
say, between two and three o'clock in the morning; it seemed at
first utterly useless to attempt to stop the flames; they were so hot
that many of our own soldiers were burnt up that night; when the
wind changed, however, it was easy to prevent any further exten-
sion of the fire; it was done; some of our men behaved badly on
account of being under the influence of drink, but they were replaced by fresh men as soon as their conduct came to the knowledge of the officer in charge; the first brigade—Stone's—was
relieved by another brigade of General Woods' division, and finally the entire division of General Hazen was brought into the
city to assist; all the men who misbehaved that we could seize
upon were kept under guard until the next day and punished;
there were quite a number of our men who had been taken prisoners and were held by the Confederates; they appeared in the
streets of Columbia soon after our arrival; I do not know myself
where they were confined; the penitentiary was also opened and
all its prisoners loosed; I found during the night a reckless mob
very often, sometimes insulting ladies, and sometimes rushing
into houses and pillaging; I did not see anybody setting fires; General Sherman himself stayed up with us for most of the night;
General Logan and General Woods were on the ground all the
time until the fire abated, and I believe did everything they could
to prevent it.[38]

Sherman wrote Halleck from Savannah on January 12: "I deeply
regret that I am threatened with that curse to all peace and
comfort—popularity; but I trust to bad luck enough in the future
to cure that, for I know enough of 'the people' to feel that a single
mistake by some of my subordinates will tumble down my fame
into infamy."[39] Less than three months later he reviewed his
troops—in triumph and tattered uniforms—in Goldsboro, N. C.
The general arrived in Goldsboro on March 24. On March 27 and
28 he had long talks with President Lincoln aboard the *River
Queen* lying off City Point, Va. Four weeks later Lincoln was dead,
and Sherman, not by acts of his subordinates but by acts of friends
in high places, had most truly been tumbled from fame into infamy.

Sherman tried in the surrender terms he allowed Gen. Johnston
on April 18 to reflect what the President had told him on the *River
Queen.* The terms were generous. They would accomplish the

purposes Lincoln had proclaimed and Sherman had fought for. They would end the war and make it possible for the seceded states to rejoin the Union.

To the victorious North they seemed far too generous. The terms left civil power in the hands of officials of the Southern states during the Confederate years and tacitly accepted the end of slavery but did not affirm emancipation. To extremists they seemed to offer a legal loophole that would require the Union to assume the debts of the seceded states. Even such stalwart supporters of Sherman as his brother the senator and Maj. Hitchcock thought they were too generous. The coalition of Stanton, Halleck, and Grant put down Sherman, and President Andrew Johnson turned down the terms Sherman had arranged.

The events from Lincoln's assassination through April 26, the day on which Gen. Johnston accepted new surrender terms, the same as those for Lee at Appomattox, constitute a very complex story. Sherman's fame was about to overtake Grant's. Halleck left his desk in Washington to try—without success—to establish a reputation as a field commander. Stanton, immediately more than Andrew Johnson, succeeded to Lincoln's power. He had at best been an arm's-length friend of Sherman and now, according to McFeely, it seemed that "an ambitious and dangerous secretary of war . . . tried to take advantage of the emergency to exercise martial authority over the nation."[40]

Sherman and Johnston in the terms they set forth on April 18 were, so McFeely says, "hurrying history." He continues:

> The kind of arrangement the two men envisioned in their surrender agreement came about when other men compromised in 1877. . . . All that Johnston had conceded to Sherman in the surrender agreement was that his Confederate soldiers would fight no more. The civilian governments of the states that had sent these men off to fight the Union were not required to lay down their arms. Instead, they were charged with the responsibility of continuing to govern—of maintaining order—and the guns of Johnston's soldiers were to go back into the state arsenals, ready for use by state officials to repress any kind of uprising. Sherman could never understand why he was criticized for agreeing to these terms."[41]

He was fully ready for the war to end and concerned most about restoring peace. He wrote in a long letter to James E. Yeatman of the United States Sanitary Commission on May 21:

You will have observed how fiercely I have been assailed for simply offering to the President "terms" for his approval or disapproval, according to his best judgment—terms which, if fairly interpreted, mean, and only mean, an actual submission by the rebel armies to the civil authority of the United States. No one can deny I have done the State some service in the field, but I have always desired that strife should cease at the earliest possible moment. I confess, without shame, I am sick and tired of fighting—its glory is all moonshine; even success the most brilliant is over dead and mangled bodies, with the anguish and lamentations of distant families, appealing to me for sons, husbands, and fathers. You, too, have seen these things, and I know you are also tired of the war, and are willing to let the civil tribunals resume their place. And, so far as I know, all the fighting men of our army want peace; and it is only those who have never heard a shot, never heard the shrieks and groans of the wounded and lacerated (friend or foe), that cry aloud for more blood, more vengeance, more desolation.[42]

And in a letter he sent about the same time to Chief Justice Salmon P. Chase he commented: "I have had abundant opportunities of knowing these people [the Southerners]. . .and believe that by one stroke of the pen, nine-tenths of them can be restored to full relations with our Government. . .I would not hesitate to mingle with them and lead them to battle against our national foes. But we must deal with them with frankness and candor, and not with doubt, hesitancy, and prevarication."[43]

After Johnston's surrender the Confederate collapse was full and complete, though isolated fighting continued in the Trans-Mississippi South until the first week of June. Jefferson Davis was captured in southern Georgia on May 10. The fall of the Confederacy had been inevitable since the capture of Atlanta. The Confederate generals knew it before the soldiers; the soldiers knew it before the civilians; the women, the little boys, and the old men were the last to know.

And so, as they had ridden together into Columbia, Gens. Howard and Sherman rode together down Washington's Pennsylvania Avenue in the Grand Review on May 24. For each man it was a bittersweet display. Howard would have preferred to be leading his soldiers, now under the command of Gen. Logan. Sherman was still smarting from his treatment at the hands of Halleck, Grant, and Stanton. Sherman seemed not to realize that Grant had participated in putting him down. He advanced to the reviewing

Grand Review at Washington—Sherman's veterans marching through Pennsylvania Avenue. *Harper's Pictorial History of the Civil War,* II.

stand amid the cheers of the crowds, shook hands with the President, pointedly declined to shake the hand of Secretary Stanton, and greeted Grant with, apparently, the same feeling he had expressed in a letter of December 31, 1864, from Savannah: "I am fully aware of your friendly feeling toward me, and you may always depend on me as your steadfast supporter. Your wish is law and gospel to me."[44]

What happened after the war to Howard and to Sherman is well known. Tom Osborn received long delayed promotions to lieutenant colonel and colonel. He was appointed by Howard as assistant commissioner of the Freedmen's Bureau for Alabama. Before proceeding south, Osborn visited his family in upstate New York and was injured in a railroad wreck. On his recovery from this accident he was reassigned to Florida where he served as assistant commissioner until August 1866. Osborn then entered the practice of law in Tallahassee and was soon made register in bankruptcy for the Northern District of Florida. "Immediately after the passage of the Military bill," he wrote in a sketch for Charles Lanman, "I moved in the matter of organizing a party in the State to carry out the principles and terms of reconstruction under the provision of the Bill. Dividing my time between my profession & politics and I am sorry to say the latter received the most of my attention."[45] His politics were of the partisan carpetbag variety and, according to his contemporary, John Wallace, the black politician and historian of that era, were more of a self-serving sort than of benefit to the freedmen.[46]

A generation later the professional historian William Watson Davis in his *The Civil War and Reconstruction in Florida* described Osborn as "a man of considerable energy and of executive ability far above average."[47] Davis wrote:

> In October [1865] soon after the arrival of T. W. Osborn in Florida another secret and benevolent society for blacks was launched—the "Lincoln Brotherhood." Osborn was probably founder and head of the organization. It spread rapidly throughout the northern portion of the state. The parent group was in Tallahassee. Initiation into these secret societies was made sufficiently mysterious to favorably impress the black with their importance and satisfy his longing for some sort of hoodooism. Amid the rattle of gun-locks, the giving of solemn oaths, and a sufficiency of mumble jumble, the candidate stood in a dim light

and swore fealty to the Union Republican party and the United States constitution.

The native whites looked askance upon these societies. They were primarily political organizations. Their projectors, white men from abroad, deliberately aimed at the political control of the state by means of the negro vote. . . . In arraying race against race, the record of the Lincoln Brotherhood and Union League was damnable and generally at wide variance with the advice of the higher federal officials, Governor Marvin, and even General Howard of the Freedmen's Bureau.[48]

Osborn was a member of Florida's reconstruction Constitutional Convention and the principal author of the constitution it adopted. He was elected a member of the Florida Senate and by that body to the United States Senate. He was sworn in as a senator on June 3, 1868—less than three months after his thirty-second birthday. He served in the Senate until March 4, 1873, but did not succeed in his efforts to be re-elected. After his term in Washington he practiced law in New York City. His only further public service was as United States commissioner for the Centennial Exposition in Philadelphia in 1876, a post to which he was appointed by President Grant.

The editors of the present volume became acquainted with Tom Osborn through the copy of his journal of Sherman's campaign in the Carolinas that is among the papers of Gen. O. O. Howard in the Bowdoin College Library. Intrigued by that document, the editors investigated further the work of the young artillerist. That investigation soon led them to Osborn's own records in the Colgate University Library. Not only, they realized, is the document at Bowdoin a copy made for the use of Gen. Howard (probably during Osborn's term as a United States senator), but there are additional papers at Colgate that round out Osborn's story from his service in the battle of Atlanta till the end of the war.

Osborn's letters written from the field in the papers housed at Colgate proved especially helpful. These letters add information not in the long journal and also provide a change of pace to a style of writing that is more informational than scintillating. The journal however, occasionally repeats information in the field letters. In this book, some repetition has been deleted and is so noted by ellipsis marks. To edit out all of these brief repetitions would mar the text more than improve it. As far as the editors have been able to determine, the originals of Maj. Osborn's letters no longer exist. This edition of Osborn's story is derived from the copy at Colgate, but differences between the Bowdoin and Colgate copies are merely copying mistakes by his amanuenses. The Major's text has been tampered with as little as feasible. Occasional quirks in punctuation have been normalized, and the use of "[sic]" has been avoided as much as possible. Misspelled proper names are shown as Osborn spelled them on their first occurrence with the correct spelling following within brackets, silently corrected thereafter.

A list of References cited is provided; for a comprehensive bibliography on Sherman's campaigns in Georgia and the Carolinas see Joseph T. Glatthaar, *March to the Sea & Beyond: Sherman's Troops in the Savannah & Carolina Campaigns* (New York: New York Univ. Press, 1985).

As with any book involving historical research the editors have been helped in many ways and by many people. Our special thanks are due Arthur Monke, Dianne Gutscher, and Susan Ravdin of the Bowdoin College Library; Bruce Brown and Peter Haskell of the Colgate University Library; Frank Anderson, Lewis Jones, and Larry McGehee of Wofford College; Mary Ellen Brooks, Nelson Morgan, Dorothy Shackelford, and Robert M. Willingham Jr. of the University of Georgia Libraries; Miles Blackwell of Oxford, England; Thomas Winston Broadfoot of Wilmington, N. C.; Thomas W. Connelly of Columbia; Stacy Day of Spartanburg; Charles East of Baton Rouge; Shirley Jane Fogle of the Florida State University Library; Marion B. Harwell of Covington, Ga.; Cynthia Maude-Gembler and Katherine Holloway of the University of Tennessee Press; Winston Lane and Nancy Barr of Atlanta; Anthony Price of Horton-cum-Studley, Oxfordshire; Frances Melton Racine of Spartanburg; Stephen M. Rowe of Raleigh; Allan Stokes of Columbia; Robert Summer of Macon; and Dan Weinberg of Chicago.

Support for time for a portion of editor Racine's research was made possible by a sabbatical leave from his teaching duties at Wofford College, using funds provided by the Andrew W. Mellon Foundation.

NOTES

1. James A. Connolly, *Three Years in the Army of the Cumberland*...ed. by Paul M. Angle (Bloomington, 1959), 286.

2. William Tecumseh Sherman, *Memoirs* (New York, 1875), II, 170.

3. Sherman, "Report of Major General William T. Sherman to the Hon. Committee on the Conduct of the War," in U.S. 38th Congress, 2d Session. Joint Committee on the Conduct of the War, *Supplemental Report*... (2 vols. Washington, D.C., 1866), 268. George Ward Nichols, in his *The Story of the Great March*... (New York, 1865), 36, gave this message as "All is well," which was its intent, but the official wire to Thomas said "Despatch received. All right."

4. Nichols, 37.

5. Connolly, 298.

6. Nichols, 38.

7. Henry Hitchcock, *Marching with Sherman*...ed., with an introduction, M. A. DeWolfe Howe (New Haven, 1927), 58.

8. The holograph copy of this "Autobiographical Sketch" of Thomas W. Osborn is in the Library of Florida State University, Talahassee. Other biographical information about Osborn has been drawn from the records of the Bureau of Pensions of the Department of the Interior, certificate no. 143019 of October 21, 1898; from the sketch of him in *The National Cyclopaedia of American Biography*... (New York, 1904), XII, 394; from a typed note describing and accompanying his "Autobiographical Sketch"; and from other references as cited in additional notes.

9. Charles S. Wainwright, *A Diary of Battle: The Personal Journals of Colonel Charles S. Wainwright, 1861–1865,* ed. Allan Nevins (New York, 1962), 26. A marker on the battlefield at Gettysburg noting where Gen. John F. Reynolds fell on the second day of the battle credits Reynolds and Osborn with the silencing of the Confederate guns on that day. *Ibid.,* 262.

10. U.S. War Department, *The War of the Rebellion: A Compilation of the Union and Confederate Armies*... (128 vols. Washington, D.C., 1880-1900), Ser. I, vol. 11, pt. 1, p. 470. Further citations to the *Official Records* are abbreviated to *OR.*

11. *OR,* 472.

12. *OR,* Ser. I, vol. 11, pt. 2, p. 110.

13. *OR,* Ser, I, vol. 25, pt. 1, p. 483

14. Shelby Foote, *The Civil War: A Narrative from Fredericksburg to Meridian* (New York, 1963), 547.

15. *OR,* Ser. I, vol. 27, pt. 1, p. 750. In addition to this official report, Osborn wrote "The Artillery at Gettysburg," *Philadelphia Weekly Times,* May 31, 1879.

16. *OR,* Ser. I, vol. 27, pt. 1, p. 757.

17. *OR,* Ser. I, vol. 44, p. 74.

18. William S. McFeely, *Yankee Stepfather* (New Haven, 1968), 15.

19. *Ibid.,* 66.

20. Osborn's letter of January 29, 1865, to S. C. Osborn.

21. *OR,* Ser. I, vol. 38, pt. 5, p. 777.

22. *OR,* 793.

23. Sherman, *Memoirs* (New York, 1875; rpt. (4th ed.) New York, 1892), I, 31-32.

24. *OR,* Ser. I, vol. 38, pt. 5, p. 793.

25. *OR,* Ser. I, vol. 39, pt. 2, p. 381.

26. *OR,* 395.

27. *OR,* 395-96. The Georgians referred to were Augustus R. Wright and Barrington King. Wright was a former member of Congress. On October 24 Sherman sent President Lincoln a letter from Gaylesville introducing Mr. Wright as "a man of high character and true faith in the future." *OR,* Ser. I, vol. 39, pt. 3, p. 412.

28. Nichols, 34-35.

29. *Ibid.* 37.

30. *The Sherman Letters, Correspondence Between General and Senator Sherman from 1837 to 1891,* ed. Rachel Sherman Thorndike (New York, 1894), 241-42.

31. March 24, 1865.

32. Lloyd Lewis, *Sherman, Fighting Prophet* (New York, 1932), 495.

33. *OR,* Ser. I, vol. 47, pt. 2, pp. 505-506.

34. Richard Taylor, *Destruction and Reconstruction.* . . , ed. Richard Harwell (New York, 1955), 236-37. The emphasis is Taylor's.

35. The title of the British edition, 1930, of Liddell Hart's biography of the general, is *Sherman, the Genius of the Civil War* (London, 1930).

36. Sherman, *From Atlanta to the Sea,* ed., with an introduction, B. H. Liddell Hart (London, 1961), 5.

37. *Ibid.,* 10, 13.

38. Howard deposition, Mixed Commission on British and American Claims under Article XII of the Treaty of Washington, 1871, *Who Burnt Columbia?* (Charleston, S.C., 1873), 26-27.

39. *OR,* Ser. I, vol. 47, pt. 2, p. 36.

40. William S. McFeely, *Grant* (New York, 1981), 227.

41. *Ibid.,* 227-28.

42. S. M. Bowman in Col. S. M. Bowman and Lt.-Col. R. B. Irwin, *Sherman and His Campaigns* (New York, London, 1865), 488.

43. *Ibid.,* 488-89.

44. *OR,* Ser. I, vol. 44, p. 841.

45. Osborn, "Autobiographical Sketch."

46. John Wallace, *Carpetbag Rule in Florida* (Jacksonville, 1888), *passim.*

47. William Watson Davis, *The Civil War and Reconstruction in Florida* (New York, 1913), 380.

48. *Ibid.,* 375-76.

The Journal and Letters of
Thomas Ward Osborn

I *Atlanta*

Head Quarters Artillery
Department and Army
of the Tennessee,
Before Atlanta, Ga.
August 1, 1864.[1]

[To A. C. Osborn][2] Again I have been changed in my assignment to duty and this time with still larger responsibilities than I have before had. After the death of General McPherson,[3] General Howard[4] was assigned to the command of this Army. I had reported for duty to the IV Corps two days before General Howard received the order of assignment and remained with that corps two days after he came here. I therefore actually served with that corps four days only. But on each of those four days I was at the front with the batteries in an engagement of more or less severity.

I am good for nothing in the field except when on horseback. I cannot get about in the trenches or in the woods on foot. I had the assistance of a good officer, Captain Bridges.[5] Still I served with the batteries each day, but with considerable inconvenience to myself.

At General Howard's request General Sherman assigned me as Chief of Artillery of this Department of the Army. The Department has more artillery, heavy and light, than any one of the geographical departments. I now find myself laboring under the misfortune of a low grade in the Army and at the same time taking possession of an office having no records at all. It is possessed of no information concerning the troops, equipment, material, condition, or even where any of the batteries, heavy or light, are excepting the fifteen light batteries serving here in the active army.

There are many more light batteries in the Department, not in the active army, than there are in it. No one at these headquarters knows where these batteries are or what they are doing.

In addition to the light batteries are all the fortified cities from Natchez on the Mississippi River, north and east, around to Fort Henry on the Tennessee River, that is, on the east bank of the Mississippi, south bank of the Ohio and west bank of the Tennessee. Also all the forts along the same banks of these rivers, along the railroads, in the mountains and throughout the territory of this Department. In a word, there is not at these headquarters a scratch of a pen available, or a well defined recollection of any thing connected with this branch of the service.

From this starting point General Howard says he "expects in a very short time a complete report of all the artillery in the Department, so that I can tell him where every gun is, its calibre and what ammunition must be provided for it." I have no staff here but this report will soon be provided.

Officers are continually complimenting me on my return to the field and devotion to the service, as it is self evident that I have returned altogether unfit for duty as it is usually performed.

The artillery officers who are now holding corresponding positions to my own are General Hunt[6] of the Army of the Potomac, General Brannan[7] of the Army of the Cumberland, General Horne[8] of the Defenses of Washington and General Stilson[9] of the Department of the Ohio, all of West Point and the regular army, except General Stilson, who is from the volunteer forces. I have the largest department and by far the greater amount of troops and artillery and am a major in the volunteer service. General Barry[10] of General Sherman's staff has the superior position of any of the artillery officers. He is of West Point and the regular army, and in extent of command is the only one superior to myself.

I have this work now on my hands to perform and I will do it regardless of how much there is of it. So far in the Army I have succeeded in whatever work I have been assigned to do and I do not hesitate now.

Late orders from the War Department forbid the mustering out of officers, except they have served three years since their last muster. I shall, therefore, probably remain in service until the end of the war or until killed.

Fighting is going on more or less every day. We shall probably be engaged this evening and again tomorrow. The Army is lying in an arc around the west side of Atlanta and within easy artillery range of the city. The enemy are determined not to give the city up and it can only be taken by hard fighting or by strategy or both, probably both. The enemy's line corresponds with our own and lies between our own line and the city. General Hood[11] is believed at army headquarters to have about 40,000 men and General Sherman has about 80,000. General Sherman[12] is continually sliding around the city to his right, entrenching as he goes. Hood slides to his left and entrenches as he goes in our front. He occupies a position which, in this case, has all the elements and advantages of a fortress thus making his force fully equal to ours for all purposes of this semi-siege.

All railroads leading into Atlanta are cut except the one running south. That one branches six miles south of Atlanta. The main line goes to Macon and the branch to West Point. We are now after this road and branch.

Several pitched battles have been fought since I have been here, in all of which we have been successful. We estimate the loss of the enemy at 20,000 men and 6,000 of our own since the Army crossed the Chattahoochee River. This large difference in the loss of the two armies rises from the fact that the enemy has continually been the attacking party while in the greater part of the battles we were in position or entrenched, or both. How long these operations will continue around Atlanta I have no idea. It may be for some time, but we are too strong for the enemy to drive us out and if we stay we shall win.

The Army of the Ohio—General Schofield[13]—is now moving from the extreme left around to the extreme right, to operate against the West Point railroad. At present the Army of the Tennessee holds the extreme right. When the Army of the Ohio gets into position, the Army of the Tennessee will hold the center and the Army of the Cumberland the left.

The enemy will fight General Schofield tomorrow morning when he attempts to reach the railroad or gets into position near it. The Army of the Ohio has nothing to fear from the result. It will be what a prisoner taken yesterday called "another killing time." Supports will be kept close up to General Schofield so that if he should require assistance he will have all he needs. I have no idea he will be able to reach the railroad, but he will entrench near it.

NOTES

1. Maj. Osborn's correspondence was regularly datelined in this fashion. Except that the full entry is given in his first letter in which the designation "Department and" is dropped (Nov. 11, 1864), all further letters and journal entries note only place and date.

2. The Reverend Abraham C. Osborn of St. Louis, a Baptist preacher.

3. Maj.-Gen. James B. McPherson. McPherson was killed June 24 in the battles before Atlanta. He was immediately succeeded by Maj.-Gen. John A. Logan.

4. On July 27 Maj.-Gen. Oliver Otis Howard was assigned to command the Army of the Tennessee. In his *Memoirs* Gen. William T. Sherman wrote: "It first became necessary to settle the important question of who should succeed General McPherson? General Logan had taken command of the Army of the Tennessee by virtue of his seniority, and had done well, but I did not consider him equal to the command of three corps.. We discussed the merits and qualities of every officer of high rank in the army, and finally settled on Major-General O. O. Howard as the best officer who was present and available for the purpose.... I wanted to succeed in taking Atlanta, and needed commanders who were purely and technically soldiers, men who would obey orders and execute them promptly and on time; for I knew that we would have to execute some most delicate manoeuvres, requiring the utmost skill, nicety, and precision. I believed that General Howard would do all these faithfully and well, and I think the result has justified my choice." Sherman, II, 85-86.

5. Capt. Lyman Bridges.

6. Maj.-Gen. Henry Jackson Hunt.

7. Maj.-Gen. John Milton Brannon.

8. This name is an error on Osborn's part.

9. This name is an error on Osborn's part.

10. Brig.-Gen. William Farquhar Barry.

11. Lieut.-Gen. John Bell Hood.

12. Gen. William Tecumseh Sherman.

13. Maj.-Gen. John M. Schofield.

Before Atlanta, Ga.
August 5, 1864.

[To A. C. O.] General Howard's command in this Department numbers, as shown in the last report, 145,000 men. Of these only 21,000 are present for duty here in the army operating against Atlanta. The remainder are on duty elsewhere in the Department or sick and absent on leave. In this army before Atlanta I have fifteen light batteries. All told in the department I have thirty-eight light batteries. Also I have five regiments of heavy artillery distributed among the various forts throughout the department. I have participated in several fights already, since I came to this command and I do not doubt I shall see more fighting soon.

In the effort to prevent our army moving to the right the enemy fights us about three o'clock every afternoon. Evidently General Sherman intends to keep up this movement until the enemy abandons the city, or if they will not do this, then to get at the railroads south of the city and cut them, thus compelling the enemy to abandon the city for want of supplies.

Our cavalry has been unfortunate. We have lost General Stoneman[1] and one half of his command, captured in a raid they were making south of Atlanta. They were captured at Clinton, a few miles north of Macon.

The works built here by each army are very strong. The average works for the infantry are abundant protection against 20 pd. rifle guns. Along the entire front of both armies all the means of defense and protection known to modern military engineering in the field are applied. The forts along the line are well built, large for field works and good specimens of military engineering. Whenever our troops go into position the men immediately entrench sufficiently to cover themselves from the enemy's fire and this without waiting for orders to do so. Every man does the work necessary to cover and protect himself. After the men have had a few minutes to throw up their breastworks, a strong skirmish line will repulse without difficulty a full line of battle moving against it. The enemy now only fights us on the flank as we encroach upon the open ground in our efforts to reach the railroad and before our men have time to throw up breastworks.

We have continually expected General Hood would be reinforced by troops sent from Virginia, but none appear to have come, neither do we take any prisoners from the armies west of the Mississippi River and assume that none have been or can be sent from there.[2]

I have made the request that, in the event of my being killed, I should be buried on the field and have said plainly I do not desire that my body shall be sent north. It is the custom to send the bodies of those staff officers who fall on the battlefield north for burial and so I have made this request as more in harmony with my feelings. Indeed I have always made this request wherever I have served, though I think I have never written the fact to you. If I am wounded you will of course be notified.

The following order has been issued by General Howard and as I assume you will like to see it I send it to you. It is in the general form of field orders. . . .

Head Quarters
Department and Army
of the Tennessee.
Before Atlanta, Georgia
August 1, 1864

General Field Orders, No. 6

The following officers are announced as members of the staff and staff corps, of this Department and Army. They will be obeyed and respected accordingly: Lieutenant Colonel C. H. Howard, Senior Aide-de-Camp; Major T. W. Osborn, 1st New York Artillery, Chief of Artillery; Captain H. M. Stinson, Aide-de-Camp; Captain F. W. Gilbreth, Aide-de-Camp; Captain W. M. Beebe, Forty-first regiment Ohio Infantry, Acting Aide-de-Camp; Captain E. H. Kirlin, Volunteer Aide-de-Camp.

By order Major General O. O. Howard

Wm. T. Clark
Assistant Adjutant-General

You will notice the foregoing order transfers the personal staff of the General from the IV Corps of the Army and also assigns me as Chief of Artillery.

NOTES

1. Maj.-Gen. George Stoneman led a cavalry raid on Macon July 27 to August 6. There were combats at Clinton July 30 (with heavy losses), at Hillsborough July 31, and Jug Tavern (now Winder) August 3. Stoneman's intention had been to threaten Macon but to by-pass it and free Federal prisoners at Camp Sumter (Andersonville). Stoneman's orders were to attack the railroad from Atlanta south toward Macon. He requested July 26 to be allowed to extend his raid and "make a dash on Macon and by a vigorous stroke release the prisoners (officers) there and afterward go on to Americus and release those (privates) there." U. S. War Department, *The War of the Rebellion: A Compilation of the Official Records of the Union and Confederate Armies,* Ser. I. vol. 38, pt. 5, p. 264 (hereinafter cited as *OR*).

Maj.-Gen. Edward M. McCook was dispatched on a coordinated raid against the Atlanta and West Point and the Macon and Western railroads. He broke the West Point road at Palmetto, crossed to the Macon road, and tore up two miles of track about Lovejoy's Station but was turned back by the Confederates when he headed toward Newnan. It was planned that Stoneman and McCook should meet at Lovejoy's, but Stoneman's defeat by Gen. Alfred Iverson's forces prevented that.

In his dispatch of August 3 to Maj.-Gen. Henry W. Halleck in Washington, Gen. Sherman reported on the raids still in progress: "I think General Stoneman has a chance of rescuing those prisoners. It was a bold and rash adventure, but I sanctioned it and hoped for its success from its very rashness. I think that all Georgia is now in my front, and he may meet but little opposition and succeed in releasing those prisoners." *OR* Ser. I, vol. 38, pt. 5, p. 340.

2. There were constant expectation and concern that the Confederates would be reinforced. Gen. Grant wrote Gen. Sherman from City Point, Va., Aug. 9; "The enemy having drawn to your front most of his forces west of Alabama, can you

not re-enforce from the Mississippi? . . . Everyday exhausts the enemy at least a regiment, without any further population to draw from to replace it, exclusive of losses in battle. I would suggest the employment of as many negroes as you can get for teamsters, company cooks, &c, and keep every enlisted man in the ranks . . . . Deserters coming in daily keep us well posted as to the position of Lee's forces. Stories of deserters are not to be relied on, but . . . I think no troops have gone from here to Hood." *OR*, Ser. I, vol. 38, pt. 5, pp. 433-34.

Before Atlanta, Ga.
August 16, 1864

[To S. C. Osborn][1] The Army has not changed its position for ten or twelve days. Skirmishing goes on continuously and a little fighting every two or three days. We are lengthening out our line and drawing our works closer to the enemy. I think General Sherman intends to husband his strength at present and until he can use it effectively on some given point. I am confident an extraordinary movement will be made in a few days by which we shall be successful in gaining possession of the city. The increasing rattle of musketry and artillery along the lines continues, but the damage done by the fire upon our men is next to nothing. I find my associations and surroundings at these headquarters very pleasant. I have asked for additional assistance in the management of the artillery of the Department and will soon have it.

NOTE

1. S. C. Osborn, like A. C., was a brother of T. W. Osborn and a preacher in St. Louis.

Before Atlanta, Ga.
August 16, 1864

[To A. C. O.] Nearly all of the enemy's cavalry has gone north of us and is breaking the railroad here and there. It is doing, however, no serious damage and is generally driven off before reaching the railroad and whenever it has reached it was driven off before serious damage was done.

The battles which have been fought since I have been here have been wonderful successes. We know what our losses are and we have buried more of the enemy's dead than all our losses killed, wounded and missing combined. We have taken more prisoners than our combined losses have been. In this we do not estimate the enemy's wounded which they have been able to remove from the field, and those so removed by them and lost to the service must aggregate a large number. Our generals think General Hood has lost nearly or quite half of his entire army since General Johnston was removed and he assumed command of it. Still the strength of the works about Atlanta is so great that we should be repulsed if a direct assault should be made at any point upon the enemy's line.

In proportion to the force he had with him General Stoneman's losses were very great. The greater part of his 700 men were captured. General McCook's losses were not so great as has been represented in the north.

The Generals commanding our armies make accurate reports to the War Department, consequently the president and proper officials know the exact status at the moment though, of course, nothing ever goes to the public. But the country at large gets its information from the newspapers and these from their correspondents in the Army. Of course neither the generals in the field nor the War Department can put valuable information in the hands of so unreliable a body of men as the reporters connected with the armies in the field. There are honorable men among them, men who can be trusted not to make illegitimate use of information furnished, but such men are exceptions. No reporter ever sees a battle and what they write to their papers is procured secondhand from officers, and they furnish such information as they think proper or prudent.[1]

NOTE

1. "Newspaper correspondents were a special abomination in his [Sherman's] eyes, provoking him to great wrath, and spasmodic profanity of a highly original pattern. 'They are,' said he, 'as a rule mischievous. They are the world's gossips; they pick up and retail camp scandal, and gradually drift to the headquarters of some general who finds it easier to make a reputation at home than with his troops. They are also tempted to prophesy events, and state facts, which reveal to an enemy a purpose in time to guard against it.' " F. Y. Hedley, *Marching Through Georgia* (Chicago, 1890 [c. 1884]), 67.

David P. Conyngham described himself in the preface to his *Sherman's March Through the South* (New York, 1865) as "volunteer aid-de-camp and war corres-

pondent." He is listed on his book's title page as a captain. He was a correspondent of the *New York Herald,* and his account is generally reliable. He was not, as
his book implies, a member of Sherman's staff and is not mentioned in the appropriate volumes of *OR.*
　Theodore R. Davis, artist for *Harper's Weekly,* did travel with Sherman's staff
and became a close friend of Hitchcock. Hedley wrote of Davis, pp. 118, 121: "He
was frequently under fire, but his work at such times bore little resemblance to
the actual scenes he intended to depict. He merely outlined the ground and position, and then filled in guns and troops from memory, when and where he could
work with less strain upon the nerves."

Fairburn, Ga.
August 29, 1864

[To S. C. O.] We are on an expedition which will necessarily
result in some fighting. In General Sherman's efforts to dislodge
General Hood from Atlanta, he determined to cut the two railroads south of Atlanta.

General Howard is leading this raid on the right of the advance,
and as the enemy must today be aware of the movement and its
object we may expect to be attacked tomorrow. General Sherman
is moving with great caution and from all I can see now we shall
be successful. If we are forced to fight it will not be at a disadvantage.

Fairburn, Ga.
August 29, 1864

[To A. C. O.] We are now near Fairburn on the Atlanta and West
Point railroad, two miles southwest of East Point. Our right is resting on the railroad a little south of Fairburn and our headquarters
three miles north. We are destroying the railroad as rapidly as possible by bending and breaking the rails, burning the ties, digging
down embankments and filling up cuts with earth, timber, fence
rails, and a few torpedoes.

We reached here yesterday and will leave in the morning to
strike the Atlanta and Macon railroad at or near Jonesboro and destroy it.

The enemy has not yet been able to get at us, but I think they will do so tomorrow and if so they will make the best fight they can. We shall feel our way carefully and be ready to stop and entrench at any moment and anywhere to save the men as much as possible. I do not think they will be able to get us at great disadvantage though it is more than likely we shall have a serious battle.

Generals Thomas[1] and Schofield are both on our left, so that flank is protected against any serious attack, while our right is in the open field unprotected and the enemy will probably try to reach us on the extreme right. We have fifteen days rations with us and it is General Sherman's intention to stay out until he forces General Hood to leave Atlanta. If he will not go, I presume we will fall back and replenish and in due time try this or some other extraordinary movement again. The Augusta and Atlanta railroad is destroyed for forty miles east of Atlanta. General Hood may now attempt to repair that but with his present force he cannot do it and at the same time hold us back. Even if he can, his army meanwhile will eat up whatever supplies he may have in Atlanta and he will be forced to leave to feed it.

The XX Corps is protecting the railroad bridge across the Chattahoochee River, north of Atlanta.[2] We are not through this job of capturing Atlanta yet and we may see a different side of the matter before we do get through. Still I have no fears of a repulse, but when we remember Chancellorsville we know that any thing is possible in war.[3]

NOTES

1. Maj.-Gen. George Henry Thomas.

2. This bridge had been destroyed by the Confederates. Col. W. W. Wright reconstructed it in six days "and our garrisons and detachments to the rear so effectually guarded the railroad that the trains from Nashville arrived daily, and our substantial wants were well supplied." William Tecumseh Sherman, *Memoirs* (New York, 1875), II, 92.

3. Gen. Howard's reputation as a soldier was marred by his failure to protect an exposed flank at Chancellorsville. His command was therefore routed by Gen. T. J. ("Stonewall") Jackson's assault.

Lovejoy's, Ga.
September 3, 1864

[To S. C. O.] We let go of our works near Atlanta and have made a quarter circuit of the city. We have occupied and destroyed both of the railroads south of the city, have had two good fights which we won. That at Jonesboro was very severe and was fought by General Howard. The other near Atlanta was fought by General Thomas. We have skirmished a good deal and in every way, in this movement, beaten the enemy and we have taken the city of Atlanta.

After the fight at Jonesboro we followed the enemy thirteen miles, to this point, where they have made a stand in a position long ago strongly fortified and intended to be used in case of an emergency. As General Sherman in this movement only wished to get possession of the city and dislodge the enemy from the strongly fortified position and military stronghold, he will not fight again here, but return to Atlanta. I am confident the enemy will not molest us on our return to Atlanta. Just now they are too badly crippled for that. I have borne my usual part in the movement and in the fighting.[1]

NOTE

1. On September 3 President Lincoln issued this order: "The national thanks are tendered by the President to Maj. Gen. W. T. Sherman and the gallant officers and soldiers of his command before Atlanta, for the distinguished ability, courage, and perserverance displayed in the campaign in Georgia, which under Divine favor, has resulted in the capture of the city of Atlanta. The marches, battles, sieges and other military operations that have signalled the campaign, must render it famous in the annals of war, and have entitled those who have participated therein to the applause and thanks of the nation."

East Point, Ga.
September 10, 1864

[To S. C. O. I presume you may know before this more about the late movement than I can tell you. Taken altogether it was a very brilliant one and was a successful termination for the campaign of the summer.

When we left our works before Atlanta, General Hood supposed or believed we were retreating across the Chattahoochee River and that General Sherman had left one corps on the south side of the river to make a raid on the railroads. In fact all the army, except the XX Corps, made a wide circuit to the west and south of the city striking one railroad at Fairburn and the other at

Destruction of the depots, public buildings, and manufactories at Atlanta. *Harper's Pictorial History of the Civil War,* II.

Jonesboro. General Hood, assuming this movement was a raid by one corps, sent half his army to drive it back. This misapprehension resulted in General Thomas fighting one half his army near Atlanta and whipping it, and when General Hood discovered his mistake he sent the other half of his army to Jonesboro, where it fought General Howard, and it was whipped. After the fight at Jonesboro the enemy drew off to the south about thirteen miles to Lovejoy's where they had a strong position previously fortified.

This fight at Jonesboro was a bitter little battle and our army showed especial gallantry and great confidence in itself as well as in its officers. I never saw any officer, except perhaps General Hooker,[1] exhibit as great and reckless daring and gallantry on the battlefield as General Logan[2] did at Jonesboro, and his entire corps partook of the spirit which moved him.

General Hood in his attempt to head off and turn back what he believed to be a corps only, divided his army. General Hardee's[3] command fought us at Jonesboro and after the battle retreated south. General Hood with that part of the army which fought General Thomas was still in Atlanta, and General Sherman with General Thomas and his forces on the railroad between the divided Army. The forces under General Hood in Atlanta destroyed all the military stores there including railroad rolling stock[4] and then in order to join General Hardee made a wide circuit to the east around us, keeping so far away from us we could not intercept him. A slight effort to do so was made, but with so little energy that it failed. I am inclined to think that if it had been made with as great vigor as it should have been, General Hood's column could have been struck and a part, or all of it captured. However, it is now understood, that General Sherman did not desire to do any more fighting than was positively necessary to gain possession of the city.

The city has been, and still is, considered by military men the key to the entire south for all future operations. The city is much damaged, being much injured by the artillery and by being so long occupied as a military post. The shelling of the city as ordered by General Sherman was mainly under my direction and in addition to doing much damage must have been a very great annoyance to the both the enemy and to the citizens.[5]

General Sherman now intends to send all the citizens out of the city and occupy it purely as a military post and depot. This sending the people out of the city will be a little rough on them.[6]

General Howard's headquarters is at East Point, four miles from Atlanta. His army is camped about East Point. The General preferred to have his headquarters in the field. The headquarters of General Sherman and the other army commanders are in comfortable houses in the city. Personally I like this better.

NOTES

1. Maj.-Gen. Joseph Hooker.

2. Gen. Howard commented on Logan's conduct at the battle of Ezra Church: "Major General Logan was spirited and energetic, going at once to the point where he apprehended the slightest danger of the enemy's success. His decision and resolution everywhere animated and encouraged his officers and men." Oliver Otis Howard, *Autobiography* (New York, 1907), II, 24.

3. Lieut.-Gen. William Joseph Hardee.

4. Sherman's Special Field Orders No. 62 of September 3 declare: "The general commanding announces with great pleasure that he has official information that our troops under Major-General Slocum occupied Atlanta yesterday at 11 A.M., the enemy having evacuated the night before destroyed vast magazines of stores, and blowing up among other things, eighty car-loads of ammunition." *OR*, Ser. I, vol. 38, pt. 1, p. 86.

On the same day he wrote Halleck: "So Atlanta is ours, and fairly won. I shall not push much farther in this raid but in a day or so will move to Atlanta and give my men some rest. Our losses will not exceed 1,200 and we have possession of over 300."

5. Sherman wrote Grant on 10 August: "I have just got up four 4½-inch rifled guns with ammunition, and propose to expend about 4,000 rifled shot in the heart of Atlanta. We have already commanded it with our lighter ordnance." *OR*, Ser. I, vol. 38, pt. 5, p. 447.

6. "I was resolved to make Atlanta a pure military garrison or depot, with no civil population to influence military measures. I had seen Memphis, Vicksburg, Natchez, and New Orleans, all captured from the enemy, and each at once was garrisoned by a full division of troops, if not more; so that success was actually crippling our armies in the field by detachments to guard and protect a hostile population.

"I gave notice of this purpose, as early as the 4th of September, to General Halleck. . . . I knew, of course, that such a measure would be strongly criticized, but made up my mind to do it with the absolute certainty of its justness, and that time would sanction its wisdom. I knew that the people of the South would read in this measure two important conclusions; one, that we were in earnest; and the other, if they were sincere in their common and popular clamor 'to die in the last ditch,' that the opportunity would soon come."

On September 8 Mayor James M. Calhoun published this Notice:

"*To the Citizens of Atlanta:* Major General Sherman instructs me to say to you that you must all leave Atlanta; that as many of you as want to go North can do so, and that as many as want to go South can do so, and that all can take with them their movable property, servants included, if they want to go, but that no force is to be used, and that he will furnish transportation for persons and property as far as Rough and Ready, from whence it is expected General Hood will assist in carrying it on. Like transportation will be furnished for people and property going North, and it is required that all things contemplated by this notice will be carried into execution as soon as possible.

All persons are requested to leave their name and number in their families with the undersigned as early as possible, that estimates may be made of the quantity of transportation required." Sherman, II, 111-12.

East Point, Ga.
September 19, 1864

[To. A. C. O.] I have written several letters since I joined this army relative to the siege of Atlanta, as it is generally called. In fact General Sherman never attempted to take Atlanta by a siege proper. He made several approaches by establishing one line in advance of another, but did not go beyond this in siege operations proper. When he arrived in the vicinity of the city he found it strongly fortified, but did not know until he was in possession of it how strong the works are. He was not aware until the last how determinedly and persistently General Hood had made up his mind to hold the city.

As General Sherman crossed the Chattahoochee on the 20, General Johnston was relieved[1] and General Hood attacked him with great violence, but having received severe punishment drew back. Again he attacked in the same manner and with the same results on the 22. And again on the 28 of July. In these and in the intermediate and lesser attacks which he made on our lines General Sherman estimated his loss at 20,000 men, while our loss was between 5,000 and 6,000 men. Still by remaining in his works Hood could hold the city. General Sherman, being unable to determine whether General Hood had concluded to risk all his fortunes in endeavoring to remain, attempted to develop his plan by shelling the city.

This work was placed in my charge and was carried out with mathematical accuracy. One 30 pound shell was dropped in the city every five minutes between sun rise and sun set and each fifteen minutes from sun set to sun rise. I used a $4\frac{1}{2}$-inch wrought iron gun from which, in this way, over 1,500 shots were fired, and the gun was in good condition when we discontinued it, to leave the works, with the exception that the vent had become enlarged.

The ordnance officers of the regular army tell me this is several hundred rounds more than has ever been fired from any gun in this country, and in fact any country, before the guns exploded. Occasionally the light rifled guns were directed to throw shells into the city.

Meanwhile General Sherman continued to draw closer to the city and at the same time move by the right flank towards the railroads south of it, until he was persuaded General Hood would not leave it until he was forced out, and he believed he had staked his all on holding Atlanta.

By the 20 of August General Sherman had perfected his plans and apparently without consulting his generals. I think he is quite as confidential with General Howard as with anyone of his subordinates but to him he said little more than to express his impatience at the delay in getting possession of the city. He frequently spoke of the influence the capture of Atlanta would have on the November election and that he was determined to have the city in time to secure this influence.[2]

He frequently said that his instruction for the campaign required him to go only to the north bank of the Chattahoochee. I am told he felt of his subordinates at a sort of general conference sufficient to know they would not endorse his plan for taking the city, that is, they would not recommend it. After this he kept his own counsel while he prepared for the work. I am also told that even at the last General Schofield would not believe General Sherman would cut himself off from his trenches and swing out into the open country, and that there must be an error in the orders directing it.

The earth works of each army were so strong that an assault by either would have resulted only in failure and the loss of men, without any corresponding benefit being gained.

The movement to the open country, south of the city, commenced on the night of the 24 of August, and, commencing with the Army of the Cumberland on the left flank. That Army was drawn back and massed on the left and rear of the center occupied by General Howard. The XX Corps, Army of the Cumberland, was sent to guard the railroad bridge across the Chattahoochee, where it entrenched. General Howard's left corps swung back to the rear, making a right angle with the right corps and a fixed flank for the army. That evening General Hood announced to his army that General Sherman was retreating across the river.

We were then ready to move after dark. New roads had been cut through the forest as far as possible and wood gathered to light the troops with small fires.

At eight o'clock in the evening of the 26 we started on this expedition. The enemy threatened a little, but gave us no serious inconvenience. At ten o'clock the Army of the Tennessee was fairly in motion and crossed the front of the Army of the Cumberland, taking the right of the entire army. At day light we had moved fifteen miles and halted. General Schofield had not left the works and then occupied the left of the Army of the Cumberland which moved in between General Schofield and General Howard. That army then occupied the center. The entire army then faced south with the right fifteen miles southwest from Atlanta, where it halted to give General Hood time to scratch his head and think. His skirmishers found the XX Corps at the railroad bridge and his scouts found the picket line in front of our army, but could not reach our main line to report in what strength we were moving. He was left with very little information upon which to base his defense. He learned, however, that no part of the army had crossed the river and that General Schofield was still holding his works in too strong force to be moved.

The following morning General Howard moved seven miles to Fairburn and struck the railroad at ten o'clock in the forenoon. The Army was distributed along the track, of which they tore up and destroyed ten miles most thoroughly. The same morning General Schofield left the works and moved to the right, keeping the connection with General Thomas.

On the morning of the 30 General Howard moved towards Jonesboro, fifteen miles distant. It appears that at this time General Hood had again concluded the main part of General Sherman's army had crossed, or were about crossing, the river and that a single corps was making a raid in the rear of his army to cover that movement. He, therefore, made no sufficient disposition of his army to stop us. After General Howard left Fairburn and moved two miles towards Jonesboro we encountered a force which made a good show of resistance. We halted and made our disposition for a fight and lost two hours in doing so, when we found we had a small brigade of infantry, one battery and a detachment of cavalry in front of us. This force skirmished all day stubbornly and delayed our march considerably. At Renfroe [Renfrew] and the Flint River they contested the ground with great spirit and we lost several men at each of these places.

At Renfrew the enemy posted their battery by the side of, and partially in the rear of, a dwelling house in which some of the enemy's sharp shooters also took their positions. I therefore put in three batteries bringing a converging fire upon the battery and the same thing upon the house. Several shells passed through the house, generally breaking up things inside. One shell exploded under a bed upon which a woman had lain down. The instant birth of a child resulted. A few minutes later we occupied the ground and one of General Howard's staff surgeons cared for the mother and infant and left them both doing well. This style of midwifery I do not think is found in the books.

At sun set and after a bitter skirmish and the capture of several prisoners we crossed the Flint River about one mile from Jonesboro. On the east bank of the river the bluffs rise abruptly between one and two hundred feet. Not being conversant with the locality or the exact whereabouts of the railroad, General Howard crossed a sufficient force to make a strong bridgehead and had them entrench on the plateau above the river. This force was thrown forward to within a half mile of Jonesboro and the flanks reversed so they rested near the river making, when filled out, a line of battle more than a mile long. We secured a position between the railroad and the river and not more than a half mile from the railroad from which we could not be divided.

The enemy skirmished around us during the night, to locate our line. In the several little dashes they made we took some prisoners from whom we got a good deal of information regarding the proposed movements of the enemy. It was dark when our line got into position.

While the head of the column was crossing Flint River, General Howard with his staff rode up, or attempted to do so, to the top of the bluff. Just before reaching the crest a volley from the rear guard of the enemy was fired at us. There were not less than a hundred muskets and they were not more than two hundred feet from us when they fired. Their aim was a trifle high and the bullets passed within a few inches of our heads. It was a rather startling reception. Fortunately no one was hit.

We learned from the prisoners that General Hardee, with his own corps and that of General Lee,[3] was moving from Atlanta by rail to intercept us. Everything indicated that the enemy would attack us on the afternoon of the day following our taking position and preparation was made to meet the attack. Generals Thomas and Schofield were between us and Atlanta, but had not yet reached the railroad. General Sherman was with that wing of the Army.

During the day General Hood attacked General Thomas and after a sharp battle was repulsed. In the evening troops were being sent rapidly to Jonesboro by rail and the night was passed with each army getting ready for a fight at Jonesboro the next day.

On the 31 at three o'clock in the afternoon General Hardee attacked our entrenched line striking it at two points. The attack was very severe, the great weight of it falling on General Hazen's[4] Division of the XV Corps. Three attacks on General Hazen were made and repulsed. At the other point, two attacks were made and repulsed. The attacks were very severe but were repulsed with comparative ease. The contest was so unequal that our men talked of it as a "killing time" of the enemy. I felt, as I understood all others did, that there was no possibility of failure, even had General Hood's entire army been present. We could only have been beaten in the position we held by some gross blunder on our own part.

In round numbers our loss was 250 in killed, wounded and missing. We took 250 prisoners and buried 400 of the enemy's dead. The enemy were not molested in the removal of their wounded. From prisoners we gathered that General Hardee had 22,000 men, all veterans, with him. That 10,000 veteran troops and 15,000 state troops were left in Atlanta. In all 47,000 men, or 32,000 of regular troops.

The following morning September 1 an effort was made to destroy the force under General Hardee by striking it on the right flank and rear. A sharp battle resulted, but with not as good results as were anticipated or as should have been secured. On account of some misunderstanding of orders or failure to execute orders given the effort in the main failed of good results. General Sherman appeared to blame General Stanley[5] of the IV Corps. General

Stanley said he had complied with all the orders he received and would have done more had he been informed where the enemy were.

This is to be regretted, as General Hardee's force was at our disposal if the necessary movements had been rightly and quickly executed. As it was, General Govan's[6] brigade and two batteries were captured. General Hardee moved out very rapidly, or as the soldiers express it, "he lit out" and we lost him. During the night General Hood evacuated Atlanta, having first destroyed the public property and stores. He then passed our army, going south via McDonough, several miles east of the railroad and of Jonesboro.

On September 2 we started south following General Hardee until we found him entrenched at Cedar Bluff, near Lovejoy's Station. These bluffs have long been talked of as the next strong military position south of Atlanta and they had been strongly fortified so as to be used in case of a necessity arising. They occupy a slight elevation of country, protected in front and on their flanks by a swamp which is crossed by the railroad. The swamp covers the entire face of the hill. We reached the swamp at ten o'clock in the forenoon intending to attack as soon as the column closed up. After closer inspection, however, by a strong skirmish line, it was found that an attack would be attended with difficulties not worth our while to encounter. The loss would be too great for the benefits gained.

An artillery duel took place while we were in front of the enemy at Cedar Bluffs which for clean work I have not seen surpassed. General Sherman with several of the prominent generals, with their staffs gathered, were together under a large persimmon tree and in plain view and easy range of the enemy's batteries. The enemy opened from a couple of batteries in the open field on this group and pulled their solid shot uncomfortably near. At General Sherman's suggestion to "silence those batteries" I put in four batteries, giving them, probably, a quarter mile point from the right to the left battery, so as to get a converging fire on the enemy. In a very few minutes, not more than five, after the firing was commenced by my batteries I drove the enemy gunners from their guns and to the open field beyond their batteries and kept them there until we knocked their batteries to pieces and until we were disposed to let them return. They annoyed us no more with their guns.

After General Sherman thoroughly inspected the enemy's position at Cedar Bluffs and determined not to attack he made such arrangements as he thought necessary for the occupation of Atlanta and turned his entire army back to go into camp in and about the city. He gave special instructions for the Army to make itself comfortable for a month.

The officers and men are in excellent health and spirits and are enjoying the rest most decidedly.[7]

NOTES

1. President Jefferson Davis's decision to relieve Johnston and place Hood in command of the defense of Atlanta remains one of the most controversial points in the history of the Civil War. Davis had the situation thoroughly investigated by Gen. Braxton Bragg. Bragg felt that Johnston would not fight Sherman except on his own terms and was oversecretive about his plans, even in declining to discuss them with him as the President's representative. Bragg wrote Davis from Atlanta on July 15 the letter crucial to the change in command. In a postscript he says: "As General J. has never sought my advice, nor ever afforded me a fair opportunity of giving my opinion, I have obtruded neither on him." Bragg recommended the promotion of Hood, if a change in command be made: "If any change is made Lieutenant General Hood would give unlimited statisfaction, and my estimate of him, always high, has been raised by his conduct in this campaign. Do not understand me as proposing him as a man of genius, or a great general, but as far better in the present emergency than any one we have available." *OR,* Ser. I, vol. 39, pt. 2, p. 714.

With his letter to Davis, Bragg enclosed one to himself from Hood dated July 14. Hood declared: "During the campaign from Dalton to the Chattahoochee River it is natural to suppose that we had several chances to strike the enemy a decisive blow. We have failed to take advantage of such opportunities, and find our army south of the Chattahoochee, very much decreased in strength.... Our present position is a very difficult one, and we should not, under any circumstances, allow the enemy to gain possession of Atlanta, and deem it excessively important, should we find the enemy intends establishing the Chattahoochee as their line, relying upon interrupting our communications and again virtually dividing our country, that we should attack him, even if we should have to recross the river to do so. I have, general, so often urged that we should force the enemy to give us battle as to almost be regarded as reckless by the officers high in rank in this army, since their views have been so directly opposite. I regard it as a great misfortune to our country that we failed to give battle to the enemy many miles north of our present position." *OR,* Ser. I, vol. 38, pt. 5, pp. 879-80.

On July 17 Adjutant and Inspector General Samuel Cooper telegraphed Johnston: "Lieutenant General J. B. Hood has been commissioned to the temporary rank of general under the late law of Congress. I am directed by the Secretary of War to inform you that as you have failed to arrest the advance of the enemy in the vicinity of Atlanta, far in the interior of Georgia, and express no confidence that you can defeat or repel him, you are hereby relieved from command of the Army and Department of Tennessee, which you will immediately turn over to General Hood." *OR,* Ser. I, vol. 38, pt. 5, p. 885.

Sherman noted that, on learning of the change of command on the morning of July 18, he inquired about Hood of Gen. Schofield, who had been his classmate at West Point "and learned that he was bold even to rashness, and courageous in the extreme; I inferred that the change of commanders meant 'fight.'. . . This was just what we wanted, viz., to fight in open ground, on anything like equal terms, instead of being forced to run up against prepared intrenchments." Sherman, II, 72.

The fullest and best account of Johnston's replacement by Hood occurs in Thomas L. Connelly's authoritative *Autumn of Glory, The Army of Tennessee, 1862-1865* (Baton Rouge, 1971), 391-426.

2. Maj. Henry Hitchcock joined Gen. Sherman's staff at Rome, Ga., on October 31 and quickly became his most trusted and confidential aide. He wrote his wife from Kingston on November 2 (six days before the presidential election): "I asked his [Sherman's] staff at Rome whether he was for Lincoln or McClellan. None of them knew; he has never said, and quietly ignores all discussion of either. But from a few words he said to me tonight,—not in any sense of a 'political' character, however,—and which he prefaced, no one else being in the room, by saying 'Now that we are alone I'll tell you,' etc., etc.,—I have no hesitation in concluding that he is not a votary of 'little Mac.'" Henry Hitchcock, *Marching with Sherman,* ed. M. A. DeWolfe Howe (New Haven, 1927), 29.

Sherman wrote Halleck more freely than he talked to his staff. In his letter of September 4 from Lovejoy's he commented: "I have not yet heard from the Chicago nominations, but appearances are strange indeed that McClellan will be nominated. The phases of 'Democracy' are strange indeed. Some fool seems to have used my name. If forced to choose between the penitentiary and the White House for four years, like old Professor Molinard, I would say the penitentiary, thank you, sir." *OR,* Ser. I, vol. 38, pt. 5, p. 794. But Sherman strongly supported the draft and feared Lincoln would give in to influences opposing it. He wrote Halleck on September 17: "Mr. Stanton tells me the draft will be made on Monday next. If Mr. Lincoln modifies it to the extent of one man, or wavers in its execution, he is gone. Even the army would vote against him." *OR,* Ser. I, vol. 39, pt. 2, p. 396.

3. Lieut.-Gen. Stephen D. Lee.
4. Brig.-Gen. William B. Hazen.
5. Maj.-Gen. David S. Stanley.
6. Brig.-Gen. Daniel C. Govan.
7. In his long letter of September 4, to Halleck, Sherman wrote: "I ought to have reaped larger fruits of victory. . . . Though I ought to have taken 10,000 of Hardee's men, and all of his artillery, I must content myself with 500 dead, 2,000 wounded, 2,000 prisoners, 10 guns in the field and 14 in Atlanta, 7 trains of cars captured and burned, many stragglers fleeing in disorder, and the town of Atlanta, which, after all, was the prize I fought for."

"The army is in magnificent heart, and I could go on, but it would not be prudent. . . . I stay here a few days for effect, and then will fall back and occupy Atlanta, giving my command some rest." *OR,* Ser. I, vol. 38, pt. 5, p. 792.

East Point, Ga.
September 26, 1864

[To S. C. O.] There is no change here in the general status of military affairs. The Army is hard at work preparing for the next campaign whenever and wherever that may be.

Since I came to this army I have made a complete revaluation in the artillery organization of this Army and Department. I found its organization bad, or more exactly I found it without organization. What I have done has been against the wishes of the division and corps commanders. The several batteries were attached to the division, two or three to each division. A division chief of artillery was attached to the staff of the division commander. The returns and reports of the several batteries were generally made to the adjutant general of the division and were returned to the corps and army headquarters as part of the division returns. The chief of artillery of the division seldom took further interest in the batteries than to keep a personal watch over them. He maintained no independent office. Naturally the division commanders desired to retain the command and control of these batteries and from long usage the corps commanders rather favored this plan. I determined to make the change and brigade the artillery of each corps of this army, as it was in the Army of the Potomac and as had been brought to the Army of the Cumberland by the XI and XII Corps and as now exists in the XX Corps composed of the consolidated XI and XII Corps.

When I came here I believed it would require six months to perfect the change and to get the new organization working smoothly. But it is already accomplished and the new order will soon be working as well or even better than that in any one of the armies. The commanding general in each one of the armies, so far as I know, has always placed many restrictions upon his chief of artillery and has thus prevented him from perfecting the individual batteries and the artillery organization so as to bring it to its greatest state of perfection and effectiveness in the field. On the other hand General Howard has fully endorsed my plans and given me full authority to carry them out. As a result the artillery of this army has a complete organization of its own. Each corps has a brigade of artillery under a competent and energetic commander. The artillery of the department, light and heavy, now sends all reports to this office and through it to the Adjutant General's office.

The artillery of the U.S. Army is by far its worst or most slipshod organization of any branch of the service. This arm has in the regular army always been considered the aristocratic one and sought for assignments by the old officers, yet from the beginning of the war it has been permitted to remain without an organization of its

Confederate prisoners being conducted from Jonesboro to Atlanta. *Harper's Pictorial History of the Civil War,* II.

own, except such as it has received as the result of incessant beg-
ging and intercession by its officers for a recognized position. The
artillery owes most of its effectiveness in the field in all the armies
and all of its organization to the earnest and effective work of
General Hunt, Chief of Artillery of the Army of the Potomac. In
his labors in this interest he has received the endorsement and en-
couragement of General Barry. But for these two officers the batteries would have still been scattered about, attached to divisions
and brigades any where and every where that a general officer had
sufficient personal influence to get a battery assigned to his command.

The ignorance of some of our general officers in regard to the
proper uses of artillery is simply stupendous. I have seen a well appointed light battery ordered by a general officer 300 yards in advance of his skirmish line for the protection of that skirmish line,
and that when the enemy was expected to attack any minute. That
is one specimen and I will give one more. At one time I went to
look after one of my batteries which had been ordered on picket
duty with a brigade commanded by a brigadier general. I found it
in a heavy forest filled with a dense undergrowth. The brigade
was entrenched across the road. A quarter of a mile in advance
were his advanced pickets, also well entrenched, and between 200
and 300 yards in advance of this picket was the battery standing
ready for action with not a musket nearer than the picket, without
a shovel full of earth thrown up or even a rail or other barricade to
give the battery the slightest protection. I called the general's attention to the position of the battery and he asked with all serious-
ness, "What is artillery for if not to protect the infantry?" I could
give many more illustrations of like foolishness of general officers
and colonels who have only had experience in the command of
infantry, but these are sufficient to show how necessary it may be,
and often is, to have men in command of artillery who have made
it their special study.

The great fault in this particular lies in the primary organization
of the Army. It is one of the unfortunate results growing out of the
building up of an army of three-quarters of a million of men upon
the frame-work of a toy army of twenty thousand men. As a whole
the increase of the Army upon this diminutive frame-work has
been successful, but in some of its parts it has been woefully de-
fective. With the infantry and cavalry it has worked well, but with
the artillery and army staff it has been a dead failure.

Exodus of Confederates from Atlanta. *Harper's Pictorial History of the Civil War,* II.

The War Department officers at Washington who have had charge of this part of the work of army organization have fallen very, very far short of being intellectual giants.

East Point, Ga.
September 29, 1864

[To A. C. O.] The enemy are attempting to break the railroad north of the Chattahoochee.[1] General Sherman has sent troops to protect it. We have here 40 or 50 days rations for the men, not so many for the horses. The army will move again in a few days. The enemy has burned one large mail for us soldiers a few days past.

A young artillery officer, Captain Francis DeGress, leaves today for Saint Louis and will call on you. He has no superior as a battery commander.

NOTE

1. In a wire to Halleck on September 9 Sherman commented: "I have ordered renewed activity, and to show no mercy to guerillas or railroad breakers. It makes a world of difference if 'my bull gores your ox, or yours mine.' " *OR,* Ser. I, vol. 38, pt. 5, p. 839.

Near Marietta, Ga.
October 10, 1864

[To A. C. O.] Our present headquarters are four miles north of Marietta. We hold Altoona [Allatoona]. The army is stretched out from Marietta to Rome covering the railroad. General Hood's headquarters are west of us. We have had no word from the north in two weeks.

Ship's Gap, Ga.
October 17, 1864

[To A. C. O.] We have been following General Hood since the 4 inst. and have marched about 110 miles. General Sherman has failed to overtake Hood and bring on a general battle as he had hoped to do.

A very severe battle was fought at Allatoona and we were successful. General Corse[1] who was in command was severely wounded in his face, but fought the battle out. He sat in the fort and commanded until the enemy drew off.[2]

General Hood threatened Resaca, but did not attack.[3] At Tilton the little garrison surrendered after a desperate defense and the block house in which they were was knocked into pieces about them.[4] At Dalton the commandant sent a flag of truce two miles and asked permission to surrender, which General Hood kindly permitted him to do. This was one Johnson, Colonel of the 44 Colored troops.[5]

Seven miles of the railroad was torn up between Big Shanty and Acworth and about sixteen between Resaca and Dalton. A small garrison at Acworth was captured. The garrison of 12,000 men left at Atlanta is in no danger.

General Sherman has 50,000 men with him and General Hood 30,000. General Hood's army being less in numbers and more lightly equipped can move faster than we, through these mountains. This at all events has been the case so far. General Sherman has succeeded in driving the enemy from the railroad and now the country and the railroad north of us is clear. Today Hood is at Summerville and is supposed to be going to the railroad at Blue Mountain.

Yesterday we came upon the enemy's rear guard and had a severe skirmish. Today we are getting clear of all encumbrances in hopes of overtaking Hood and making him fight. We will move this evening or in the morning, taking the same roads he has taken. So, at least, all the orders indicate. I do not think Hood will permit this army to overtake him.

The success General Sherman has had on the last campaign and especially in the taking of Atlanta has given the officers and men so great confidence in him that no one appears to have the least care or anxiety about the tearing up of the railroad or where General Hood goes or what he does.

NOTES

1. Brig.-Gen. John M. Corse.

2. Confederate Gen. S. G. French invested the garrison at Allatoona in an effort to capture large supplies of rations there. He asked Corse's surrender "to avoid a needless effusion of blood." Howard recounts the traditional story: "There were

Hood's attack on Allatoona. *Harper's Pictorial History of the Civil War,* II.

several dispatches which passed between Sherman and Corse during this engagement, among them the famous signal which came over the Confederate heads from the top of Kenesaw sixteen miles away at 6:30 A. M.: 'Hold fort; we are coming.' From this incident the famous hymn 'Hold the Fort, for I Am Coming,' was written by Major D. W. Whittle, my provost marshal and personal friend." Howard, *Autobiography*, II, 59, 62. The exact signal quoted by Howard does not appear in *OR*, but the messages in *OR*, Ser. I, vol. 39, pt. 3, and those quoted by Howard overlap and supplement the record; such a signal might well have been sent. Howard issued a special field order praising Corse and his men for their victory and "for the glorious manner in which they vetoed 'the useless effusion of blood.' " Corse received a promotion to Brevet Maj.-Gen. of Volunteers for his work at Allatoona. Howard, II, 62, 63.

Corse's stand at Allatoona further figures "in song and story" as one of the principal events in the delightfully crazy play *The Blue and the Gray; or War Is Hell,* revised and edited by Christopher Morley from an old script by Judson Kilpatrick and J. Owen Moore (New York, 1930). Kilpatrick and Owen's play was originally called *Allatoona.* In Morley's version it opened at the Old Rialto Theater in Hoboken in the fall of 1929 and ran for fifty-two performances. In it, according to its jacket, "Northern homes in the grave hysterics of mobilization . . . Southern belles and war and Sherman in Georgia, are presented to the reader in a kaleidoscope of humor and exaggerated sentiment."

3. Hood demanded on October 12, the unconditional surrender of the post and garrison at Resaca, declaring "if the place is carried by assault no prisoners will be taken." To this Col. Clark R. Wever replied: "In my opinion I can hold this post; if you want it come and take it." Shortly afterward reinforcements arrived and Hood did not attack. *OR*, Ser. I, vol. 39, pt. 1, pp. 753-54.

4. Gen. Alexander P. Stewart offered the garrison at Tilton the same terms Hood offered at Resaca. Lieut.-Col. Samson M. Archer's reply virtually duplicated Col. Wever's, but Archer was overwhelmed and forced to surrender. *OR*, Ser. I, vol. 39, pt. 1, p. 759.

5. Osborn puts this in a very different light from that in Col. Lewis Johnson's report to Col. R. D. Mussey, Commanding Officer, U. S. Colored Troops, Nashville, Tenn. Hood made the same demand he had made at Resaca. Johnson refused. Some skirmishing ensued. The demand to surrender was again made and again refused. Johnson then sent three officers under a flag of truce "with instructions to demand permission to inspect the rebel forces" to determine if resistance would be possible or if the post should be evacuated. Permission for such inspection was, of course, refused by aides on Hood's staff. They said the Confederates were determined to take the place and that no quarter would be given. Johnson declared: "To fight any more than had been done was madness, in the face of such barbaric threats which I was fully satisfied would be carried out, as the division of Cleburne . . . was over anxious to move upon the 'niggers,' and constantly violated the flag of truce by skirmishing near it, and to fight was also hopeless, as we were surrounded and could not be supported from anywhere." He reported that Hood declared he would return "all slaves belonging to persons in the Confederacy to their masters" and refused Johnson's insistance that his men be surrendered as soldiers. "The colored soldiers," he said, "displayed the greatest anxiety to fight, although all could plainly see what an immense force threatened us, and that there was no hope whatever. It grieved me to be compelled to surrender men who showed so much spirit and bravery." In a supplemental report of October 17 to Brig.-Gen. William D. Whipple, Johnson recounted indignities heaped on the Negro officers and soldiers. Several, including men taken

from the hospital and unable to travel, were shot and killed. *OR,* Ser. I, vol. 39, pt. 1, pp. 718-23.

On Little River, Ala,
October 24, 1864

[To A. C. O.] General Hood has drifted off to the west and General Sherman gave up the pursuit three days ago. Every thing now looks as if we should turn back and undertake a new campaign independent of him. This is enough to say at present.[1]

NOTE

1. Conyngham, *Sherman's March,* wrote (p. 233): "The pursuit continued... until Hood slipped from Sherman at Gadsden, and crossed the Tennessee River. Sherman exclaimed, 'Let him go north; our business is down south.' "

"There has been much conjecture," declared Conyngham (p. 232), "as to whether Sherman planned the programme of his great marches through Georgia and the Carolinas himself, or whether they were planned by Grant, and merely carried out by Sherman. From my own observation, I know that the programme of the campaign originated with Sherman himself, at Gaylesville, but, of course, was submitted to Grant's approval.... Travelling with Sherman, seeing all his movement, my firm impression is, that he was the originator, as well as the operator. Grant always said that the Confederacy was a shell. Sherman knew that, and intended to prove it, too."

Cedar Town, Ga.
November 1, 1864

[To A. C. O.] We are returning to Atlanta, moving but a few miles each day.

Smyrna Camp Ground, Ga.
November 6, 1864

[To A. C. O.] I am very busy now. Will write to you more at length as soon as I can get the time. I go to Atlanta tomorrow. This has been a very singular campaign. For several days General Hood has been going north and General Sherman going south. These two armies have practically been fighting each other since the beginning of the War. It is doubtful now whether they have not bid each other a final adieu and will never meet again.

Smyrna Camp Ground, Ga.
November 10, 1864

[To S. C. O.] We have had another campaign which has resulted in much more marching than fighting. When General Hood moved round our army at Atlanta and marched north General Sherman followed him, going in all about 180 miles, but was unable to overtake him and bring on a general engagement.

One of our depots of reserve supplies was at Allatoona, a partially fortified post, where the railroad passes through the mountains. This was commanded by General Corse, who had with him one of his own and part of another brigade. The enemy under General French[1] attacked this place with the intention of capturing the garrison, but mainly to get the rations stored there. A desperate fight followed and General Corse succeeded in holding the place and driving the enemy off. The enemy was so certain of taking the place that they had their supply train with them closed up to take away rations. General Corse was badly wounded by a bullet striking his cheek carrying a part of it away and passing through his ear. He did not give up the command, but held it until the enemy was driven off.

General Hood had a smaller army than General Sherman and moved lighter and consequently could move more rapidly. It was to General Hood's interest to avoid a fight and to General Sherman's to bring one on, but the greater rapidity with which the enemy could move and being favored by the mountainous character of the country, General Sherman was not able to force a battle. The enemy succeeded in destroying more than twenty miles of railroad which was repaired and trains running again in a week. They also attacked and captured several of the smaller garrisons along the railroad, in this way taking several hundred men prisoners. Our round trip occupied one month and one day. We marched between 280 and 300 miles.

While we were in the neighborhood of Resaca General Sherman placed General Thomas in command of all the country north of us, with headquarters at Nashville, and detached a large force from his own army and sent them north to Nashville. The object was to get a competent commander and a sufficient force north of Hood's army, to defeat him if he continues to move north, as he announced to his army he intended before he undertook this raid. General Sherman with the main body of his army returned to Atlanta, where we shall be in two or three days.

Wherever we have been on this campaign we have, so far as the country afforded supplies, lived off of the country and have pretty effectively cleaned it of all that man or beast could eat. The people who were so unfortunate as to live on the line of march of either of the armies will be sufficiently hungry this winter to regret that Hood ever made this raid. But this is one of the misfortunes of war, and war, at the best, is scientific cruelty.

The election is over but we have not heard a word of the result. It will be a calamity if General McClellan[2] is elected and becomes President with the copperhead party of the north at his back. However, I have no fear that he has been elected.

From present indications I do not think you will hear from me again in a month or six weeks. I think we shall be cut off from all mail facilities.

NOTES

1. Maj.-Gen. Samuel Gibbs French.
2. Gen. George Brinton McClellan.

Smyrna Camp Ground, Ga.
November 11, 1864

[To A. C. O.] I will give you a little account of what we have been about lately and what it has amounted to. As to future movements, I presume it would be imprudent to write while the mails are so uncertain. These I will write about when we get through with the next campaign. This last one has been interesting to me as it has taken me over most of the country the Army passed through while I was laid up with the broken ankle, which, by the

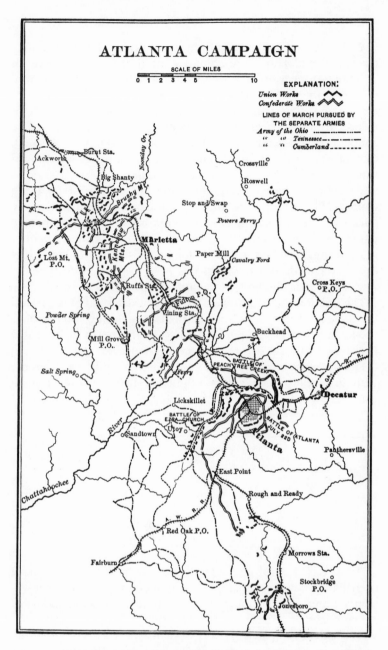

Map 1. Atlanta Campaign. From *General Sherman,* by Manning Force.
New York: D. Appleton and Company, 1899.

way, is not yet so far recovered but that I still use one crutch and one cane, though I will soon now throw away the crutch.

For several days before we left Atlanta we knew that General Hood was moving his army from Lovejoy's to Palmetto and Campbellton, on the Chattahoochee River. Apparently he had determined to execute the threat so often made by himself and which was confirmed by Jeff Davis, in a speech made at Palmetto, to pass above us, cut our communications and then move north. The southern newspapers continually reiterated this statement, but such statements are frequently made to attract attention only.

General Sherman, however, prepared Atlanta for any contingency which might arise and waited developments. About the first of October it was known that General Hood was at Villa Rica and north of it, west of the Chattahoochee. On the 1 and 2 General Stanley crossed the river at the railroad bridge and on the 2 General Davis[1] joined him connecting with his left and rear. On the 3 Generals Howard and Schofield crossed, and on the night of the 3 General Howard's army camped on the ground where we now are. It is an old camp meeting ground. At the same time General Hood with the greater part of his army was camped at Powder Springs, while General Stewart[2] of his army, with his own corps, was west of Lost Mountain and nearer Allatoona. On the 4 General Stanley moved north and camped south of the mountain.

The whole Army then, with the exception of 12,000 men left in Atlanta, were north of the Chattachoochee and in position to resist an attack if General Hood saw fit to make it and also to operate in any direction when it should become necessary.

The fact very soon developed that General Hood's cavalry was stronger then General Sherman's. Our cavalry was not able to reach the enemy's infantry or procure the information concerning their strength or movements, which it was absolutely necessary to have. This was a hindrance all through this campaign. On the other hand the enemy's cavalry was strong enough to secure information concerning our movement and strength and was very active.[3]

On the 5 General Stanley moved to Pine Top and General Schofield to Lost Mountain. The same day General Stewart attacked Allatoona. General Hood was lying at Powder Springs, waiting to hear the result of the assault on Allatoona. General Stewart's corps, aided by some cavalry, had taken Acworth and captured its little garrison and torn up several miles of railroad before it reached Allatoona. French's division of this corps went into position about Allatoona the night of the 4 and attacked at day light on the 5. Allatoona is a mountain pass and was partially fortified for a depot for reserve supplies. There were there at the time 1,500,000 rations. The garrison was small and the place meanly fortified. It had two small forts and a few trenches for infantry, none of which were completed. The natural position is strong, the engineering bad and the works unfinished.

During the night General Sherman signaled from Pine Top to General Corse who was at Rome, thirty miles away, to go to the assistance of the post at Allatoona. This he did taking with him by train 900 men—one small brigade. He had but barely got the men to the post and sent the train back when the enemy occupied the road in his rear. In the night he prepared for the attack and at daylight both he and French were ready. The fighting was very severe and the enemy made a lodgement within 300 yards of the fort and at a greater elevation than the fort, so that they commanded the inside of the fort, both with artillery and musketry. Our men were but slightly protected. With these advantages the enemy did their best and yet failed to get possession of the post and retired, or, more properly, they were repulsed.

The assault commenced at daylight and lasted until between nine and ten o'clock, but they did not withdraw from the neighborhood of the post finally until about noon. We lost in round numbers about 600 men of whom 260 fell in the fort which was only eighty feet in diameter. The one battery in the fort fired its last round as the enemy fell back. The captain of this battery[4] told me the dead and wounded in the fort were so thick he could not prevent the wheels striking them by the recoil of the guns and no one had time to move the dead and wounded. . . .

On the 5 General Howard was in camp in Culp's [Kolb's] Farm, six miles from Marietta. While so near Kenesaw Mountain I visited it and made an inspection of the works of the two armies and especially that part of the works where the battle was fought. I was much gratified by having an opportunity to see these works. But you have read so much about them I need not go into any detailed description of these. I was not with the Army when it passed through here on the Atlanta campaign.

The battle of Kenesaw Mountain will figure somewhat in the

history of the war and the works will then be considered as a military position. Kenesaw Mountain and the flanking hills is wonderfully strong. The view from the top of this mountain cannot be surpassed for beauty. In looking from the summit, one can judge how little of this country, comparatively, is cultivated. In the valleys the forests predominate over the cleared fields as at least twenty to one and on the hills one hundred to one.

On the 11 we moved from Kenesaw where we were watching General Hood's movements to Kingston. He held off so far to the west that his movements could hardly be determined or a guess made of what he proposed to do. At length it was known he was crossing the Coosa River at Cedar Bluff, near Cedar Town below Rome. On the afternoon of the 11 his main force was concentrated at this point and we moved to Kingston. We marched all night and made thirty-four miles with the entire column.

The following morning General Sherman, having concluded General Hood would attack Rome, moved his whole force there, but when he reached Rome he learned the enemy had moved too and reached the immediate neighborhood of Resaca, that our corps was skirmishing at Resaca and the remainder of the army was in easy supporting distance. General Raum,[5] commanding at Resaca, telegraphed that his surrender had been demanded, that skirmishing was going on and that he would hold out as long as possible. We were at once ordered to Resaca and made it, thirty-three miles in one day. We marched all night but the enemy had gone having made no general attack, but kept General Raum quiet while they destroyed the railroad north, nearly the entire distance between Resaca and Dalton.

At Dalton the enemy demanded, or rather accepted, the surrender of the post with 800 colored and 200 white troops. At Tilton two companies of old troops held a blockhouse and fought until the enemy knocked the blockhouse to pieces with artillery and then surrendered.

October 15 we left Resaca and passed through Snake Creek Gap. The enemy had fallen back across Taylor's Ridge to Lafayette and south to Subligna. They were holding the gap with two brigades and General Sherman wished to capture a part of all of this force. He directed General Howard to hold the eastern end of the gap and General Stanley to cross the ridge by a trail with his infantry and occupy the western end. Had these last orders been executed the capture would have been certain. The pass is a narrow ravine with a road running through it. The force in it was estimated from 1,000 to 2,000 men. It was a perfect trap. General Howard went into position and opened a sharp skirmish fight for the purpose of holding them in the gap until General Stanley could get over the mountain.

After he was heard from on top of the mountain and sufficient time was given for him to reach the western end of the gap, General Howard drove the enemy through. Meanwhile we had lost seven killed and several men wounded. While we were holding the eastern end of the gap, the enemy had filled the ravine with fallen timber and most effectually blockaded it. The engineer corps commenced to clear the road at two o'clock in the afternoon and at eight o'clock in the evening we had passed through with the artillery, but the enemy had gone and General Stanley had not been heard from. He afterwards reported that when he reached the summit with one brigade he waited for his corps to close up and it not coming, he had not thought it safe to attack. He made a weak and foolish failure and the enemy escaped, i.e. all except one or two companies which were captured.

I intended, when speaking of the operations about Rome and Resaca, to say that General Sherman was a good deal annoyed on account of his own movements. He thought that going from Kingston to Rome was a mistake. From Kingston he should have moved direct to Resaca, which he could have done in from 24 to 36 hours. He would have then been in time to have struck General Hood's column and turned it back, or having gone to Rome he should have crossed the Etowah and struck the enemy in flank and cut the column in two, separating the corps operating on the railroad from the main body. General Howard at Rome recommended this latter course. General Sherman fears that the operations of these three days will be considered in history as showing poor military judgement.

From Snake Creek Gap we moved to Taylor's Ridge for the purpose of crossing the mountain at Ship's Gap. In the gap we found the enemy's rear guard in considerable force and a disposition shown to contest the pass with the greatest tenacity. Indeed we could not dislodge them until we deployed a whole brigade as skirmishers and surrounded them. We took a half regiment prisoners. They were South Carolina troops. After getting clear of these men we found the road over the mountain and into the valley beyond open. There we camped for the night and most of the next day and until the columns on other roads had come up abreast, preparatory to concentrating at Summerville.

Our next camp was at Lafayette, a town of some military importance in this region on account of the many roads and mountain passes leading to it. Colonel Hawkins[6] of the calvary early last spring took refuge in the Court House at this place, where, with 400 men, he repulsed General Pillow[7] with 2,500. Colonel Hawkins was with us and pointed out to me the several places of interest connected with this fight. From the appearance of the Court House and the town he must have been hard pressed and have made a good fight.

General Hood was then moving ahead of us at the rate of twenty miles a day and we following at the same speed. This country is a series of mountains parallel to each other. The valleys are rich and afforded abundant rations and forage. In this pursuit we passed through Summerville, Alpine, Gaylesville, Cedar Bluff and Turkey Town, at which last place General Sherman gave up the chase on the 22. The enemy drifted to and beyond Gadsden.

We went into camp at Cedar Bluff and Gaylesville, where we remained about a week. As far as it was possible to do so, General Sherman put his Army into condition to return to Atlanta preparatory to a further campaign. He gave General Thomas the command of all the country and troops north of where we were, with headquarters at Nashville. He sent large bodies of troops north by rail to report to General Thomas.

Major J. W. Powell, Inspector of Artillery for the Army and Department of the Tennessee, went with General Thomas as his Chief of Artillery. General Thomas and the troops at his command are to operate against General Hood, if he shall attempt to go north beyond the Tennessee River.

Gaylesville had a peculiar charm for General Sherman as the place where, in his early days, he visited a young lady, the daughter of one of the former governors of the state and for whom the town is named. He took pleasure in pointing out the places of interest, even the old log house where he had visited, and of the scenes and incidents of the old time.

From Gaylesville we moved by easy marches back to this camp where we arrived on the 5 of November. In returning we passed through Cave Spring, which has been a splendid little town, Cedar Town, Dallas, Lost Mountain post office, to this camp.

Since we have been here General Hood's army has been lying at Tuscumbia and Florence while his cavalry has been bobbing around that part of the country.

Considering the extent of this raid by Hood, the damage done has not been great. The enemy destroyed several miles of railroad and captured some men. They have done some fighting, but in doing so have lost much heavier than we, having generally attacked entrenched positions. General Hood's main object, that of compelling General Sherman to abandon Atlanta and consequently this country, he has failed in. He also failed to capture any considerable amount of supplies and in fact failed in all the main objects of his raid so far as we can see and up to the present hour.

Yesterday morning the enemy attacked us in this camp with a brigade of cavalry, apparently to feel whether we still occupy this position. We lost one man killed and picked up seven of the enemy's dead.

We are looking every hour for orders to move to Atlanta and may yet leave this camp today.

NOTES

1. Brig.-Gen. Jefferson C. Davis.
2. Lieut.-Gen. Alexander Peter Stewart.
3. Brevet Maj.-Gen. James H. Wilson reported to Sherman at Gaylesville, Ala., October 24 to take command of the Cavalry Forces of the Military Division of the Mississippi. He reviewed the situation he found with the cavalry of Sherman's army in a long letter to Brig.-Gen. J. A. Rawlins, Gen. Grant's chief of staff, on October 26. He outlined the comparative strength of Federal and Confederate cavalry forces and commented: "If General Thomas is left in Tennessee the infantry forces must necessarily be more or less divided between him and General Sherman; if the cavalry force is divided equally between them, we shall effect nothing. Cavalry is useless for defense; its only power is in a vigorous offensive; therefore I urge its concentration south of the Tennessee and hurling it into the bowels of the South in masses that the enemy cannot drive back. . . . [He continues, asking great reinforcements and, particularly, the assignment of experienced officers.] All I wish is to get my tools in an efficient condition. I shall answer for the consequences. I have read this letter to General Sherman, and he concurs in what I have said. I would like, therefore, to have the officers sent to me whom I have designated, and horses, arms, and equipments sufficient to put my troops in the field, and the policy of concentration adopted, so, finally, that I may be able to exceed Forrest in numbers and organization." *OR,* Ser. I, vol. 39, pt. 3, pp. 414, 442-44.

The Fourteenth and Twentieth Corps moving out of Atlanta. *Harper's Pictorial History of the Civil War,* II.

4. Capt. Frederick Welker.
5. Brig.-Gen. Green B. Raum.
6. Col. Isaac R. Hawkins.
7. Brig.-Gen. Gideon J. Pillow.

Head Quarters Artillery
Army of the Tennessee.
Smyrna Camp Ground, Ga.
November 11, 1864

[To A. C. O.] I sent you today the usual letter after any considerable movement. I have been both busy and tired since our return
from the chase after General Hood or I should have written you
earlier.

It is now ten o'clock in the forenoon and the last train will pass
by here at twelve noon after which the railroad will be destroyed.
After that we will be at sea from 300 to 500 miles from anywhere.
I do not think you will hear from me again in less than six weeks.[1]
The Confederate newspapers will probably keep the country
pretty well informed of our whereabouts and of what we are
doing.

By telegraph we learned that Lincoln is elected. This is gratifying news. I hope there is no mistake about it and I do not think
there can be.[2]

In the orders for this movement and detaching of General
Thomas and sending him to Nashville places him in command of
all of the country in which Hood's, Forrest's[3] and other Confederate forces are operating. This includes all of the Department of the
Tennessee. By this new disposition of commands General Howard
retains the command of the active Army of the Tennessee in the
field, consisting of only the XV and XVII Corps, in all about
30,000 men. I am retained with him as Chief of Artillery of this
moving Army and in command of the batteries belonging to it.
This relieves me of the oversight and responsibility of the artillery,
light and heavy, of the Department as it relieves General Howard
of the command of all troops except of those with him here. I am
now Chief of Artillery of the Army of the Tennessee, not of the
Department of the Tennessee.

NOTES

1. Howard wrote his wife: "From present appearances we shall be cut off from communication for some little time. I don't know myself where we shall go, but we have stripped for a trip in the enemy's country." Oliver Otis Howard to Mrs. Howard, ALS(Autograph Letter Signed), Smyrna Camp Ground, Nov. 11, 1864. Howard Collection, Bowdoin College Library.

2. "From what we hear Lincoln must be elected as we have the report that all States so far as heard from have gone for him. McClellan's pro-slavery proclivities, have ruined him, for providence had to go on with the great work and leave him behind. I don't think he has a black heart, but he has made a mistake to ally himself with malcontents at such a time as this." Ibid.

3. Maj.-Gen. Nathan Bedford Forrest.

II The March to the Sea

Before Savannah, Ga.
December 13, 1864

[To S. C. O.] Communication has just been opened with the Naval Fleet after we have been cut off 33 days from all communication with the known world. The Army has come through from Atlanta all right.

The city of Savannah is held by about 20,000 men who must be either dislodged or captured. General Hazen carried Fort McAllister today by assault and has thus opened the Ogeechee River to the naval fleet and the transports. All is progressing well now, but for three or four days we have been very short of rations.

Before Savannah, Ga.
December 14, 1864

[To A. C. O.] This is the first opportunity to send a letter north and I will at once. Fort McAllister was carried by assault at five o'clock in the afternoon yesterday and this opened the Ogeechee River to the ocean and the fleet. Generals Sherman and Howard have now gone down to the blockading fleet. Our last rations were eaten today and I presume the army cannot be supplied inside of two days.

Savannah is completely invested on this side of the Savannah River and I presume will be carried by assault. We have no word yet from the north, or any where else outside our own lines.

Before Savannah, Ga.
December 17, 1864

[To S. C. O.] A ship load of mail has arrived for this Army and this headquarters received absolutely nothing. A strange oversight somewhere.

Since I wrote you from Marietta this army has marched about 300 miles, through the enemy's country, and that without serious difficulty. We have torn up and destroyed about 200 miles of railroad, burned all bridges and cleaned up the country generally of almost every thing upon which the people could live. The Army in this movement covered a strip of country about forty miles wide. We burned all cotton, took all provisions, forage, wagons, mules, horses, cattle, hogs and poultry and the many other things which a country furnishes and which may be made available for the support of an army. If fact, as we have left the country I do not see how the people can live for the next two years. Much of the country was very rich and a good deal of it very poor. There has been some fighting, but not much, except what the cavalry has done. We brought all our wounded with us in the ambulances and army train and what is surprising about this is we have never known men to do as well in hospital as they have done in the train on the road.

When we reached here we had driven 15,000 or 20,000 of the enemy into the city. The enemy had taken every possible precaution to prevent us from reaching the fleet. Troops, forts, torpedoes and all else their engineers could devise or furnish were employed. To get to the fleet, Fort McAllister on the Ogeechee River had to be taken. This is one of the oldest war forts and was considered safe from the possibility of capture. General Hazen with his division of 5,000 men took it in twenty minutes after he moved to the assault. It was desperately defended and besides being well garrisoned and mounted was protected by torpedoes buried in the sand outside the fort and also by strong and complete lines of abatis covering the entire front of the fort. The fort itself is a well built and strong work. General Hazen lost twenty-four men killed and 110 wounded. The most of this loss was from torpedoes which exploded as they were stepped on by the men just in front of the fort. The enemy's loss was forty-eight killed and wounded and in all about 280 prisoners. The taking of this fort was one of the most brilliant incidents of the war.[1]

Our communications are now open and we can be supplied. The Army was very hungry for a few days and lived on corn, rice and fresh beef and very short rations at that.

I have no positive knowledge of what our future movements are to be. If we remain here we shall capture the city. But there is a current rumor running through head quarters that General Grant has work for us elsewhere and that operations will cease here very soon. Whatever we are to do we shall probably do soon.

NOTE

1. Fort McAllister is on the right bank of the Ogeechee. Sherman, Howard, and a few other officers watched Hazen's attack on the fort from Cheves' rice mill across the river. Howard gives a detailed account of its progress in his *Autobiography* (II, 91). He describes its climax: "We all noticed an increased fire toward the fort, and our flags in men's hands, passing the obstructions. They crossed the ditch, then over the parapet; when we next saw them, the men were firing upward into the air from right to left, and the sound of their cheering came to us across the water. That, indeed, was a gallant assault!"

George Ward Nichols, an aide-de-camp of Sherman, wrote of Hazen: "General Hazen, the hero of Fort McAllister, is a West Point graduate, and not yet thirty years of age. In person, he is rather squarely built, is above the medium height, and has a fine, open, manly face; resolute, withal, but that kind of resolution which does not seem to need constant assertion.... His manner is that of an accomplished and refined gentleman. On the field of battle he is alert, self-assured, concentrated, brave and capable." *The Story of the Great March* (New York, 1865), 92.

Savannah, Ga.
December 21, 1864

[To S. C. O.] The enemy evacuated this city and crossed the Savannah River last night[1] and we entered and occupied it this morning. Thus the immediate object of the campaign is completed. This army has been transferred from the middle of the country to the sea coast, this city captured and all the lines for supplies for General Lee's army south of here are destroyed. The Confederacy proper is now southern Virginia and North and South Carolina. It has no other territory now at its disposal for military operations and this campaign has shown there is not much more left to it, ex-

Treasure seekers. G. W. Nichols, *The Story of the Great March.*

cept General Lee's army and the small force in our front. The fall
of Augusta, Columbia and Charleston are not far distant. They, like
Atlanta and Savannah, are great military depots.

We hear that General Thomas has defeated General Hood at
Nashville.[2] If this is correct it is a long step towards the end. General Hood had a brave, well disciplined Army. None better in the
Confederacy.

NOTES

1. Henry Lea Graves, a Confederate marine, wrote from Charleston to his
mother, Mrs. Sarah D. Graves, in Newton County, Ga., December 28: "The order
to retreat came at dark Tuesday the 20th. I have no words to picture the gloomy
bitterness that filled my breast on that dreary march through water, mud and
darkness. Independent of the various feelings of a soldier abandoning his native
State, of a patriot witnessing a disaster to his country's cause, and last but not
least, of the instincts of humanity thinking of the certain and terrible suffering
entailed on thousands in that devoted city, independent I say of all these, there
pressed upon me the consciousness that some of the best and truest friends I have
on earth were about to be abandoned in their utter helplessness to the power of
the enemy. . . . We started from the trenches at dark and reached the city at 12
o'clock midnight, halted an hour and then fell into the long line of silent men
who were pouring in a continuous stream over a pontoon bridge which had been
erected between the city and the Carolina shore."

His brother, Iverson Dutton Graves, was slower in writing their mother. He had
served in Savannah as a warrant master's mate aboard the CSS Savannah. On January 20 he wrote from James Island, S. C.: "You should have seen me as I started
out; to have appreciated the woe begone face and dismal groans that would have
greeted you as we sloped. On Tuesday night the city fell. . . . On Wednesday night
commenced our troubles. An order was issued to leave by 8 o'clock so forthwith I
buckled on my armor, made a little knapsack, put in two changes of clothes,
strapped on a blanket and shawl, and announced myself in readiness. How light
the load felt then, I thought I could walk a thousand miles with it and not tire.
The Yankees were kind enough to stop the shelling they had been treating us to
during the day, just as night fell, so we effected a landing on the South Carolina
shore in small boats without molestation. We were about six miles distance when
our ship blew up, and you have no idea what a sad blow it was to me. Thinks I,
there goes my pleasant quarters, my good clothes, my warm overcoat, and I am
forever cut off from Savannah and the hope of making myself agreeable to the
Sav. girls; my heart sank within me, my limbs ached, my load was terribly heavy,
and my eyelids had a mutual affection for each other. But I thought of my canteen
which I had been provident enough to fill with whiskey, and taking a good swig, I
felt the generous fluid to course through every vein and fill me with fresh
strength and spirit." Richard Harwell, ed., A Confederate Marine (Tuscaloosa,
Ala., 1963), 125, 127-28.

2. Gen. Thomas soundly defeated Hood at Nashville on December 15 and 16.

Savannah, Ga.
December 21, 1864

[To A. C. O.] We are at last in Savannah and without a fight. General Hardee evacuated the city last night and crossed the river going into South Carolina. We crossed the works at sun rise and occupied the city. We should have carried the works if we had assaulted them and captured the force inside, but we should have lost many men we now have. I think General Sherman is better satisfied as it is. We have 2,000 prisoners taken here....

Savannah, Ga.
December 26, 1864

[To A. C. O.] As this has been a somewhat remarkable campaign and you could not have learned much about it from the newspapers I will give you the outlines of it as nearly as I can by letter writing.

The orders preparatory to the campaign, as issued by General Sherman, all admitted of a double construction. Had any of them fallen into the hands of the enemy, they would have been at a loss to determine what he intended to do or where he intended to go. Before we left Atlanta General Sherman, apparently, talked very freely about his intended campaign and yet no two men could reach the same conclusion as to his final destination. Different officers who had heard him talk fixed his objective point all the way from Memphis by the south around to Charleston while still others thought he would go to Richmond via East Tennessee. So much for what the generals knew when the Army was concentrated at Atlanta to commence this campaign. The field and line officers knew just as much as the generals. No more and no less. Every one guessed what the General was intending to do and no one had any misgivings about the success of whatever he might attempt.

On the 12 of November this Army, the Army of the Tennessee, moved from the neighborhood of Marietta to Atlanta and camped at White Hall, south of the city. The army trains were loaded, but not in the regulation proportions of rations. Of coffee and sugar we took forty days and of salt eighty days. The ammunition taken was 200 rounds per man of infantry and 350 rounds per gun of artillery. This was equivalent to four or five days steady fighting for the entire army. The Army had been rapidly brought together at Atlanta and the railroad was then broken up between Atlanta and Chattanooga. That portion of the iron north of Etowah was carried to Chattanooga and that portion south of Etowah was destroyed. Forty miles of railroad each, south and west of Atlanta, had previously been destroyed.

The Army laid at Atlanta two days, during which time certain portions of the city were destroyed by burning.[1] All the storehouses, manufactories, railroad buildings and such large blocks as might readily be converted into storehouses were burned. Also a few dwelling houses were burned, but these were only such as took fire from other burning buildings. Still the center of the city was pretty thoroughly burned out.

I rode through the city while the fire was at its height. It seemed a pity that so many fine buildings should be destroyed. The principal buildings in Marietta were destroyed in the same manner.[2] I did not see those burned. This is in keeping with General Sherman's view of conducting the war. He believes it best not only to break up their armies, but also to make the country feel it and to destroy everything which can be employed directly for military purposes, such as their lines of transportation, store houses, factories, accumulated supplies and every other available military resource.

While at Atlanta General Sherman organized the Army of Georgia comprising the XIV and XX Corps, to which General Slocum[3] was assigned as commander.

In this campaign the Army of the Tennessee was designated as the right wing, and the Army of Georgia as the left wing.

At that time General Hood was at Tuscumbia. General Wheeler,[4] with a cavalry corps, was watching us and General Hardee, with a small corps of veterans, militia and other trash, such as he could get together in an emergency, was at Macon.

On the 14 of November we received General Sherman's plans for the "First Stage of Campaign." In substance they were, the right wing was to move south from Atlanta on the east side for the Atlanta and Macon railroad, threaten Griffin, then turn east and cross the Ocmulgee River at Planters' Factory, then south threatening Macon, strike the Central [of] Georgia railroad and destroy it, concentrating this wing at Gordon. This to be accomplished in seven days.

General Kilpatrick[5] was to cover our right with the cavalry.

General Slocum with the left wing was to follow the Atlanta and Augusta railroad to [the] Oconee [river] then south to Eatonton and Milledgeville, all to be accomplished in seven days. No fortified towns were to be attacked and no considerable body of troops molested, but only threatened by either wing.

On the 15 of November the Army broke camp and moved out on this campaign. General Sherman made his headquarters with General Slocum, with the XIV Corps, left wing. Of General Howard's command the XV Corps had the right and the XVII the left. General Howard made his headquarters with the XV Corps. We met with no disturbing force the first day until near evening when we encountered a few of the enemy's scouts watching us. We camped for the night at Stockbridge. While we were going into camp the enemy opened on us with musketry and artillery but a brisk skirmish was all that came of it. General Kilpatrick found the enemy at Jonesboro in too strong force to be moved by him.

When we moved on the morning of the 16 the enemy had left our front.[6] It proved to have been only a detachment of cavalry watching us. The head of our column reached McDonough at noon and halted for the army to close up. The country to this place had been stripped of every thing which could be made of use to the army. At Lovejoy's General Kilpatrick attacked a force in position and after a sharp fight and a charge captured fifty prisoners and one battery, two guns of which had belonged to General Stoneman at the time he was captured. The enemy, mostly militia, were routed and abandoned, or threw away most of their arms. The General reported that his men picked up and destroyed 500 muskets which had been thrown away along the road.

On the 17 we moved to Jackson. Having left the country which has for a long time been traversed by the enemy's forces we found it well supplied with provisions, forage and animals. When we left Atlanta we were pressed for animals, ours having been reduced in numbers by the long march after General Hood, and what we had were thin in flesh from the want of sufficient forage, arising from the rather frequent breaks in the railroad north of Atlanta.

At Jackson we began the system of foraging which we employed until the close of the campaign. The plan of operations adopted were, a detail was made of men from each regiment and sufficient officers from each brigade to command them. These were then organized into companies. Both the officers and men detailed were selected on account of their reliable and soldierly qualities. These companies were then sent out into the country ahead of and on the flanks of the columns to gather up whatever provisions, forage, and animals the country afforded. They spread themselves over the entire country and every thing available for the use of the army was gathered in. The food animals were slaughtered where found, the horses and mules were brought to the Army, or rather to the brigade to which the detachment bringing them in belonged. The provisions and forage were brought in by army wagons or in such vehicles as the men could pick up in the country. The orders of General Sherman directed that private property at the houses, not available to feed the army, should not be disturbed. I think this order was generally complied with, though probably not always. Whenever cotton was found it was burned. I think but a few houses were destroyed.[7]

We went into camp at noon at Jackson. This was a beautiful little place and evidently occupied by the most prosperous people of that region. The white population has not exceeded 300 people. Most of them left before we visited their town. In fact all along the line of our march the white population in advance of us ran away from home. As these people did not know which way to go they generally ran from one column into another where they were then stopped, their animals taken and the people left at the nearest house or shelter, whether it was large or small, until the Army passed and the country was clear for them to go where they chose. When we left Jackson the people were a sadder if not a wiser community. Little was left them besides themselves and their houses.

Our orders required us to go to Planters' Factory on the Ocmulgee River, twenty miles from Jackson. This is a rolling red clay, well cultivated country. We found a good deal of cotton and under General Sherman's instructions burned it.

The weather being clear and no wind we could determine the march of the several columns by the smoke rising from the burned cotton. Frequently as many as twenty-five of these columns of smoke could be seen at the same time. The men we met in this section were civil but the women were not inclined to take our innovation so good naturedly.

While the name Planters' Factory designated a locality it was in fact a cotton factory only, with the necessary dwelling and other buildings about it. It was a fine factory on the Ocmulgee River, had seventy-five looms and all the necessary machinery for taking raw cotton and turning out cloth. The owner said he had purchased it a month before we destroyed it. He told us that he paid $450,000 for it of which $20,000 was gold, a considerable sum in English stocks and the remainder in Confederate bonds. The revenues from it must have been large. The owner had had a factory burned at McDonough by General Stoneman, after which he had purchased this.

We laid our pontoon bridge near the factory without difficulty, the enemy making but little resistance. It required thirty-six hours for the XV Corps with 16,000 men, its artillery, supply train and driven stock to cross this bridge. While we were crossing the river a severe storm set in, which, by the way, lasted several days, and gave us much trouble. At the eastern end of the bridge the bank rose quite abruptly, making a steep hill. The falling rain softened the clay ground and made the crossing difficult. The wagons and artillery carriages were helped up the hill by over 1,000 men stationed along the road between the river and crest of the hill.

Before we crossed this bridge, at my request, General Howard directed the artillery officers to select from the horses gathered in the country such and so many as their batteries required and also that all officers who were entitled to be mounted should select what horses they needed and the same to the quarter masters for their trains.

A detachment was then stationed at the bridge with orders to take all surplus animals from the column. When this was done a small regiment of infantry was mounted as cavalry from the horses taken out and the worthless animals remaining, about 1,000 of them, were shot. Since then the artillery, wagon trains, cavalry and mounted officers have been well supplied with horses.

When we left the river an officer with a squad of men was directed to burn the factory and all its belongings. This was done, including the factory, store house, 700 bales of cotton and other property. The able bodied negroes found at this place volunteered to enter the service and were put into the Engineer Corps.

On the 19 we passed through Monticello, a pretty little village, and, as we saw it, remarkable for the great number of young ladies. No men except a few old ones were to be seen, all others being in the army or in the swamps hiding from the conscription officers. This is a force, by the way, these people appear to dread more than they do our army. If one can judge correctly from what these people say, this is surely so.

An incident happened here which had a decidedly ludicrous side to it. Some one of the citizens—young lady in fact—told our men that a Captain Bradly of General Iverson's[8] staff was hiding in the town and where he could be found, and that it would be agreeable to her if we would take him along, also that he was a notorious rough and boasted that he could whip any man in Georgia. Our men took him in, but gave him the personal liberty granted in such cases to officers, upon which he fired a pistol at the man who captured him, but missed him. Upon this notice of hostilities the soldier handed his musket to a comrade and went at Bradly with his fists, knocked him down and bruised his face badly. He was then turned in with the other prisoners and told to move along. This he refused to do, saying he must have a horse or he would not go. Therefore one of the guard gave him, from the rear, about an inch of his bayonet, after which the Captain concluded to walk. I saw him an hour later and he was a sorry looking specimen. The point of it all was the citizens deliberately turned this stupid fellow over and both the men and ladies appeared to enjoy his troubles intensely.

We camped on the 19 at Hillsboro which is a place in name only. General Kilpatrick was still on our right. We had not yet heard from General Slocum.

On the 20 we moved from Hillsboro to Clinton. The march was easily made. The only item worthy of note on this march was our passing over the field where General Stoneman was captured on the bank of Sunshine Creek, six miles from Clinton. This country abounds in peaches and much peach brandy is manufactured from them. The citizens told us that General Stoneman's men were deliberately made drunk on this brandy and while they were still drunk were crowded and captured. We were told also that the General was under the influence of liquor, but as the General never drinks intoxicating liquors of any kind this is an error. It is not impossible this accounts for the misfortune of that command. Some of the men captured with General Stoneman were now with General Kilpatrick and it was with much difficulty he restrained them from burning the town of Clinton. I believe they succeeded in burning a few houses.

Clinton is twelve miles from Macon. Every precaution was taken to induce the enemy to believe we were moving directly on Macon and we succeeded in making them believe it and to concentrate their entire force there. General Kilpatrick cut the railroad near the city to prevent the force in Macon from moving quickly to the east or making an attack on our right flank. When General Howard was satisfied that the enemy had concentrated their whole force in Macon and would wait for us to attack there, he turned the head of the column to the left.

On the 21 we moved direct to Gordon. One division kept far enough to the right to strike the railroad midway between Macon and Gordon. The XVII Corps moved directly to Gordon where it found a brigade of the enemy and drove it east. The XV Corps halted five miles before reaching Gordon and camped for the night. General Kilpatrick assaulted the enemy's works east of Macon and charged over the outer line, but finding the inner works well manned fell back.

On the 22 the Army was moved to and along the railroad and the wagon train closed up. The roads were bad, the horses worn and it was with difficulty the train was brought up.

General Sherman's orders to General Howard was to march to Gordon in seven days. This he had done. General Slocum's army, with which General Sherman was, was to have been at Milledgeville the same day, but nothing could be learned concerning it from citizens or otherwise. The General attempted to communicate with General Sherman by sending Captain Duncan,[9] of the headquarters scouts, with four men to Milledgeville. When the captain reached the outskirts of the town the Mayor[10] came out and formally surrendered the city, the capital of the state. The captain accepted the surrender and the mayor's hospitality, going to his house and taking a glass of wine with him and his friends. He made it convenient however to make his call short for fear the strength of his army would be discovered. He burned the depot and a train of cars as he left the city. As was afterwards learned several soldiers were in the city, but they had all gone to cover and

Sherman and his generals. From left: *seated,* John A. Logan, William T. Sherman, Henry W. Slocum, *standing,* Oliver O. Howard, Judson Kilpatrick, William B. Hazen, Jeff C. Davis, Frank P. Blair, Jr., Joseph A. Mower. *Harper's Pictorial History of the Civil War,* II.

did not come out until he left. He neither found or heard of General Slocum.[11]

We learned in Gordon that the convicts in the penitentiary in Milledgeville had been organized into a company of 140 men, under officers of their own selection. They were in service in General Wayne's[12] command which General Blair[13] found in Gordon, but we soon had the most of them as prisoners, deserters and such like.

On the 23 the headquarters remained at Gordon while the most of the army and trains moved to the east of it. The railroad was destroyed from the farthest point west which our troops had occupied, east as far as our troops went that day.

The incident of the day was the battle of Griswoldville. General Walcutt's[14] brigade of General Woods'[15] division crowded up towards Macon to feel of the enemy and having advanced as far as was prudent entrenched. He was then attacked by the entire force occupying Macon which was just at that time making an attempt to pass to the east and get in our front before, as they supposed, we could occupy the railroad in sufficient force to stop them. General Walcutt had 1,400 men and the enemy's force was estimated at from 5,000 to 6,000 men under General Philips.[16] The enemy charged over an open field and was repulsed. This was repeated several times and each time with the same result. Our entire loss was ninety-four, including killed, wounded and missing. We buried in round numbers 300 of the enemy's dead. The Confederate papers put the enemy's loss at 640. It was certainly not less.

All the wounded from that fight were put in our train and brought with us. At this time not one of those men has died. Among the wounded is one man with both legs off and one with one leg and one arm off. Both would have died with ordinary hospital treatment, but the open air has saved them all. General Walcutt had about two ounces of flesh carried from his leg by the fragment of a shell.

On the 24 headquarters remained at Gordon and we completed tearing up the railroad to the Oconee River. The XV Corps was moved east of Gordon.

General Howard communicated with General Sherman and received the orders for the "Second Stage of the Campaign," which were substantially the Army of the Tennessee move along the railroad and destroy it to Millen, the Army of Georgia to keep to our left and make a junction with us at Sandersville.

We learned that the XV Corps had followed the Augusta (Georgia) railroad and destroyed it to the Oconee River and then turned south and with the XX Corps moved to Milledgeville. The left wing of that army foraged on the country to the same extent and in the same manner as the right wing.

On the 25 we moved with the headquarters twenty-five or thirty miles to Ball's Ferry where the main body of our army had concentrated. The pine country commences about ten miles west of the river and the quicksand bottoms [commence] about five miles west of the river.

The counterpart of this quicksand land, I believe is to be found no where else except in the coast region of the southern states. The surface of the ground is hard and apparently firm. After a few heavy wagons or half of a battery has passed over it the surface or crust breaks. This hard surface is found to be about four inches thick and is sufficiently strong to bear the domestic vehicles of the country. All under this hard crust is quicksand in which, when the crust is broken, the horses go to their knees and the vehicles to the hubs. After this nothing can be moved on the roads until the entire surface of the roads on this peculiar soil is corduroyed.

Ball's Ferry is at the crossing of the river where the road on the west side runs five miles over the quicksand. The enemy held the eastern bank and skirmished sharply, though fortunately not one of our men was hit, though the enemy had some wounded. The river was high and rapid. [Because of] these natural hindrances, together with the annoyances given by the enemy's skirmishers, we had an unpleasant job in getting the bridge down. This was finally accomplished by sending a detachment a mile or two up the river, where by using pontoon boats they made a flying bridge. With this sufficient men were put over the river to turn the enemy on the road in front of us out of position. After this the pontoon bridge was laid at our leisure. This being accomplished and the road over the quicksand corduroyed, the Army passed over without further annoyance.

Our headquarters having crossed the river, on the 26 we made headquarters at the large country house and residence of Mr. Irwin.[17] The locality is known as Irwin's Cross Roads. The owner is in some way connected with the state government. He left just before our troops reached his place. We learned that General Wheeler the day before crossed the river fifteen miles south and with his command had just passed Irwin's before our column arrived. He gave out that he was going after General Kilpatrick who had moved over to the front and left of General Slocum's command. The great railroad trestle over the low lands and the bridge over the river were burned.

On the 27 the headquarters remained at Irwin's to see everything over the river and well on its way east before we broke camp.

Leaving Irwin's on the 28 we struck out into the great pine forest of eastern and southern Georgia. On the large state maps are indicated, by lines, what purport to be the roads through this country. These roads are generally mere trails and in many cases they are barely, if at all, distinguishable by a person unaccustomed to the country in riding on them. The people of the country speak of this road and that, as roads are spoken of in densely settled communities at the north, and yet a person not accustomed to them can scarcely follow them. Out of this peculiarity of the roads we had that day a singular experience.

In making the order of march for the day the map of Georgia was consulted and the right division was directed to move to "Johnson's." General Howard and staff moved with this division. We soon found the column was moving more to the south than appeared proper, and no man we could find, white or black, had ever heard of Johnson's. We were in Johnson county and assuming the county site was intended, we found that was Wrightsville and moved the column there. We reached it at noon and found a little village of a dozen families.

General Howard with an aide and a few scouts started out to find where he was and how far from the other columns, and after riding three miles met a squad of headquarters scouts looking for him. From them he learned the remainder of the Army was at Griddlesville, fifteen miles to our left. Starting at once for the other column he sent word for his staff to follow at once and the division in the morning.

The General rode a horse of remarkable speed and endurance and we knew we could not overtake him. We started at sunset to ride fifteen miles in the night by these trails. I was called upon to take the lead or act as guide in a country I knew nothing about and

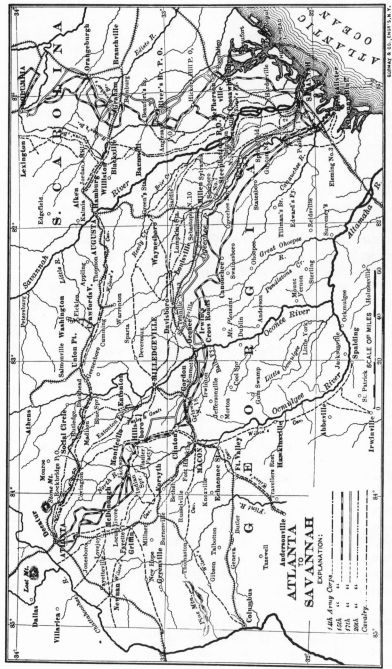

Map 2. Atlanta to Savannah. From *General Sherman*, by Manning Force. New York: D. Appleton and Company, 1899.

in the night, and in addition I rode a half broken colt, though a very powerful animal. When it became dark there was nothing to do but go on. I had no alternative but to take the general direction and trust to the instincts of this horse to keep the trail and pilot us through. I gave her the rein and she, dropped her nose close to the ground, started off in a swinging trot and kept that pace going almost like the wind and in less than three hours we had made the journey.

There was but one halt in this ride. After we had gone about five miles we found a fence across the road in front of a dwelling house, called people out and found them not disposed to give any satisfaction until we led them to believe we belonged to the Confederate cavalry and were at once given all the information we desired.

After reaching the camp of our troops we learned we still had five miles to go to General Howard's headquarters. We reported to him at half past ten having made in all twenty miles in about four hours.

The pine forests in that part of Georgia are immense. In some respects campaigning in them is pleasant. The roads are hard and solid to move the trains on, except where the quicksand bottoms are found near the rivers and creeks. The general character of the country made the moving of the army easy, but the country afforded very few supplies for the Army itself and the foragers had hard work to furnish it with provision and forage.

On the 30 General Blair moved his command to station $9^{1}/_{2}$[18] on the railroad and relieved General Slocum's command in destroying the road, which work for a few days the Army of Georgia had been doing. In this movement the right wing again came upon the railroad and the left wing moved north of it. At this time General Sherman made his headquarters with the XVII Corps, which was then on the left bank of the Ogeechee River and the XV on the right bank.

The 1 of December presented nothing of interest, except the vast extent of these pine forests. I think it was on that day, General Sherman wrote to General Howard to keep the head of the XV Corps on the right bank of the river well ahead of the XVII Corps on the left bank of the river and on the railroad, in order that the XV Corps could be crossed over to the left bank and turn General Hardee out of position whenever he became troublesome in front

Destruction of Millen Junction. *Harper's Pictorial History of the Civil War,* II.

of the XVII Corps. General Hardee had put all the troops at his disposal in front of General Blair to annoy and hinder him while he was destroying the railroad. After this order was received, if General Hardee[19] would not move when the head of the XV Corps passed him General Howard laid a bridge over the river and began to move his column over it. This always started the enemy at once. They did not wait to fight.

General Howard with the XV Corps reached station 8[20] on the railroad. The XVII did not quite reach the station.

On the 2 we had the same disposition of the two corps. The XV Corps crossed Sculls Creek, a deep stream, which it was necessary to bridge. At this point the forests begin to show a more southern character. We saw the cypress, magnolia and live oaks as well as the spanish moss.

The XVII Corps, with which General Howard was, was too far ahead of the XVII Corps and the left wing was falling behind the right. General Sherman, in his letter of that day to General Howard, complained of the slowness of General Slocum's movements. The two corps moving on either side of the Ogeechee River were only a little way separated, each following the road parallel to the river and nearest it.

On the 3 the XVII Corps continued to destroy the railroad, while the XV did not move forward but laid a bridge across the river sending one division over and turned General Hardee out of position. This division destroyed several miles of the railroad thus helping General Blair along with that work.

General Blair occupied Millen, burned the depot[21] and ware houses and did such other work as was necessary. The town amounts to nothing. There is a prison pen there and General Sherman made an effort to rescue the prisoners confined in it, but of course failed. As soon as there was real danger, the enemy moved them out of reach. Millen, as the junction of the railroads, is of military importance and in the same sense as Branchville in South Carolina is of military importance. I am told there is only a water tank there and yet both armies are speculating on the possibility of our making an effort to get possession of it and of its value in this contest. It certainly is, in the military sense, of value.

The enemy developed no considerable strength but still had force enough to annoy the head of the column.

On the 4 there was no change from the usual routine of the march and the work.

On the 5 General Sherman directed General Blair to destroy the railroad to station 3½[22] or 35 miles from Savannah and there its destruction was to be abandoned. The XV Corps was to go to Statesboro.

On the 6 the right wing remained in camp for the left wing to come up abreast. The enemy began to show temper and skirmish sharply, and it was now evident they had all along been undecided in their minds as to our intentions or destination. The XV Corps being south of the Ogeechee looked as if we might be going to Brunswick, the XVII on the railroad looked as if we were heading for Savannah and the left wing appeared to be starting for Augusta and perhaps Charleston.[23]

Here, however, we stopped to bring the Army up abreast and cover the peninsula between the Ogeechee and the Savannah rivers, so as to drive every thing in front of us into Savannah. There were two bridges over the Ogeechee twelve miles ahead of us, with good roads leading to them. We made an attempt to get possession of them, but the enemy was too quick for us and burned them and then for some hours held the road with strong skirmish lines. The uncertain movements and operations of the enemy had convinced us that up to this time our destination was a matter of conjecture only and they assumed we would go to any point rather than to Savannah. But as the Army was now brought up across the peninsula, they realized we were going direct to that city.

On the 7 Army was closed up so as to cover the peninsula and the XV Corps moved down to the bridge opposite station 2.[24] We cleared the enemy from the river and laid the bridge. General Sherman thought it was then necessary to keep the Army well in hand in order that, if General Lee[25] should send a strong detachment down to make a fight, it would not be able to strike one corps when out of reach of support.

On the 8 the XV Corps was again ahead of the XVII, but the disposition of the Army was such, that it could all be made available in case of an attack. The XVII Corps was ordered to move to station 1,[26] 10 miles from Savannah. One division of the XV was sent beyond the Ogeechee to cut the canal, while two divisions were sent across the country to cut the Atlantic and Gulf railroad at station 2.[27] The skirmish lines holding the streams prevented this force from reaching that railroad. The canal was cut. General Slocum was expected to cut the Savannah and Charleston railroad. if both of these roads had been cut we should have captured all the rolling stock in Savannah. The enemy skirmished stubbornly and we learned they were planting torpedoes and had planted them in the roads. The prisoners were ordered to dig them up under the direction of their own officers. They remonstrated sorely but were compelled to do it nevertheless.[28]

On the 9 the XVII Corps moved as before, but made only four miles. The enemy in its front showed much temper. At one point General Blair was compelled to develop a division and send a long skirmish line through the swamp to dislodge the force in his front. The country in this region is swampy and very difficult to operate in. The roads cut through the swamps are generally straight and the road bed is raised a few inches above the swamp water level. The enemy's plan of resistance was to place a battery on the road so as to sweep it and support the battery with a strong infantry support. These tactics made our operations in the swamps tedious.

General Corse with his division struck the enemy well entrenched and apparently determined to fight. The General drew back a little and made the necessary disposition to attack. The enemy saw an attack was coming in sober earnest and promptly withdrew.

In this little affair, the enemy placed two guns on the road in such a position as to do us some damage. They were but a few hundred yards away. I ordered two guns forward to silence them. This section of guns moved rapidly down the road to a sharp turn where they came in plain view of the enemy's guns about a quarter of a mile away. Quickly going into position, they fired one shot from each gun and seeing the enemy's men run from the guns fired no more. We soon reached the guns and found to our great surprise that one had been struck in the muzzle and knocked off the carriage and the axle of the other was broken. These were Blakely guns just imported from England and were never before used. The shippers' mark in white paint on the guns and carriages was not soiled.

Immediately after the above incident General Howard accompanied by an escort of mounted men, rode to the Altantic and Gulf railroad and broke it. As he did this a train of cars from Savannah came up but seeing our men on the track the train commenced to back. At that minute Captain Duncan of the headquarters scouts struck the track back of the train. Not having time to break it, he led a mule on the track and shot it, so it fell across the rail. In an instant the rear car struck the mule and was thrown from the track. This was a passenger train carrying prominent people out of Savannah.[29]

General Sherman was exceedingly anxious to inform the fleet known to be lying off the coast he had arrived in the neighborhood of the coast, and every device was tried to attract their attention. Rockets were fired at night, and I attempted to attract attention by throwing shells as high as possible in the air and exploding them there. This I did both day and night but without effect. We failed to let them know we were there, or rather they failed to recognize our signals.

Having failed in this General Howard sent Captain Duncan down the Ogeechee River to communicate with the fleet. At dark the Captain left King's bridge in a dug-out, accompanyed by two of his men, to float down the river on the tide. Before reaching Fort McAllister he found morning was too near to pass the fort before light. He stopped at the house of a negro and letting him know he was a Union soldier, the family promised to take care of him. He remained through the day, but the men at the fort had in some way had their suspicions aroused that some one was trying to pass and made a search for him. They entered this house but Duncan and his men were hidden under the floor and the negroes denied any knowledge of them.

The next night our old negro piloted the dug-out past the fort, the torpedoes and the picket boats. The morning was foggy and when the fog rose, they were ten miles out in the bay. The Captain acknowledges he was then frightened. The enemy would be as likely to see him as our people and the slightest wind would swamp the boat. Seeing what he supposed was a gun boat ten miles away he commenced to paddle for it. He had just struck out when an armed boat came out from behind an island and made for him. He believed this one of the enemy's boats until they were near, when the men raised our flag. This boat came from a gun boat which the captain did not see, but from which he had been seen.

Assault on Fort McAllister. *Harper's Pictorial History of the Civil War,* II.

He was first taken on board the gun boat and from it sent to Admiral Dahlgren's flag ship. He took the first news of the arrival of General Sherman on the coast to the fleet. Every attention was shown him and the three days he remained with the fleet he received a continued ovation.[30]

Captain Duncan is twenty-six years of age, medium size, fair hair and complexion, moderate ability, great energy and wonderful personal recklessness.

On the 10 General Sherman determined to get his army up and develop the enemy's defenses. So far General Blair had taken but little part in the skirmishing near the city. He then moved up and with his left resting on the river he felt his way up to the works about the city which he found located three miles from it. He suffered some from one or two heavy guns which swept the main road. The XV Corps moved up on the right of the line to find the enemy's works. This it did. We found on our right if the works had been held by veterans, instead of by militia, as they were, we should have been badly hurt, but as it was we escaped without injury. Twice the head of our column came within pistol range of the enemy's entrenched artillery and they did not fire. Veterans would not have been so considerate of our welfare.

This line extended from the Savannah River to the Little Ogeechee. The rice fields and the marsh lands were considered sufficient protection for their left flank. The indications were that the works had been constructed to be garrisoned by about 20,000 men. General Sherman did not wish an assault made or desire to take any chances. Our rations were running short and it was desirable to hear from the fleet before any thing further was done.

On the 11 the Army of Georgia relieved the XVII Corps and part of the XV and occupied the trenches on about two thirds of the line. The greater part of the Army of the Tennessee fell back in reserve to be employed in opening the Big Ogeechee River to the ocean. All attempts to attract the attention of the fleet failed. We continued our effort to get their notice. Each night rockets were sent up, but elicited no response. I again tried with artillery. Taking a battery to Cheves rice plantation, the farthest point east we could reach, I opened fire on Fort McAllister. The range was very long but I still was able to throw shells in the fort and did so but the garrison would not reply probably because no one of their guns was so mounted that it could be brought to bear on us. In the night I threw shells into the air exploding them a half mile high, but this did no good.

The fleet was reported on the coast two days before we arrived here, but we could not find it. We had plenty of beef, but other food was nearly gone. We found some threshed rice, but it was in the hull. This was issued to the men. There was plenty of rice in the straw within reach, so we should not starve, but this was poor food to feed an army on.

General Sherman concluded Fort McAllister must be taken, that being done the river would be open to the ocean. The only other alternative was to go south of the Ogeechee River and out to the coast. General Kilpatrick had already been to the coast to find a suitable harbor to go to if the taking of Fort McAllister should fail.

On the 12 General Hazen was selected by General Howard to take the fort with his division and to move as soon as the King's bridge could be repaired so he could cross the Big Ogeechee River. The work of repairing the bridge was urged on as rapidly as possible. Otherwise the Army did nothing.

On the 13 the conditions along the line were rapidly assuming those of a siege. Most of the time the camp remained quiet, but this quiet was now and then broken by sharp artillery firing.

Before daylight General Hazen started for Fort McAllister. By the road it was nineteen miles. It was thought he would reach the fort at noon. Generals Sherman and Howard went to the Cheves rice mill which commands a view of the fort across the river to watch the assault. The timber in rear of the fort had been cleared off so, not only the fort, but the movements of the troops in rear of it, could be seen from the mill. About noon a gun boat appeared in the river below the fort and stopped before reaching the torpedoes. I was with General Howard and the following signal dispatches were as near as I now recall them.

General Sherman signaled the boat and it answered "Who are you." The General replied "Generals Sherman and Howard. Who are you." Answer "Admiral Dahlgren[31] and General Foster,[32] what can we do for you. Is Fort McAllister ours?" Answer "No but it will be in a few minutes."

Just as they had gone so far General Hazen moved to the assault. The musketry from the assaulting force and the musketry and artillery from the fort showed it was being made in earnest. Our troops fired but one volley, the enemy fired continually. Our line moved around the fort, the flanks resting on the river above and below. Our men made no halt, but moved directly to the fort, clambered up its sides and over it into the fort. In reaching the fort they went over two or three lines of abatis and a complete circle of torpedoes between the abatis and the fort. From our position we could see every movement. There was no cessation in fighting from the moment the line moved until our men were in the fort and the garrison was driven to one side of the fort itself. When General Hazen's men who had not gotten into the fort saw that it was taken they fired their muskets in the air and gave a cheer which we heard. Generals Sherman and Howard at once took a skiff and went to the gun boat, taking the chances of running against the torpedoes in the river.

Our loss was 24 killed and 110 wounded. The enemy lost 48 and the entire garrison of 280 men was captured. A large percentage of our killed and wounded were by the torpedoes exploded by the men stepping on them after the fort was taken. These torpedoes were planted in the sand outside the fort and inside the lines of abatis. There were mounted in the fort twenty-five heavy guns. This was the strongest and best built sea fort on the coast. Capture opened the river to the entrance of the supply transports and we could get rations and forage for the Army.

No finer piece of military work has been done anywhere than was that of taking Fort McAllister.

From the 13 to the 20 there occured nothing to vary the monotony of ordinary siege operations. All of this time I was on court martial duty. The Army was supplied with rations and forage by the way of the Big Ogeechee River. About the 18 General Sherman demanded of General Hardee the surrender of Savannah making in his demand, as an alternative, if he should be compelled to carry the city by assault, that he would give the city up to the men for two days without resistance. He sent with this a copy of the communications of General Hood to the Commander at Dalton, in which he says he will show no quarter, if he is compelled to carry the place by assault. General Hardee replied that he declined to surrender, and that in the conduct of the war he had always been governed by the usage of civilized nations. They were both "only talking," and both knew it.

As soon as General Sherman received General Hardee's reply he ordered, that under no circumstances should an assault be made and then went to Hilton Head. All the preparations for an assault were completed on the 20. The enemy's position in our front was thoroughly reconnoitered and an abundance of places found where the works could be carried.

Light bridges were made to throw across the creeks. The troops were distributed to make the assault when General Sherman should return.

On the night of the 20 an active artillery fire was kept up by the enemy along the whole line till mid-night and along our front till two o'clock. We were sure the enemy was leaving, but the orders to not attack were positive and we let them go without annoyance.

At daylight our pickets were over the works and reported the enemy gone, and by eight o'clock in the morning we were moving the heads of the columns into Savannah. We concluded General Sherman wanted the enemy to leave and not make a fight necessary. What was wanted was the city and the route by the Savannah River open to the sea. This we secured without a fight.

The people of Savannah were much frightened, but were in no way disturbed by the soldiers, who moved through the city to their camps apparently caring neither for the city or the people. Since General Sherman's return the citizens are very anxious he should issue some definite instructions for the government of the city and instructions to the inhabitants. This he refuses to do. They fear every thing their active imaginations can cunger [conjure] up and his refusal to issue such orders annoys them more than any orders he could give would do.[33]

For the use of the Army a general order was issued, that the soldiers could go where they pleased without passes and making them responsible only to their immediate officers. General Sherman tells the people that what is required of them is that they shall be loyal and that he does not expect that of them, but that they will keep on fighting until the present generation is wiped out and the quicker it is over with the better for all.

The city is substantially a fortress. The works were mounted with 225 heavy guns, many of them splendid pieces and from eight to twelve inches calibre. These are ordered dismounted, and I am ordered to carry out the order and have sent to Hilton Head

Sherman's headquarters at Savannah. *Harper's Pictorial History of the Civil War,* II.

for the necessary machinery to do it. The Army is being rapidly re-fitted for another campaign, but what or how extensive it will be is as yet, a matter for conjectures only. We learn here of General Hood's defeat. He made nothing by his northern raid, but lost much. It appears to me now that next spring will finish this war, but there will be some very heavy fighting to be done yet. Please send this letter on this campaign to S. C. He will be anxious to know what I say about it and I have not time to repeat.[34]

NOTES

1. "Today (15th) the destruction fairly commenced, though yesterday some large buildings were destroyed. Capt. Poe has charge. Orders are to destroy all R. R. depots, large R. R., etc., warehouses, machine shops, etc., including all buildings of use to the enemy: but no *dwellings* to be injured. This P. M. the torch applied, also sundry buildings blown up, with shells inside—heavy explosion, several lesser ones for several minutes following. Clouds of smoke rise and hang like pall over doomed city.

"At night the grandest and most awful scene. . . . From our rear and E. windows, 1/3 of horizon shows immense and raging fires, lighting up whole heavens—probably, says Sherman, visible at Griffin, fifty miles off. First bursts of smoke, dense, black volumes, then tongues of flame, then huge waves of fire roll up into the sky: presently the skeletons of great warehouses stand out in relief against and amidst sheets of roaring, blazing, furious flames,—then the angry waves roll less high, and are a deeper color, then sink and cease, and only the fierce glow from the bare and blackened walls, etc. Now and then are heavy explosions, and as one fire sinks another rises, further along the horizon. . . ." Hitchcock, *Marching with Sherman,* 56-57.

2. "Behind us we leave a track of smoke and flame. Half of Marietta was burned up—not by orders, however." Nichols, 37. Hitchcock watched this fire also in the company of Sherman and was much upset by it. He recorded in his letter to his wife from Marietta on November 13: "When Court House fairly broke out, H. H. remarked—'Twill burn down, sir?' 'Yes, can't be stopped.' 'Was it your intention?' 'Can't save it—I've seen more of this thing than you.' 'Certainly, Sir.' Went out then together to house . . . taken for Headquarters.—Passing some soldiers— 'There,' said Sherman, 'are the men who do this. Set as many guards as you please, they will slip in and set fire. . . . Dare say the whole town will burn, at least the business part. I never ordered burning of any dwelling—didn't order this, but can't be helped. I say *Jeff. Davis burnt them.* " Hitchcock, 52-53.

"When we reached Marietta we found all the business part of town was burned by Kilpatrick's cavalry last night. Marietta was a very pretty town and its private residences are still beautiful."[35] James A. Connolly, *Three Years in the Army of the Cumberland*, ed. Paul M. Angle (Bloomington, 1959), 299.

3. Maj.-Gen. Henry Warner Slocum.

4. Maj.-Gen. Joseph Wheeler.

5. Brig.-Gen. Judson Kilpatrick.

6. "About 7 A. M. of November 16th we rode out of Atlanta by the Decatur road. . . . Behind us lay Atlanta, smouldering and in ruins, the black smoke rising high in air, and hanging like a pall over the ruined city. Away off in the distance,

on the McDonough road, was the rear of Howard's column, the gun-barrels glistening in the sun, the white-topped wagons stretching away to the south; and right before us the Fourteenth Corps, marching steadily and rapidly, with a cheery look and swinging pace, that made light of the thousand miles that lay between us and Richmond. Some band, by accident, struck up the anthem of 'John's Brown soul goes marching on;' the men caught up the strain, and never before or since have I heard the chorus of 'Glory, glory, hallelujah!' done with more spirit, or in better harmony of time and place." Sherman, II, 178-79.

7. Foraging proceeded with such liberality and enthusiasm that Gen. Howard tried to restrain it. "The attention of corps commanders and the commanders of unattached regiments and detachments," he ordered, "is called to the irregularities existing in foraging, and the manner in which this privilege is often abused. It is noticed that many men not belonging to proper foraging parties are allowed to straggle from the ranks and forage themselves without any authority whatsoever. It is by such men that the greater part of the pillaging is done, and depredations committed, of which there is so much complaint. Officers in charge of foraging parties must be continually instructed to keep their men well in hand, never allowing them to precede the advance guard of the column, and to use more discretion in taking from the poor, being careful to leave them sufficient for their immediate subsistence. It is also noted that the number of mounted men is very largely increasing, and that the ranks are correspondingly diminished. Means will be at once taken to check this growing evil. The number of mounted foragers to each brigade should be limited and regulated in orders, which, if not done, mounted foragers will be no longer allowed. We are now nearing the enemy, and foraging parties should be cautioned against preceding the advance of the column." Howard, *Autobiography,* II, 77-78.

"I have used the word 'bummer' in my accounts—it now has a recognition in the army lexicon. Fancy a ragged man, blackened by smoke of many a pine knot fire, mounted on a scrawny mule, without a saddle, with a gun, a knapsack, a butcher knife and a plug hat, stealing his way through the pine forests far out on the flanks of a column. Keen on the scent of rebels, or bacon, or silver spoons, or corn, or anything valuable and you have him in your mind. Think how you would admire him if you were a lone woman, with a family of small children, far from help, when he blandly inquired where you kept your valuables. Think how you would smile when he pryed open your chests with his bayonet or knocked to pieces your tables, pianos and chairs; tore your bed clothing in three inch strips, and scattered the strips about the yard. The 'bummers' say it takes too much time to use keys. Color is no protection from these rough-riders. They go through a negro cabin in search of diamonds and gold watches with just as much freedom and vivacity as they 'loot' the dwelling of a wealthy planter. They appear to be possessed of a spirit of 'pure cussedness.' " George W. Pepper, *Personal Recollections of Sherman's Campaigns in Georgia and the Carolinas* (Zanesville, Ohio, 1866), 275-76.

8. Brig.-Gen. Alfred Iverson, Jr.

9. Capt. William Duncan.

10. Boswell B. de Graffenreid.

11. On November 22 Gen. Slocum's headquarters were at the Milledgeville Hotel. *OR*, Ser. I, vol. 44, p. 524. Sherman arrived there the next day and occupied the governor's mansion. Sherman said the fleeing governor, Joseph E. Brown, "had hastily stripped it of carpets, curtains, and furniture of all sorts, which were removed to a train of freight-cars, which carried away these things—even the cabbages and vegetables from his kitchen and cellar—leaving behind muskets, ammunition, and the public archive." Sherman, II, 188.

Hitchcock reported that the depot burned on November 23. He wrote on that date: "Had a talk with Jeff. C. Davis and Slocum today about discipline, etc. J. C. D. says the belief in the army is that General S. favors and desires it, and one man when arrested told his officer so. I am bound to say I think Sherman lacking in enforcing discipline. Brilliant and daring, fertile, rapid and terrible, he does not seem to me *to carry out things* in this respect. . . .

"Kilpatrick tells me (and reports to General) that the rebs *killed after surrender* the prisoners they took from him, except four who took oath of allegiance to C. S. A. If this proves true Sherman will retaliate, *and we must not be taken prisoners*. I confess I don't expect any mercy if captured: and the worst of it is that the 'foraging' or pillaging of our men is bound to bring this about. It is all wrong. . . . I am very anxious to see and know Gen. Howard and talk to him freely about all these things. Yet his Report today mentions 'with regret' just such outrages by his men as what I condemn and deplore. Certainly an army is a terrible engine and hard to control. And J. D. & Co. *are* primarily responsible for all this!" Hitchcock, 85-88.

12. Maj.-Gen. Henry Constantine Wayne. A brief reference in Sherman's *Memoirs* to Gen. Wayne's resistance at Bull's Ferry elicited a long response from the Georgian. It is dated "Savannah, Georgia, October 23, 1875" and is a remarkably able, yet brief, account of Confederate opposition to Sherman from that point to Savannah. It appears in the 1890 and later edition of the *Memoirs,* II, 566-69.

13. Maj.-Gen. Frank P. Blair, Jr.

14. Brig.-Gen. Charles C. Walcutt.

15. Brig.-Gen. Charles R. Woods.

16. Maj.-Gen. P. J. Philips.

17. Jared Irwin, Jr. Irwin's Cross Roads is now Irwinton, which is not the same as Irwinville farther south.

18. L. M. Dayton, Sherman's aide-de-camp, sent a message to Gen. Slocum of November 30: "We are at Station 9½—marked Barton on our map" (O R, Ser. I., vol. 44, p. 581). This point would be between Sebastopol (No. 10) and Herndon (No. 9). It does not appear on modern maps nor on the map accompanying Sherman's *Memoirs.* It does appear on the map of Georgia reproduced in the atlas of *OR* and corresponds to the present Midville.

19. Actually, Gen. Hardee was in Savannah; Gen. Wayne was commanding these Confederate troops.

20. Millen.

21. "The extensive depot at Millen was a wooden structure of exceedingly graceful proportions. It was ignited in three places simultaneously, and its destruction was a brilliant spectacle; the building burning slowly, although there was sufficient wind to lift the vast volume of smoke and exhibit the exquisite architecture traced in lines of fire. This scene was so striking that even the rank and file observed and made comments upon it among themselves—a circumstance which may be counted as unusual, for the taste for conflagrations has been so cultivated of late in the army that any small affair of that kind attracts very little attention." Nichols, *Story of the Great March,* 80.

Hitchcock commented on this fire without registering an objection. "The depot," he said, "made a superb fire, even at noonday." Hitchcock, 133.

22. Brewer.

23. The destinations guessed in the Confederate correspondence in *OR* ranged every possible spot from Mobile to Charleston, but Savannah was the most frequently mentioned.

24. Eden.

25. Gen. Robert E. Lee.

26. Pooler.

27. Way's Station.

28. "The enemy having endeavored to wreck railroad trains by planting torpedoes on the track, he wrote to a subordinate: 'Order the point suspected to be tested by a car-load of prisoners or citizens implicated; of course an enemy cannot complain of his own traps.' " Hedley, *Marching Through Georgia*, 67.

29. Gen. Wayne told his cousin, Col. George Gordon, in Savannah: " 'I hear that your uncle, Mr. Cuyler, the President of the Central Railroad, intends leaving by a special train this evening on the Gulf Railroad for Macon. Beg him, for me, not to attempt it, for if he does he will run into Sherman's lines.' He went, however, and was captured." Sherman (1890), II, 569.

30. "I selected Captain William Duncan, who had escaped from capture and had returned to my escort, and told him to take with him Sergeant Myron J. Amick and Private George W. Quimby and proceed down the Ogeechee, passing Confederate stations, the King's Bridge, Fort McAllister, and all obstructions, and go out to sea and communicate with the fleet. It seemed next to impossible that the feat could be accomplished, but Captain Duncan's already distinguished career as a scout and his confidence that he could accomplish the enterprise led me to try him. He secured a long dugout, rather narrow and somewhat weatherbeaten; then putting in rations, he took my dispatch and another from my signal officer and set out. He went along very well by night, having passed the bridge and carefully worked through the torpedo obstructions.

"When the day dawned the morning of the 10th, he found some negroes who befriended him and his men. The party kept pretty well under cover until evening. During the night they made considerable progress but did not succeed in getting past Fort McAllister. They went ashore to get a Negro guide and some provisions; they tied up their boats and made their way through some bushes and thin groves till they came near a roadway. Here they heard the voices of some Confederates passing along the road. By lying down and keeping very quiet, they were not discovered.

"Soon after this they came to quite a sizable negro house, went in, and were well treated and refreshed with provisions. While they were eating they were startled by hearing a party of Confederate cavalry riding toward the house. Of course they expected to be instantly captured, but the negroes coming quickly to their rescue concealed them under the floor. The coolness and smartness of the negroes surprised even Captain Duncan, though he believed in and trusted them. The cavalry stopped but remained only a short time, and the negroes guided our men back to their boats [boat].

"In such operations as these, with hairbreadth escapes, they hid through the 11th in the daytime. When night came, to avoid one danger, they crossed the wide river; but hearing some voices, they feared a recapture from the bank, so they quietly pushed away, avoided a boat filled with oarsmen who were passing over the Ogeechee from a Confederate gunboat at anchor below Fort McAllister. They ran so near the gunboat that they were in terror for some noise that they had to make in paddling, or some flashlight from the vessel, would discover them; but surprising to say, they passed all obstacles, and soon after daylight on the morning of the 12th they drifted out into the broad bay.

"There the *Dandelion*, a dispatch boat of our navy, discovered the dugout with its three weary scouts. They were taken on board and carried to Port Royal Harbor . . . and saw my brief dispatch put into the hands of Rear Admiral Dahlgren, to whom it was addressed.

"Admiral Dahlgren reported on this expedition: 'It may be perhaps exceeding my province, but I cannot refrain from expressing the hope that the department will commend Captain Duncan and his companions to the Honorable Secretary of War for some mark of approbation for the success of establishing communications between General Sherman and the fleet. It was an enterprise that required both skill and courage.' " Howard, *Autobiography,* II, 83-85.

31. Adm. John A. Dahlgren.

32. Maj.-Gen. John G. Foster.

33. "As the division of Major-General John W. Geary, of the Twentieth corps, was the first to enter Savannah, that officer was appointed to command the place, or to act as a sort of governor. He very soon established a good police, maintained admirable order, and I doubt if Savannah, either before or since, has had a better government than during our stay. The guard-mountings and parades, as well as the greater reviews, became the daily resorts of ladies, to hear the music of our excellent bands; schools were opened, and the churches every Sunday were filled with most devout and respectful congregations; stores were reopened, and markets for provisions, meat, wood, etc., were established, so that each family, regardless of race, color, or opinion, could procure all the necessaries and even luxuries of life, provided they had money. Of course, many families were actually destitute of this, and to these were issued stores from our stock of supplies." Sherman, II, 236.

"I have now been in the vicinity of this beautiful city since the 21st inst . . . . I am living in the house of an old English consul: A magnificent establishment." Howard to Mrs. Howard, Savannah, Dec. 26, 1864. Howard Collection.

On January 6 he wrote his seven-year-old daughter Grace Ellen: "You hardly know what a really pleasant place this is. While you have snow & cold, bleak fields with the wind whistling through the trees, we have it warm & sunny. The trees here are many of them always green. One kind is called the live oak. Almost all the streets in Savannah are bordered with these oaks." Howard to Grace Ellen Howard, Savannah, Jan. 6, 1865. Howard Collection.

34. On the day Osborn dated (December 26) this letter to his brother, President Lincoln wrote Sherman from the White House: "Many, many thanks for your Christmas gift, the capture of Savannah. When you were about leaving Atlanta for the Atlantic coast I was anxious, if not fearful; but feeling that you were the better judge, and remembering that 'nothing risked, nothing gained,' I did not interfere. Now, the undertaking being a success, the honor is all yours; for I believe none of us went further than to acquiesce. And taking the work of General Thomas into the count, as it should be taken, it is indeed a great success. Not only does it afford the obvious and immediate military advantages, but, in showing to the world that your army could be divided, putting the important part to an important new service, and yet leaving enough to vanquish the old opposing force of the whole—Hood's army—it brings those who sat in darkness to see a great light. But what next? I suppose it will be safer if I leave General Grant and yourself to decide. Please make my grateful acknowledgments to your whole army, officers and men." *OR,* Ser. I, vol. 44, p. 809.

General Sherman said in his Special Field Order No. 6 of January 8, 1865: "Almost at the moment of our victorious entry into Savannah came the welcome and expected news that our comrades in Tennessee had also fulfilled nobly and well their part, had decoyed General Hood to Nashville and then turned on him, defeating his army thoroughly, capturing all of his artillery, great numbers of prisoners, and were still pursuing the fragments down in Alabama. So complete a success in military operations, extending over half a continent, is an achievement that entitles it to a place in the military history of the world." Sherman, II, 220.

Savannah, Ga.
December 31, 1864

[To S. C. O.] I think this campaign just closed will be one of the really historical campaigns of the war, much more so than some where vastly more fighting was done. It was brilliant in conception and well executed, but practically one of the easiest campaigns we have had.

Tonight, the close of the year 1864, finds me in Savannah, Ga. The close of 1863 I was in Bridgeport, Ala., the close of 1862, in Falmouth, Va., the close of 1861, in Washington, the close of 1860 in Watertown, N. Y. as a law student and the close of 1859 as a college student in Hamilton, N. Y. What next?

Just now I have more work on my hands than any one of the staff officers, but we shall not remain here long. It is plain we are to move soon.[1]

NOTE

1. Grant wrote Sherman on December 27: "Your confidence in being able to march up and join this army pleases me, and I believe it can be done. The effect of such a campaign will be to disorganize the south, and prevent the organization of new armies from their broken fragments. . . . Without waiting further directions, then, you may make preparations to start on your northern expedition without delay. Break up the railroads in South and North Carolina, and join the armies operating against Richmond as soon as you can. I will leave out all suggestions about the route you should take, knowing that your information gained daily in the progress of events, will be better than any that can be obtained now." *OR*, Ser. I, vol. 44, pp. 820-21.

III *In South Carolina*

Beaufort, S. C.
January 11, 1865

[To A. C. O.] We arrived here on the 9 by steamer from Savannah. The XVII Corps is all here and the XV is on its way. The right wing will all be here by the 15. I understand General Slocum will move by land and cross the Savannah River forty miles above Savannah, on a pontoon bridge and move up abreast of us and on our left.

I do not think it is in General Sherman's plans to move directly against Charleston, but to neutralize it by other operations. It is strongly fortified and an attempt to take it would result in a large loss of men. The information we pick up indicates that the enemy is not in large force in this part of the country, but that the main body of the troops have been shipped to some other point. I am confident that General Sherman is going inland. Indeed I know that he is, but to what point after striking Branchville I am not aware, probably we shall not be very long absent from the coast. The prominent railroad connections above us, the possession of which appear to be of value in cutting off supplies from General Lee's army are Branchville, Columbia, Florence, Raleigh, Goldsboro, Greensboro, Weldon and Danville. I have heard General Sherman talk freely of all these points and I know, that, in the coming campaign he intends to break the roads at more or less of these junctions. There is nothing now left, practically, of the Confederacy, west of the Allegheny range, or south of the Savannah River.

Beaufort, in the olden time, was a beautiful little place say of 500 polite people, who from appearances belonged to the wealthier classes. It is now the head quarters of the negroes who have congregated here from along the coast, as it has been occupied by our forces, and who have escaped from the interior.

General Saxton is in command of all this part of the coast with headquarters at Beaufort.[1]

NOTE

1. "General Rufus Saxton had his headquarters there. He was quite domesticated amid a new Northern community and multitudes of Negroes that were peopling that part of the seacoast which had come into our possession. General and Mrs. Saxton gave me a sweet home and cordial welcome with them for a few days. I visited at Beaufort, St. Helena, and other neighboring islands. . . .

"Our soldiers were so many, needed so many supplies, and felt themselves at last on South Carolina soil, that a lawless spirit came over them and many complaints came to me of their doings." Howard, *Autobiography,* II, 98-99.

Howard described his first visit to Beaufort in his letter of January 6 to his daughter: "I breakfasted with Gen. Saxton and then we rode off for ten miles on the beautiful broad straight roads. On our right and left we saw neat little huts where the negroes live. The negro men are soldiers mostly and look very nice. When we returned a negro band played on some very bright brass instruments. How clean and nice their clothing & their instruments looked! The children were clean and pretty well dressed [and] on the whole everybody in Beaufort & near there looked happy." Howard Collection.

In his brief time in Beaufort, Howard foreshadowed his postwar work as chief of the Bureau of Refugees, Freedmen and Abandoned Lands (the Freedmen's Bureau). He visited five schools in which lady volunteers from New England were teaching Negro children whom he found "sparkling with intelligence." He wrote then (in 1865): "You can't help saying, That is not the stuff of which to make slaves." Howard, II, 98.

Beaufort, S. C.
January 17, 1865

[To A. C. O.] The XVII Corps has occupied the Charleston and Savannah railroad which it succeeded in doing with a loss of about a dozen men. I am told here that at one time and another 6,000 men have been lost in attempts to occupy this railroad from this point. Of course we have more men than has at any one time been employed and the enemy are in a less confident spirit than at any time before. Yet I am disposed to think that the success with so light a loss is more owing to good military judgment than to any other cause.

We expect to be on the move again in a few days. General Sherman is much more reticent to all his subordinates now than at any time since I have known him. The indications are, that we will first go as far west as Branchville, but where from there is only guess work with any one. When General Blair occupied the railroad, General Sherman ordered him not to destroy it, as it might yet be necessary to use it as a line of supply. This looks like a movement towards Charleston which I do not believe he intends to make, unless he is compelled to do so by reason of some future contingency. General Blair is beyond the worst coast swamps and a disagreeable part of the work is done. The weather is fine.

Beaufort, S. C.
January 25, 1865

[To S. C. O.] We are about starting on a new campaign and it is not now unlikely we shall be absent from the coast as long as we were between Atlanta and Savannah. We may not be out of reach more than two weeks, quite likely six, but I guess about four. We cannot tell how much the enemy will oppose us, from present indications not very much, but probably more then in the last campaign. General Grant[1] notifies General Sherman that General Lee shall not send his army, or any portion of it, against this.[2] If that promise can be kept, the enemy has not force enough in our front to hinder us greatly.[3]

We have had a very severe rain storm and the low country along the coast is badly overflowed and the roads are exceedingly bad. When we move they will become as bad as roads can be. Those we shall have until we reach a higher country away from the coast. But we are still at work getting ready for this new campaign. The late severe storm lasted four days and has flooded the country.

The scouts report that the enemy, 15,000 or 20,000 strong, are at Branchville. If this is correct General Sherman will not fight, if he can dislodge them without doing so.

We know little or nothing about the future. General Sherman says it is to be the greatest campaign yet undertaken. So General Hooker said before Chancellorsville and he was correct. I hope General Sherman will not be correct in the same sense. But I do not anticipate he will. No Army was ever more devoted to the fortunes of its leader than this is. Wherever he goes this Army will go most willingly and faithfully.

NOTES

1. Gen. Ulysses S. Grant.

2. Despite repeated requests to authorities in Richmond from Gens. Beauregard, Hardee, and Hood, Gen. Lee did not feel that he could spare any men as reinforcements to the Confederate armies in Georgia and Tennessee. President Davis regularly left the decision on this point to Lee.

3. Late in December a group of thirty-five very prominent South Carolinians pleaded in an undated message written in Columbia and addressed to Secretary of War James A. Seddon: "The undersigned citizens of South Carolina respectfully request that at least one corps of the army be sent from Virginia to save the States of Georgia and South Carolina from being laid waste by the enemy. There is no force here to prevent it, and it is absolutely necessary to have at least one well-organized corps besides Hardee's on the coast, about which the half-trained citizens may rally. Otherwise, however brave and determined, their efforts will amount to nothing. These two States have, to a large extent, furnished the Army of Virginia with supplies. If they are wasted by raids and their railroads cut, this source of supply is lost. We are sensible of the pressure upon Richmond, and the importance of saving the capital, but it is manifest that its defense must at this moment be made here.

"A just regard for the safety of these States and of the common cause in which we are all embarked induces us to press this appeal with great earnestness upon your consideration."

On January 5 Secretary Seddon submitted their appeal to President Davis, who endorsed it: "The question presented is one of which General Lee can best judge. I suggest a reference to him." *OR,* Ser. I, vol. 44, p. 1011.

Pocotaligo, S. C.
January 29, 1865

[To S. C. O.] I write once more before we cut loose from the coast, which will be tomorrow morning at six o'clock.[1] We are to move directly into the center of the state, at the rate of ten or fifteen miles a day. That is providing we do not meet General Lee's army and if we should do so, we shall probably be prudent enough to back down to the coast again. That movement, however, would give Richmond to the Army of the Potomac and General Grant would not be long in starting on the trail of General Lee. So on the whole nothing would be lost to us by that move. This is a great game that is being played and great men are playing it. And the end is now not far off.

I think we shall be out longer than we were before as General Sherman intends to cut the railroads in the interior of the state, for the purpose of cutting off the supplies from the Army at Richmond. This we can do by cutting the lines of transportation. You will continually know of our whereabouts from the daily papers and the extracts they will give from the southern papers.

General Slocum's Army crossed the Savannah River forty miles above Savannah and in this movement takes the left. He moves farther to the west than we do.

This letter is written by the light of a camp fire as it is too cold to write inside the tent.

NOTE

1. "Tomorrow we break loose again from our base and launch forth an uncertain campaigning, but the same God is my trust and I hardly feel a misgiving. Yet anything is possible." Howard to Mrs. Howard, ALS, Pocotaligo, S. C., Jan. 29, 1865. Howard Collection.

Pocotaligo, S. C.
January 29, 1865

[To A. C. O.] We leave the coast tomorrow morning.[1] General Sherman appears to be very confident of success in his present movement. He has his army in good condition well equipped and the same strength it was when he left Atlanta, that is about 60,000 men. General Howard moves on the right and thus keeps nearest the coast. We are to move into the country west as far as Branchville and then turn north. General Slocum crossed the Savannah River above Savannah and is now moving towards Branchville near which he will make a junction with us.

The remnant of General Hood's army, left after the battle of Nashville, is moving east and will probably be in our front again, General Sherman tells us that large reinforcements for this Army from General Thomas's Army are now on their way through the northern states and by sea. It is certain they cannot join us until we reach the coast again.

So far, since last April, the fortunes of war have been heavily in our favor or perhaps more explicitly, since General Grant became Commander in Chief, and General Sherman his second in command, we have been uniformly successful.

I think when I last wrote you I said a large force was reported as being at Branchville. Later reports do not confirm the former.

Probably there are no troops stationed there, but some moving command has been mistaken by the scouts as a stationary force.

NOTE

1. Nichols recorded for January 30: "The actual invasion of South Carolina has begun. . . . The well-known sight of columns of black smoke meets our gaze again; this time houses are burning, and South Carolina has commenced to pay an instalment, long overdue, on her debt to justice and humanity. With the help of God, we will have principal and interest before we leave her borders. There is a terrible gladness in the realization of so many hopes and wishes. This cowardly traitor state, secure from harm, as she thought, in her central position, with hellish haste dragged her Southern sisters into the caldron of secession. Little did she dream that the hated flag would again wave over her soil; but this bright morning a thousand Union banners are floating in the breeze, and the ground trembles beneath the tramp of thousands of brave Northmen, who know their mission, and will perform it to the end." Nichols, *Story of the Great March*, 131-32.

"It was to me manifest that the soldiers and people of the South entertained an undue fear of our western men, and, like children, they had invented such ghostlike stories of our prowess in Georgia, that they were scared by their own inventions. Still, this was a power, and I intended to utilize it. Somehow, our men had got the idea that South Carolina was the cause of all our troubles; her people were the first to fire on Fort Sumter, had been in a great hurry to precipitate the country into Civil War; and therefore on them should fall the scourge of war in its worst form. Taunting messages had also come to us, when in Georgia, to the effect that, when we should reach South Carolina, we would find a people less passive, who would fight us to the bitter end, daring us to come over, etc., some that I saw felt that we would not longer be able to restrain our men as we had done in Georgia." Sherman, II, 254.

JOURNAL, JANUARY- MARCH

Pocotaligo, Beaufort, S. C.
January 31, 1865

It will be necessary to run back a little way in our operations to get at the present time and conditions of affairs, how we happen to be where we are, how we got here, and why we were not here sooner, or even so soon.

On the night of the 14 of January, at midnight, General Howard and part of the staff left Beaufort to join General Blair and with his corps, and our brigade of the XV Army Corps, to make a movement on the Savannah and Charleston Rail Road at Pocotaligo. These troops were encamped about ten miles from Beaufort and Port Royal Ferry. At daylight the ferry, which is about six hundred

yards wide, was bridged with pontoons, and the troops passed
over. None of the enemy excepting a small picket guard were on
the main land, and they decamped at once. The head of column
had moved about eight miles before it struck the entrenched position of the enemy on the further bank of one of the salt creeks by
which this coast is thoroughly cut up. This one, with its accompanying marsh, is about four hundred yards wide. The position was
a fine one, and could not be carried by a direct assault. To take it,
General Howard moved one of the rear divisions of the column to
the right, on another road, on which the enemy had burned a
bridge over this same creek, and then had the road only picketed
by a small detachment. The creek was at once crossed on this new
road, and the column moved past the enemy's main position,
who, apparently did not discover this unexpected manouver, until
the head of column had passed them two or three miles, when
they broke and made off rapidly, and we at once occupied their
works. A corresponding movement was made again at Pocotaligo,
where the enemy had an entrenched camp.

In these operations, we lost two officers killed, and two men
wounded.

The enemy now turned out of position as far as the rail road,
which was three miles in advance of the entrenched camp. The
Corps moved out and occupied the rail road before dark, having
made during the day about fifteen miles. In these operations, with
a loss all told of twelve men, we had accomplished precisely what
different commanders during the war had attempted and lost, as
shown by official records, six thousand and five hundred (6,500)
men.[1] The difference is mostly accounted for in the display of generalship on the one part, and the lack of it on the other. The
former commanders had been in the habit of throwing troops by
the head of column, over the narrow causeways against the enemy's works, while General Howard simply manouvered them out
of position. The question of fighting was not a question of great
consideration, as nearly anyone of the commanders could have
whipped the enemy usually defending this country if they could
have gotten them in an open field. General Foster, the Department
Commander, is a cripple, and cannot take the field.[2] Hatch,[3] his
fighting subordinate, is a very poor specimen of a General. Col.
P. P. Brown,[4] who knows him well, criticizes him as a personal
coward, and says he has scarcely ever seen the troops he com-

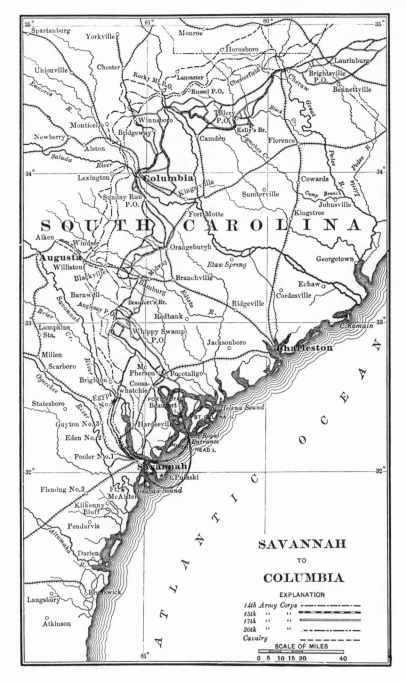

Map 3. Savannah to Columbia, S.C. From *General Sherman,* by Manning Force. New York: D. Appleton and Company, 1899.

mands on a battle field. General Sherman criticizes the Department Commanders as having frittered away all the troops ever sent to the Department.

General Howard returned to camp the following day, leaving the troops on the rail road at Pocotaligo Station under the command of General Blair. His next work was to get the Army in complete readiness to move on the prospective campaign. This was a heavy work, as one Army Corps, and most of the transportation for the Army, had still to be shipped from Savannah, the troops clothed, and supplies of all kinds procured and placed in the trains, able to move at a moment's notice. These, and other branches of army labor necessitated a great deal of preparation and labor.

From some unknown cause, or from the obstinacy or mental inability of General Easton,[5] Chief Quartermaster, and Colonel Beckwith,[6] Chief Commissary of the Military Division of the Mississippi, the supplies were not forthcoming. Each of them seemed to have taken a pique from some cause and allowed the supplies to move on slowly, as all other quarter masters were compelled to go to him for orders, it made our operations remarkably slow. It is unnecessary to mention instances upon which my opinion of General Easton is based, but as soon as Colonel Conklin,[7] the quartermaster of this Army, was freed from his supervision and had direct control of his dept., every part of the business went on with much greater rapidity, and this Army was supplied for the campaign.

On the 26 we left Beaufort nearly ready for the general movement, which was to commence on Monday the 30. On the 29 we were ready and moved one division (Giles A. Smith's) four miles beyond the rail road. On the same day, I inspected the artillery of the XVII Army Corps and found it in good condition. On the morning of the 30 the whole Army was supposed to move from the points designated by General Sherman, as starting points. The right wing—Army of the Tennessee—to move from Pocotaligo. The XV A. C. to move on the road next north of the Coosawhatchie River. The XVII A. corps on the road next south of the Great Salkihatchie [Salkehatchie] River, the Army to move directly in the country between the two rivers. The left wing to move up on the south side of the Savannah River to "Sister's Ferry" and cross at the ferry to Robertsville, being the starting point for General Slocum on the 30. General Corse's Division of the XV Corps, accompanied this wing and was to rejoin its corps at Hickory Hill,[8] on the Coosawhatchie River, while the left wing was to move over to Barnwell. Commencing operations to reach the interior of South Carolina from points so far separated, would naturally foil the enemy in any attempt to check us with troops at hand, and would also trouble him to jump at a conclusion as to the objective point of Sherman, whether it might be Branchville, Charleston, Columbia, or even Augusta, or all of them. The lines of concentration were all decidedly in our favor. I have written thus far on the evening of the 31.

On the 30 we moved inland six miles. Today—31—we are lying still waiting to hear from Slocum before we move farther inland. We have already passed the low ground of the coast, and the ground begins to look better for campaigning, i.e. higher land. There are some farms here, but they have been ruined by the occupation of the country by the Rebel army.[9] The weather thus far has been beautiful and now bids fair to remain so for some time; the roads are sandy and pretty good. The country is timbered with the universal pine, and I suppose we are now above the regions of live oak excepting here and there a few around the plantation houses. The live oaks are in great abundance on the coast, and many of them are beautiful, and the ground around the large plantation houses are beautifully shaded by them, [as] on many of the sea island cotton plantations.

The nights are chilly, in truth are very cold, and we require a large amount of clothing to make us comfortable.

NOTES

1. A month earlier Gen. Foster lost over a thousand men trying to capture Pocotaligo. Nichols, *Story of the Great March,* 127.

2. Grant wrote Sherman on February 1 that Foster, "from physical disability, is entirely unfit for command. I would like to change him for a man who can get about and see for himself." *OR,* Ser. I, vol. 47, pt. 2, pp. 193-94.

3. Brig.-Gen. John P. Hatch.

4. Col. Philip P. Brown.

5. Gen. Langdon C. Easton.

6. Col. Amos Beckwith.

7. Col. James T. Conklin.

8. Now Hampton. In 1865, wrote Hitchcock, "Like so many other Southern Post Offices, it was no town but simply the homestead of a planter. . . . We found quite a large and unusually comfortable frame house, with numerous outbuildings, on something of an elevation, but of course *no* hickory trees that I saw,

though plenty of pines. . . . This place was owned by a Mrs. McBride, a rich widow, reported by the darkies as a very hard and cruel mistress. She was gone long before we came. All the whites seem to have fled before us, except that in a few instances 'poor whites' have been left in the dwellings of their rich neighbors in hopes to save the houses." Hitchcock, *Marching with Sherman*, 237-39.

D. H. Trezevant quoted a Yankee correspondent, presumably Conyngham: "At McBride's plantation, where Sherman had his headquarters, the out-houses, offices, shanties, and surroundings were all set on fire before he left. I think the fire approaching the dwelling hastened his departure. . . . In Georgia few houses were burned; here few escaped, and the country was converted into one vast bonfire. The pine forests were fired; the resin factories were fired; the public buildings and private dwellings were fired. The middle of the finest day looked black and gloomy, for a dense smoke rose on all sides clouding the very heavens—at night the tall pine trees seemed so many huge pillars of fire. The flames hissed and screeched, as they fed on the fat resin and dry branches, imparting to the forest a most fearful appearance. . . .

"The ruins of homesteads of the Palmetto State will long be remembered. The army might safely march the darkest night, the crackling pine woods shooting up their columns of flame, and the burning houses along the way would light it on, while the dark clouds and pillars of smoke would safely cover its rears. I hazard nothing in saying that three-fifths of value of the personal property of the counties we passed through were taken by Sherman's army." *The Burning of Columbia, S. C.* (Columbia: 1866), 7-8.

9. Gen. Wheeler issued a forceful general order, dated "Beaufort District, S. C., December 29, 1864," which began "The continued and grave complaints made by citizens against this command require that the most stringent efforts be used by all officers to prevent the slightest depradations of any character in future." *OR*, Ser. I, vol. 44, p. 1002.

Whippy Swamp Creek,
Colleton District, S. C.
February 1, 1865

This morning we broke camp at seven o'clock and moved Army Head Quarters with the XVII Army Corps along the right bank of the Big Salkehatchie River to this point, the road running about one mile from the river. The first five miles the road was good and very little obstructed by fallen timber. We then struck the enemy's skirmishers with our advanced guard, the 9th Illinois Mounted Infantry, and commenced driving them rapidly about as fast as the column moved although they skirmished at every point which afforded them the least cover, such places as small marshes, creeks, the edges of woods, which had an open field for our men to cross in front of them. Our men behaved admirably. Two miles from this creek, the road forks. The enemy, mistaking our intentions, continued on the left fork. The enemy's force consisted of two or three Regiments of Wheeler's Corps of Cavalry. The General [Howard] sent a brigade after them and turned the head of column on this road to cross the creek. It runs through a swamp three quarters of a mile wide, in seven streams while the surface of the whole swamp is covered with water from six inches to a foot in depth. The timber is as dense as it is possible for it to grow, and all sizes, from immense cypress to small brush, and vines intertwined. The bridges averaged about sixty feet in length, and were all burned. The road was filled with fallen timber, cut off from either side of the road. We cautiously felt down the road with cavalry skirmishers, which were met at the first stream by a company of rebels who skirmished stubbornly. General Howard with a portion of his staff followed the skirmishers to the stream, when the enemy opened fire striking Lieut. Taylor,[1] an artillery officer on duty with me. The ball struck on the right side of the neck, passed inside the main artery, cut the wind-pipe and out in front of the corresponding artery on the left side, barely missing either of them. He was close behind the General when wounded, and the General caught the wound with his hand stopping the blood and escape of breath. Taylor in a few moments rallied, and walked back a quarter of a mile to the surgeon to have the wound dressed. We hope he will recover. He is a brave and good boy, and a pet with all here. All feel his misfortune very deeply. He will be sent back in the morning to Pocotaligo about twenty-five miles, and from there to Beaufort by General Hatch. With all our skirmishing today only one man besides Taylor was wounded.[2]

The XV Army Corps moved up the left bank of the Coosawhatchie, with instructions to camp at Hickory Hill. General Sherman accompanied them. We have not yet heard from them this evening, but know the enemy have been in their front, obstructing the road the same as here. This country is covered with pines, and is a quicksand land. There are but few roads, and they cut through, or as the expression is used here, "the bottom falls out," long before a Corps and its trains can pass over, and much of it must be corduroyed; two hours use of the road absolutely ruins them, and we are compelled to depend on rails and timber to get the trains along. Our superior pioneer organization is of great value to us now. It is composed mostly of negroes and is probably superior to that of any other Army. There are very few plantations here and a few poor houses. The houses are mostly abandoned. A great share of the abandoned houses are being burned by the soldiers, while those with the families are not molested further than to take the forage and provisions for the Army. We hear Wheeler has ordered that all supplies in the country be taken or destroyed excepting twelve days rations for the people. This is to prevent its falling into our hands. The Rebel orders are that all stock be driven off.[3] Still we are already getting a little of each.

NOTES

1. Lieut. William N. Taylor.
2. "As we halted at a point a little higher than the road, an artillery officer of my staff standing near me was struck with a bullet just under his chin. The bullet cut his windpipe and one of his arteries. Fortunately for him, I caught the wound with my hand and stopped the flow of blood. The officer, Lieutenant Taylor, at first stunned by the blow, quickly came to himself, and, aided by his comrades, succeeded in getting to the surgeon and securing prompt relief. A companion said of Taylor: 'We hope he will recover. He is a brave and good boy and a pet with all here. All feel his misfortune very deeply.' He did recover after some months." Howard, II, 105-106. This passage by Howard is quoted so fully here as one of a number of evidences of how the General made use of Osborn's accounts in preparing his *Autobiography.*
3. Wheeler had repeatedly been ordered to destroy all supplies ahead of the Federals' advance—by Beauregard and Bragg on November 18 and 25, for example. *OR,* Ser. I, vol. 44, pp. 867, 897. On December 10, while "In the Field," he issued: "Circular. Soldiers! While you have been engaged gallantly fighting the enemy a band of thieves and stragglers have spread over the country robbing and insulting wives and children of your brother soldiers who are opposing the invaders upon other fields. These soldiers expect protection from you, and I appeal to every officer and soldier of this command to assist in arresting and bringing to justice these depredators, who claim to belong to the command, and by their conduct are bringing disgrace upon you and distress upon citizens, the families of our comrades in arms." *OR,* Ser. 1, vol. 44, pp. 946-47.

Rivers' Bridge over Big
Salkehatchie River,
Colleton District, S. C.
February 2, 1865

We broke camp at 7 a.m. Lieut. Taylor was sent to Pocotaligo under a cavalry escort. He seemed to be in good spirits, and the surgeon pronounced his condition favorable. During the night the enemy had been reinforced considerably, and were now commanded by Colonel Colcox [Colcock][1] of the 5th [3rd] S. C. Cavalry.

As soon as the column moved, the skirmishing began sharply but we drove them about five miles with infantry skirmishers, and then halted for the 9th Illinois to come up and relieve them. The work was too hard for dismounted men to move with sufficient rapidity out of the way of the column.

The Infantry worked gallantly while engaged. This 9th Illinois M'td. Inf'ty. is the Regiment which crossed Flint River Bridge on the campaign from Atlanta to Jonesboro, last summer, and made one of the most gallant charges of the war for so small a body of men.[2] This regt. with its infantry supporters was placed under charge of Lieutenant Colonel Kirby[3] of General Blair's staff. A superb officer—none better. He had advanced two miles, when he found the enemy in a strong position protected by rail barricades having on each of their flanks a swamp, their position commanding a wide open field, over which our men would approach them. When Kirby came within long range of their muskets, he deployed the cavalry as skirmishers, mounted, supported by a strong skirmish line of infantry, and then charged upon the barricade, the men firing their seven-shooters as they deployed and on the charge. The enemy stood still till Kirby was in on them.

The only one of our men hurt was Kirby, a ball passing through the calf of his leg, and through the horse, killing his horse instantly. The horse was a magnificent one. Kirby's wound is not considered dangerous. Our troops crowded the enemy from one position to another, until they reached the head of the road crossing Broxton's Bridge, over the Salkehatchie River, where the enemy had expected we would cross, and had made preparation for us. The road to this bridge runs through a swamp about a half mile wide of the same nature as the Whippy Swamp. The bridge had been burned, the opposite side of the river fortified and the artillery entrenched and commanding the road through the swamp and the crossing of the river. A skirmish line was sent through the swamp to the river, and made a threat of crossing, meanwhile skirmishing across the riverbridge. The forest is so dense that the enemy could not see our column, which was moved directly past their position towards Rivers' Bridge, five miles above, where we intended to cross. Major General Mower,[4] First Division, XVII Army Corps, was in advance and as soon as possible turned the head of his column down towards Rivers' Bridge. The peculiar formation of the swamp and angles of the road led to different conclusions than should have been reached by the division commanders. The road passed through the bottom land, half way to the bridge in an air line and then turned abruptly to the left running again in an air line to the bridge. The bridge being about a mile from the bank of the swamp. The enemy showed no resistance with skirmishers, but when the head of the column moved on the last section of the road, at the head of which, and on the opposite bank, the enemy had an entrenched battery about eight hundred yards from the angle. They allowed the column to move about 200 yards in this section before they opened the battery.

Our men threw themselves at once into the swamp on either side of the road and saved themselves except a dozen or more who were either killed or wounded. Colonel Sampson⁵ of the 43rd Ohio was struck just below the knee with a fragment of shell and has lost his leg. He was esteemed very highly as an officer and a gentlemen. I am not personally acquainted with him. His term was out and he was commanding his regiment gratuitously on this campaign. A line of battle was at once formed, and skirmishers thrown out to the bank of the river to sharpshoot, and if possible, to keep the enemy's battery quiet. This angle of the road, however, was a tender point in the operations. If a single man showed himself in it, they opened fire but did comparatively little harm. They fired about ten feet too high, though a shell bursting a little short was dangerous. As staff officers had to cross this road frequently, they had the especial advantage of this battery. General Mower saved himself by one leap backwards which he made when he saw the flash of the gun, the shell burst right to have struck him. It was now near dark and the troops went into position for the night. The main part of the troops were withdrawn to the high ground. The skirmishers strengthened and moved up. The bridge is in possession of the enemy, but our sharpshooters command it so effectually they cannot burn it, though the kindlingwood can be seen on it ready for the match. The enemy has shown no skill in the use of the battery.

They have only directed their fire down the straight section of road while if they had swept an arc of ten or fifteen degrees, and so have commanded the road over which our troops passed to reach the last section they would have done us great damage. Any

Marching through the swamps. *Harper's Pictorial History of the Civil War,* II.

sensible officer would have known this, as of necessity in approaching a field of operations an Army always masses to a certain extent very near the point from which they deploy, and to get this point we would fill the second section with troops and ordnance wagons. The second section was the only one on which they should have fired, and as long as they knew the distance, it made no difference whether they could see the troops or not. The depth of water and the denseness of timber and undergrowth in this swamp partially explains why Mower moved his column without keeping out the usual line of skirmishers. He wished to move faster than men could get through this entanglement, as the men could only get through it by parting the undergrowth with both their hands.

I should have said before that in one of the forenoon skirmishes we had three men slightly wounded, and found three of the enemy's dead on the same ground. We also learned that there was a corpse carried back here on horseback supposed to be an officer. (I have since learned it was a colonel.)

Our force to night is distributed as follows. General Mower's division at the bridge. Gen. Giles A. Smith's[6] in rear, covering the trains and different head quarters. General Force's[7] Division is at Whippy Swamp, or near Anglesey's [Angley] Post Office.[8] The enemy have the advantage of us tonight if they knew it. Turning our position at Beaufort's Bridge he could strike these two positions in reserve, and be off again before General Force could get to our assistance.

Nothing less than 20,000 men could crowd us in the swamp and capture our trains, and I do not believe they have that number of men within reach of us. There is a rumor among the citizens that S. D. Lee's Army Corps is in front of us, and General Howard thinks there is no man better adapted to understand a desperate scheme than he.

There is an item I might make some comments on here, though perhaps I had better not—here goes however.

Sherman early in January sent word to the War Department that Howard should be at Pocotaligo on the 15 ult and Slocum at Robertsville on the north bank of the Savannah River near Sister's Ferry on the same day. General Howard was on time. General Slocum waited for supplies on the representation of General Easton, Chief Quarter Master for General Sherman. When the present movement commenced, General Sherman was with us and sent his orders to General Slocum, depending on him to have them carried out. Last night General Sherman sent word to General Howard that he had just heard from General Slocum, and that he had been unable to get off from lack of supplies but that he would get Kilpatrick's Cavalry across at Sister's Ferry today, and I suppose the Infantry will cross tomorrow. Rather a bad record from the 15 of January to the 3 of Feby to get in position from which to commence a great campaign.

General Sherman is in high temper and orders a halt till the left wing comes up. General Howard replied to him that the best thing to be done now is to put on a bold front and press on till we cross the rail road and fight the enemy if necessary, as a delay now would be fatal so far as giving the enemy time to guess the plan of the campaign and reinforce against us. Sherman says "go ahead."

I understand that no one can approach Sherman now without being snubbed. His high nervous temperament and sarcasm are now at their highest pitch, and all who are acquainted with him keep at a respectful distance. It makes but very little difference whether one be a major general or a private soldier, they do not tamper with Sherman during these spells of deep anxiety and care.

Some of us eastern soldiers knew Slocum better than Sherman did. In my own mind, I do not doubt but this twenty days delay comes more from lack of ability and energy to cope with what he has on his hands than from any other cause. He once failed Howard in a fight at Gettysburg, and I fear he will do it again, and if so, he will go overboard. I hope not, but we shall see. I should have said that two divisions of Slocum's command, under Williams,[9] cross[ed] the river near Savannah, and are now somewhere near Lawtonville.[10] Corse's division has not been heard from yet.

NOTES

1. Col. Charles J. Colcock.
2. The charge to which Osborn refers was made by the 92d Illinois Mounted Infantry led by Capt. Lewellyn G. Estes. *OR,* Ser. I, vol. 38, pt. 2, p. 860.
3. Lieut.-Col. Dennis T. Kirby.
4. Maj-Gen. Joseph Anthony Mower.
5. Not identified in *OR.*
6. Maj.-Gen. Giles Alexander Smith.
7. Brig.-Gen. Manning F. Force.
8. Present-day Sycamore.
9. Maj.-Gen. Alpheus S. Williams.
10. Two miles west of the present town of Estill.

Rivers' Bridge,
Colleton Dist S. C.
February 3, 1865

Our Head Quarters today have been stationary, though we have done a substantial day's work. The enemy were holding the bridge with great tenacity, and it was a severe job to get them out. Our men skirmished up to the enemy's works and succeeded in sharpshooting them down quite effectually. They could barely use their artillery or muskets at all. During the whole day there has scarcely been a cessation of fire for a moment. Early in the day a reconnaissance was made over the river between this and Broxton's Bridge, and a foothold obtained on the opposite bank. The river was found to be a wide flat or marsh, one mile wide, with the water running in thirty-five different streams, no one of them taking a man above the middle. This crossing was made through the original forest where there was no sign of a track. Gen. G. A. Smith was thrown over here with his whole division and established on the opposite bank. He accomplished this by 5 P. M. but the enemy began at once to skirmish all around him. It being near night, the brush very thick, and as he knew nothing of what was in his front he thought he had better not swing off till morning. He entrenched himself in position. The swamp is so impenetrable that we cannot get around to the enemy tonight.

About 5 P. M. General Mower pushed his division to the left, so as to pass or overlap the enemy's right, and then forward to the high ground, and at the same time made a desperate assault with a strong skirmish line on the enemy's front. The enemy resisted sharply for a few minutes then fell back. We lost several men killed and wounded. This little success gives us the line of the Salkehatchie River, and we have reason to believe the enemy expected to hold it. We have lost all told, killed and wounded, in gaining the opposite bank of the river, about one hundred men. We have contended here with the worst enemy I have ever seen, and the works were well placed, and very strong.

The enemy tonight threatens to cross the river at Broxton's Bridge in hopes of striking our trains, thinking all our force had crossed the river, at this place, leaving our trains behind. We are, however, prepared to resist such a movement. Our troops tonight have this distribution. Mower and Smith over the river. Force here, one div. of Logan's Corps at Angley's P. O. and the remainder a little south of there. Word has reached us that Beaufort bridge, six miles above us is in our possession.

We have the same word tonight from Slocum. He is on the other side of the Savannah River, which is too high to cross. Kilpatrick with his cavalry is with him.

Our day's work in a military sense is a good one. A few poor fellows here lost their lives, and several are wounded.

The conclusion today is to send back our empty wagons and fill them with supplies in hopes they can reach us again while we are moving slow to humour Slocum. All our sick and wounded are to be sent back with this train, and so spare them the hardships of the remainder of the campaign. It affords us a much better opportunity to look out for the welfare of our men who have suffered so far [more] than we had expected. General Howard's ability as a soldier is almost eclipsed by his kindness and consideration for his troops, their comfort and welfare in every particular, his persistent fighting when engaged, and determination to win; the reckless disregard of his own person; his implicit obedience to all authorized orders, and the child-like simplicity of his social character. He has in his personal address a nervous and unstudied gesture, which to people unacquainted with him, appears feminine. Still his address is elegant and his language indicates a mind of very superior cultivation.

His most marked characteristic is his especial military ability and unerring judgment in military operations. His energy of character I have never seen surpassed, and with all he is the highest toned gentleman I have ever known. It appears impossible for him ever to think amiss. He is by no means the profound thinker and learned man that General Sherman is, nor has he his large natural ability. He does not call out from his troops the enthusiastic applause that Generals Logan and Hooker do; yet every officer and man has an unbounded confidence in him, and never question that an order from him is from the highest known authority, or even think of going beyond it for a superior decision. I have never been in an Army where such implicit confidence was displayed in its leader.[1]

NOTE

1. "General Howard, who has command of our right wing during this campaign has often been called the Havelock of the army; and the parallel is not un-

natural for both the hero of the Indian campaign and our own distinguished General will rank in history as perfect types of the Christian soldier. General Howard is a man whose religious convictions are intense, positive, entering into and coloring every event of his life. When exposed to fire there is no braver man living than he. . . . He sees the whole field of operations, and has an admirable tactical knowledge of the best use to be made of its advantages. It is a high compliment to his worth as a man and a soldier that he should have been chosen by General Sherman to the command of the right wing of the army. General Sherman may not be a religious man in the sense that Howard is, but he valued and respected Howard all the more for his Christian faith and practice." Nichols, *Story of the Great March,* 141-42.

Hitchcock quoted Sherman: "Howard is a good man and a sincere Christian; he is an instance that a man may be a good Christian and *yet a good soldier." Marching with Sherman,* 235.

Rivers' Bridge,
Colleton Dist S. C.
February 4, 1865

Our train carrying the wounded left this morning at daylight. The enemy have left our entire front. This morning I rode over the enemy's position and in crossing the river, crossed *sixteen* clear and fine running streams, on an average of fifty feet wide and from one to two hundred feet apart. This seems to be the character of the rivers in this country.

The enemy's works on the north side of the river, consist of a redoubt for four guns, bearing on the section of road mentioned before, and an infantry parapet for about 2,000 men. The position could scarcely have been better. The enemy's loss proves to have been about the same as our own, i.e. 100 men. We took last evening seven prisoners, and this morning picked up a few more. We learn that the 5th, 37th, 47th Georgia Infantry Regiments were here also 5th South Carolina Artillery, 4th Tennessee Cavalry, also two companies of Texas Cavalry, in all 2700 men, commanded by Colonel Harrison,[1] 32nd Ga. Inf'ty. This Military District is commanded by General McLaws.[2]

We have often fought against McLaws in Tennessee and Virginia. The enemy also had one four-gun light battery called the Beaufort Artillery.

I scouted around on the opposite side of the river considerably [and] found the country higher and better cultivated and with plenty of supplies which had been increased by large amounts taken over from this side while we were approaching. I saw two men, "Galvanized Yankees," who had belonged to our Army and had enlisted from Rebel prisons, in the band of the 32nd Georgia Infantry.

The majority of the citizens here are of the same "cracker or sand hill" species we have found so plentiful everywhere we have been. I heard a soldier say to his comrade today the "the whole damned state was not worth the life of our Federal soldiers." He was about right. We everywhere hear the fear expressed of "Negro equality," while no one ever expressed a fear of equality with this class of "Southern white-trash."

They are lower than the negro in every respect, not excepting general intelligence, culture and morality. A man not acquainted with this larger population of the South can form an idea of it in their style of living and cleanliness, &c. They are not fit to be kept in the same sty with a well to do farmer's hogs in New England. Once in ten or fifteen miles we find a plantation owned by a *"reliable"* man, a *"first family"* who lives in Charleston or Columbia, while every half mile we find a shanty with the poles a foot apart, a stick chimney, three or four half naked children, two or three with nothing but a shirt, but with an incrustation of dirt which entirely conceals the natural color; the mother with her person partially concealed by ragged cotton cloth and dirt combined. If you ask her where her husband is, the reply is "in the Army" or "I haint never had no husband," "I'm an old maid."

General Howard to day visited General Sherman at Beaufort's [Buford's] Bridge, who gave directions for this Army to cross the river here and go to the rail road tomorrow. General S appeared much delighted with our success at the river, and gaining the crossing with no greater loss. The five brigades of the left wing have been turned toward Barnwell. We have the same report today from Slocum including Kilpatrick and Corse's division of this Army. The force with Slocum on the other side of the river cannot fall short of 25,000 men, and perhaps as high as 30,000. Sherman has determined to push on and accomplish his work, and if necessary to fight without the assistance of Slocum. From what we can learn of the enemy, we are induced to believe they are not in great force in our front.

We understand that the XXIII Army Corps has gone to New-berne [New Bern] and if this is so, it will be of great advantage to us in occupying the attention of the enemy while we are out of reach of the coast.

There is also a rumor that Columbia is being strongly fortified.

I hope this is not so, as all wish to get in the city, and we think Sherman will not attempt any fortified places. No one knows yet where Sherman intends to go, but a careful study of the map indicates that he will go above the city of Columbia, and thus avoid the great swamps nearer the coast, and those especially on the Santee and Congaree Rivers.

If we go to Columbia, or below Columbia, direct on Florence, nearly the whole country will have to be bridged, while if we go around Columbia, the country will be comparatively high. Reasoning in this way I draw my conclusion. We will see how correct I am in judging of Sherman's plans by studying strategy on the state map and the development of his movements so far.

We have made quite a mistake this morning in sending back the wagons, or rather a misunderstanding of the order by the Qr Master. He thought the Army was to remain here until the train returned. He unloaded four days' rations and sent the wagons back. General H's instructions were to make no stop but trust to fortune for the trains to overtake us again, guarded by a small escort. A portion of the train has been sent for tonight, and will probably be back tomorrow by making a forced march.

Everything remains quiet tonight.

NOTES

1. Col. George P. Harrison.
2. Maj.-Gen. Lafayette McLaws.

Rivers' Bridge, S. C.
February 5, 1865

Not much has transpired today worth speaking of. The XVII Army Corps has crossed the river and marched out on the road to Millersville P. O. towards Midway. The XV A. C. crossed at Buford's Bridge, moved out the same distance towards Lowry's Turnout. The XX A. C., i.e. the five brigades, are close by the XV A. C., and on the same road, but will in the morning turn to the left toward Barnwell, and make the RR to the left of the XV A. C.

General Sherman sends word this evening that Kilpatrick is passing through Arnondale [Allendale] Post Office making toward Barnwell. If the cavalry is over, we may soon expect the assistance of Slocum.

Scouts have been sent forward and report the enemy holding the Little Salkehatchie in the same way that this stream was held, i.e. a brigade entrenched on the opposite side of the stream covering each road.

We have now had our headquarters four days in one place but the Army has been hard at work all the time. These head quarters have been the pivot on which the Army has made a right wheel. The XVII A. C. has done its fighting and made about eight miles. The XV A. C. has marched from twenty-five to thirty miles, and is now ahead of us on the north side of the Salkehatchie River. We are now ready to move on the rail road twenty miles ahead.

Our foraging parties are now gathering on the north side of the river more material than can be consumed, and large accumulations will be left in the morning.[1] Our trains that were ordered to return to the Army after having started for stores, have returned. Fifty wagons went on with the wounded and on their return will probably be captured, at any rate the Rebels are a pack of fools if they do not capture this train. The Southern people and papers talk of peace and how it may be reached and the papers hold out to the country but little hope that they can ever whip us. They say Commissioners[2] have been sent to Washington to see what can be done &c.

We had services today and learned from the Divine that "Hagar left the household of Abraham on account of certain *little family difficulties.*" Long live the Army Chaplain.

NOTES

1. At this time Hitchcock was in charge of the mess for Sherman's headquarters. In his letter of February 2 he commented: "I am happy to say, since my duties as caterer give me special interest in these matters now, that we find more 'supplies' in this country than I had feared we might. Chickens, sweet potatoes, fresh pork and honey and fresh lard, all rewarded the zealous inquiries of our headquarters foragers today; and the dinner table tonight reminded one of Georgia in its abundance." *Marching with Sherman,* 246-47.

2. Vice President Alexander H. Stephens, Senator Robert M. T. Hunter, and Assistant Secretary of War John A. Campbell were the Confederate commissioners who met with Lincoln and Secretary of State William H. Seward at Fortress Monroe, Hampton Roads, Va., February 3 in a fruitless conference.

Cowpen Ford,
Colleton District, S. C.
February 6, 1865

We have today accomplished a fair day's work and with fair suc-cess. At 7 A. M. we left Rivers' Bridge and moved direct to this place. [We] met with no resistance till we reached this ford where we had the ordinary skirmish. The men seemed impatient and went at the work with great energy, one party skirmishing directly down the road and another deployed and moving by the flank through the swamp beyond the flank of the enemy. We dislodged them, probably 500 strong, in an hour and a half, from the oppo-site bank, but they fought well. This stream is of the same charac-ter as the Big Salkehatchie, but only a quarter of a mile wide, and the water considerably deeper than the other. This river is in *nine* streams, each bridge being about sixty feet long; in the remainder of the swamp the water is about knee deep.

The XV A. C. moved from Buford's Bridge at the same time that we moved from Rivers' Bridge and had the same work to perform. They lost *two* men, and we *none.* The XV A. C. moved to Dun-cansville, only five miles from the rail road, we are ten miles from it. The enemy is preparing to make the usual resistance at Lemon's Creek.

If our maps are correct, Logan has already turned that position, and we shall have no resistance there though our scouts have been to the bank of Lemon's Creek and find the enemy tearing up and burning the bridges. I should have said before that all the bridges on this stream were burned and a good barricade of fallen timbers [erected] near the further bank. It required only four hours to re-pair the road through. The five brigades of the XV A. C. turned to the left this morning with instructions to strike the R. R. at the best and easiest point, on Logan's left.

General Sherman says this morning that Logan will make direct for the Rail Road in the morning; the same of Williams. Kilpatrick will be on the R. R. at 8 o'clock A. M. tomorrow at Graham's Turn-out.[1]

Nothing new of Slocum; we expect he will be at Barnwell to-morrow.

The force of the enemy and his whereabouts is still a mystery. We have no knowledge of any force but what I have already men-tioned being in front of us. The citizens have all kinds of rumors.

Some say there is nothing to stop us, others say we will *see* when the time comes, others that Longstreet[2] is coming with 15,000 men (an old dodge) and all curse Davis because he don't send help to stop Sherman. Officers differ in opinion, some think we shall be met at the rail road by a considerable force, others think that the stand will be made on the north bank of the Edisto, to save Branchville and the R. R. north and east. I am inclined to think the latter plan is the one the enemy will adopt, or at least intend to. We shall soon know more.

The weather is again unsettled and this P. M. and evening it is raining slowly.

NOTES

1. Denmark.
2. Lieut.-Gen. James Longstreet.

Midway, S. C.
February 7, 1865

We left Cow Pen Ford this morning in a severe and very unpleasant rainstorm, taking the direct road to this place. The rain had softened and flooded the road so it was very bad and even before the first brigade had passed it was necessary to corduroy the road. Five miles from the ford we came to Lemon Swamp or Creek, which is of the same character as the Salkehatchie Rivers; but is crossed by only four bridges. The timber had been felled into the road and the water was very high, owing to the recent rains. The Rebels had told all the people that they would make a severe fight at the creek, but they were gone when we reached it. We had the road repaired and were crossing in two hours after we reached the stream. One regiment had been sent through on our arrival at the creek and moved out about a mile on the north side and halted. As soon as the bridges were finished, General Howard and staff rode on, and after passing the advanced Regts. a little way, we met a "Bummer" or forager on a good horse, just picked up, with a rope bridle, rope stirrups, and an old blanket for saddle, coming post haste to inform the General that the foragers had taken the rail road at Midway and were holding it for the Army to come up. The extreme ludicrousness of the idea that a party of "Bummers" had gone in advance of the Army and taken the vital rail road of the Confederacy, and were holding it for the Army to come up, coupled with our extreme anxiety as to whether we could get it at all without a pitched battle, and the novel style in which this orderly of the Bummers made his appearance was too much for the General as the idea struck him. Knowing what a keen appreciation General Blair[1] had of a "good thing" he sent the orderly to General B to report the facts to him. General Blair taking the joke at once, sent him to the division commanders, and so the poor fellow was officially shown around to the major generals; each one with genuine military dignity passing him down to his subordinate.

The foraging organization is an institution by itself. The parties or men engaged in this duty are known only as "Bummers." Even in official communications they are frequently spoken of as "Bummers."[2] I doubt whether the history of war shows an organization equal to it in scientific and authorized stealing. These squads are composed of about twenty men each, selected for their great personal bravery and reliable character as soldiers. They are always commanded by picked officers, whose duty it is to scout the country and gather everything that can be used by the Army.

Nothing escapes them; they go miles in every direction from the main column, and never hesitate to fight wherever the enemy can be found and very frequently whip ten times their own number. A column of troops always stops to reconnoitre if they find the enemy skirmishers in their front as the presumption is that the enemy will not appear at the head of a column unless in considerable force. The Bummers pitch in at once, and either whip the enemy, or as soon as they find the enemy too heavy for them, retreat.

They invariably go to each other's assistance, and whenever firing is heard, every party within hearing goes to the assistance of the party attacked. We feel more safe with these men out on every side of us than if we had ten times their number of organized cavalry; as we cannot be approached on any side without sufficient notice of the approach of the enemy, and the bold front they put on always deceives the enemy as to the force they have. There is, however, of necessity a strong demoralizing tendency connected with this work.

It cultivates a strong tendency to illegitimate plundering, and requires a firm hand on the part of commanding officers to keep this spirit under, and even then it is by no means possible to do it.[3]

The rain continued all day and the roads are horrible, requiring a great amount of labor to get the trains through.

We found on our road here that the enemy had prepared cover to fight from every half mile for several miles, but Logan's column turned them out of the position.

Our troops reached the R. R. about 2 P. M. and went into defensive position and are ready to be attacked if the enemy are near enough and strong enough to do it. Midway is a little place of five houses and a good depot, &c. There is a German Jew who has a couple hundred bales of cotton and wants protection because he is a foreigner.

He asks that his cotton be saved to pay some "beeples" [people] up in New York, who he owes some "little debts." He will hardly save the cotton.

General Logan reached the R. R. at Bamberg, at 7:30 A. M. and sent a detachment to the Edisto bridges, and General Blair sent one to a bridge lower down as soon as he reached here. The Rebels burned all bridges when these detachments showed themselves, including the R. R. bridge which was precisely what we wished. They have by this means prevented themselves from annoying us any while we remain here. Prisoners tell us that most of Stevenson's Division of S. D. Lee's Corps, Hood's Army, has gone through to Branchville. This appears to be all the reinforcements they have got. Hood passed through in person a couple of days since to Richmond. Hampton's[4] Division of Cavalry is at Columbia and is being mounted on impressed horses. The people talk of peace, reconstruction &c. I looked over the mail captured here and find the universal expression is that all are tired of the war and never expect to win, excepting perhaps a few just impressed and running around in front of us. Officers and old soldiers say they are whipped, and the sooner they get into the Yankee lines the better.

NOTES

1. Maj.-Gen. Francis Preston Blair, Jr.
2. "Early on the 7th, in the midst of a rain-storm, we reached the railroad, almost unopposed, striking it at several points. General Howard told me a good story concerning this, which will bear repeating here: He was with the Seven-

teenth Corps., marching straight for Midway, and when about five miles distant he began to deploy the leading division, so as to be ready for battle. Sitting on his horse by the road-side, while the deployment was making, he saw a man coming down the road, riding as hard as he could, and as he approached he recognized him as one of his own foragers. As he came near he called out, 'Hurry up, general; we have got the railroad!' So, while we, the generals, were proceeding deliberately to prepare for a serious battle, a parcel of our foragers, in search of plunder, had got ahead and actually captured the South Carolina Railroad, a line of vital importance to the rebel Government." Sherman, II, 273-74.

In his *The Star Corps* the Rev. G. S. Bradley, chaplain of 22d Wisconsin Infantry, wrote admiringly of Sherman's soldiers in general but derogated the excesses of the Bummers, excesses that grew in number and extent as the columns passed through South Carolina. "These 'Bummers', " he recorded, "were detailed for foragers, and upon them the army depended for subsistence; for be it known that we started with a very small stock of supplies, and our campaign was lengthened after starting from our base (Savannah), consequently the 'Bummers' were the life of the army. About 5,000 strong, not a field or house or barn, but was searched by them; not a town or hamlet but the 'infernal bummers' (as Kilpatrick said) managed to plunder before his cavalry came up. They met the enemy at Fayetteville, and drove him across Cape Fear river; they entered Columbia as skirmishers, not only for 'Johnnies,' but for meat and bread and goodies. Many outrages were committed by them. To enter a house and find the feather bed ripped open, the wardrobes ransacked, chests stripped of contents, looking glasses taken from the walls, cooking utensils gone, and all the corn meal and bacon missing, bed quilts stripped from the beds, the last jar of pickles gone, was no uncommon sight, and one to make a soldier blush with indignation. Every effort that could be made was made to check the demorilization of the foragers; but the occupation tended to demorilization, and 'the army must be fed, and the Bummers must feed us.' Thus we reasoned, but deprecated the means used to bring about the result. Some would discriminate, others would not, and thus the few have caused a great deal of unnecessary suffering." G. S. Bradley, *The Star Corps; or, Notes of an Army Chaplain, During Sherman's Famous "March to the Sea"* (Milwaukee, 1865), 275-76.

3. "We do so many things that are wrong in this living off the country in the way we do that I do not like it and I am afraid of retribution. I am particularly made to feel this when we reach a loyal place like Beaufort. It is almost impossible to keep the soldiers from seizing every horse and mule and appropriating sundry other things that don't belong to them." Howard, ALS to his wife, Near Pocotaligo, January 27, 1865. Howard Collection.

4. Lieut.-Gen. Wade Hampton.

Midway, S. C.
February 8, 1865

This morning the troops were distributed along the R. R. and the work of destroying executed in the usual manner, commencing at the bridge over the Edisto River and moving west.

General Blair's Corps destroyed seven miles, General Logan's seven, and on his left General Williams, and next Kilpatrick. The road is most thoroughly destroyed, and it will be a bad job to repair it.

We learn that Branchville is evacuated excepting a very small force nominally holding it. The report and impression today is that the enemy are concentrating at Columbia and fortifying. They are doubtless correct in leaving Branchville and concentrating somewhere, but they show in doing so so soon that they are a good deal frightened and that they are weak. They should have kept a good front at Branchville, and fallen back when they were compelled to do so, and not have stampeded now when it is decidedly to our advantage and morale to have them go. They certainly would have time to leave, but by their hasty movements, they show that their force is small, and they should not have let us know that now!

I visited today the residence of William Gilmore Simms, the South Carolina novelist and author of "Marion" &c. He has evacuated but has left a very ardent secesh family to protect the residence and library for him. He has a fine Library. I think it will be saved. I should have no objection to seeing it burned. His influence has been very great in carrying on the war.[1]

We now have word that Slocum is on the way up, a portion of his force being yesterday at Hickory Hill. The roads are very bad, and he will probably come up slow.

An escaped prisoner is just in from Florence. He reports that the suffering there is intense. Each man has a pint and a half of meal per day and a little salt—no meat. His own appearance proves that he has suffered.[2]

The weather today is clear, with a high wind. This country is the same low bottom land, or semi-quick sand we have had all the time. It is covered with pine timber. The swamps have the ordinary swamp timber, including cypress which grow to immense size. There are a great many of the sink holes, or shallow cypress swamps, in which no trees but the cypress grow. These swamps are perfectly represented by the stereoscopic views of them. We have passed beyond the region of the live oaks, and have seen no portion of the state but what was low and sandy. Excepting the coast, it is a comtemptible country.

NOTES

1. "When Sherman's army approached Woodlands in February, 1865, Simms took his daughters and younger sons and departing by train from the nearby station of Midway reached Columbia a week or so ahead of the army.... The writer has seen three claims—one from a major-general and two by colonels who served in Sherman's army—that when Sherman's army was passing Woodlands Station Simms appeared at his gate and sought the claimant officer to put a guard over his valuable library. Each of the heroes of the episode is reported to have offered an impolite rebuff and then to have replied: 'Your fame does not belong to the South, but to the nation.'
"As a matter of fact, the episode occurred in Columbia. A young lieutenant who had learned in some way of Simms's presence in Columbia...secured a guard for his Columbia abode.... The guards that had been placed at Woodlands by those old 'fourflushers' were ineffective, however. Woodlands was burned." A. S. Salley in his introduction to the second (reprint) edition of William Gilmore Simms's *Sack and Destruction of the City of Columbia, S. C.* (Atlanta, 1937), xviii-xix.
Nichols noted February 12: "To-night we are encamped upon the place of one of South Carolina's most high-blooded chivalry—one of those persons who believed himself to have been brought into the world to rule over his fellow creatures, a sort of Grand Pasha and all that sort of thing. How the negro pioneers are making away with the evergreens and rose-bushes of his artistically arranged walks, flower-beds, and drives! These black men in blue are making brooms of his pet shrubs, with which they clear the grounds in front of the tents." *Story of the Great March,* 149.
Hedley wrote: "Whether his premises were destroyed or not, the author does not know; but many books from his library, bearing his autograph, found their way into camp, and were carried away by the men as mementoes." *Marching Through Georgia,* 361.
Much later the distinguished Southern poet Paul Hamilton Hayne wrote historian Lyman C. Draper: " '*The Magnolia Mag.,*' and the back nos. of the '*So. Literary Gazette*' needed for your life of Sumter, are non-existent I fear. My friend, the late W. Gilmore Simms had copies of these works, and many individual historical pamphlets, (never to be replaced), in his great library at Woodlands, (Barnwell District, S. C.), but at that the *special* order of your Genl. Tecumseh Sherman—is not *that,* pardon me for saying so—, his *appropriate* name? the Library was burnt, and all these treasures went heavenward on the wings of fire.... If, however, you know any of the officers, or soldiers who accompanied Sherman in 'his grand march to the sea,' it is *just* possible that the works mentioned, may be procured from some one of them. I make this suggestion in no sneering spirit, believe me." William B. Hesseltine and Larry Gara, eds., "Sherman Burns the Libraries," *South Carolina Historical Magazine,* LV, no. 3 (July 1954), 141.
Woodlands was burned February 18, after the burning of Columbia. What caused this fire is a question still moot.
2. Conyngham wrote at this time: "A man named William Clark, formerly of Colonel Walford's cavalry came into our lines. He was an escaped prisoner and had been concealed for eight weeks by the poor negroes. He remained in the swamps by day, and joined his kind protectors at night. Though they would be liberally rewarded for betraying him, still they were faithful." *Sherman's March Through the South,* p. 320.

Binnaker's Bridge,[1]
South Edisto River, S. C.
February 9, 1865

We left Midway at 8 A. M. and moved to this point on the main road, about twelve miles. We have had the best roads we have found considering the late rains. The day is fine. The disposition of the troops today is for Logan to move still further down the R. R. towards Augusta and finish the destruction of the road to Blacksville [Blackville]. This was to be done with two Divisions, while Hazen was to move to Holman's Bridge[2] and effect a crossing if possible. General Blair was to move to Binnaker's bridge, and make a crossing at all hazards. The head of column reached the bridges at 1 P. M. and found plenty of Rebels on the opposite bank to make a stubborn resistance. General Mower had the advance of the XVII A. C. and when he reached the river, threw out his skirmishers to feel the position. The enemy had a section of artillery and a brigade of infantry on the opposite bank. Mower also put in artillery and commenced operations by sharp shooting. He then moved to the left about half a mile, and laid a pontoon bridge without being discovered by the enemy over the main stream and crossed two brigades to an island. The enemy did not develop while Mower was on the island, and he moved in an air line through the swamp to the opposite side.

The water continued to grow deeper as they advanced till the men undid their cartridge boxes and swung them about their necks and carried their knapsacks on their shoulders. The deepest water was a little more than waist deep but the troops reached the opposite bank and got into position just as the enemy's skirmishers found them. By the time a sufficient force was over it was too dark to operate, and the General concluded to wait till morning, and entrenched all his force which consisted of his own division and one brigade of G. A. Smith's division. Getting a little restless in his unpleasant position, at eight o'clock he moved on the enemy but they left the moment they discovered he was moving.

This gives us the bridge, or rather the road and a place to put the bridge.

General Hazen at Holman's Bridge did not accomplish so much as General Mower. Their relative positions were about the same at dark, but Hazen waited till morning while Mower moved on the enemy in the evening. The river here is a deep and rather rapid stream, and differs from the others we have crossed by passing one main channel, and wide, swampy banks, a mile wide, covered with water and filled with the usual swamp timbers. Our entire loss today has been two men killed and three wounded. The other two divisions of the XV A. C. have worked all day on the R. R.

This country is more rolling, and better than most we have passed through, and has plenty of supplies. The enemy evidently do not intend to destroy any great amount of provisions for the sake of starving us. Wheeler's order to destroy all but ten days rations for the people, for the purpose of starving Sherman, as Napoleon was starved in Russia, does not suit the South Carolina people better than the Georgians. There is no bushwhacking done; men only operate in regularly organized bodies of troop. In fact, there are no men in the state excepting the army. In one year more the South will have attained one of their original propositions—Independence or extermination, unless they quit while a few men are left to propagate the species.

Everything looks well this evening.

NOTES

1. Binnaker's was at the site where the Julius B. Ness Bridge now crosses the South Fork of the Edisto River on state highway 70.

2. Holman's Bridge stood where state highway 34 now dead ends at the Edisto River, about two miles west of state highway 321.

Binnaker's Bridge, S. C.
February 10, 1865

This morning General Blair sent one of the divisions further out on the road, and with the remainder of the command repaired the road through the swamp, and built the bridge. The water in the road for half mile is two feet deep, but the road is good and will do for the trains, so we will only require a foot bridge for the troops. Hazen this morning found this front clear, and has moved over. Scouting parties have been out, and learn that when the enemy reached the Orangeburg and Edgfield road they turned to the left. This shows that they expect us at Columbia or Augusta yet. We have picked up about a dozen men from Stevenson's division belonging to Stovall's brigade. They report the brigade as only four hundred strong, and also in coming here they marched from Milledgeville to some point on the Ga. Central R. R. This shows the R. R. is repaired from Macon to Milledgeville, but that it is not repaired so as to make a connection through Atlanta as they have reported.

The tenor of information still is that the enemy concentrating at Columbia and fortifying. General Corse, who has been with Slocum, camped last night at Rivers' Bridge, and has marched nearly twenty miles today. He sends in word that he is very tired and has hard work in repairing roads. Slocum has reached Blackville today and is getting on our left. I do not know to how great an extent his delay has changed General Sherman's plans, but I suspect considerably. I know we have done comparatively little with what we might have accomplished had he kept parallel with us and cooperated in all that has been done. I have not yet learned the alleged cause of his delay.

General Corse is tonight within six miles of the camp. The weather is magnificent. The roads are as good as the season of the year and nature of the soil will conveniently admit. One of the scouts today picked up a lieutenant Colonel by the name of Dougherty,[1] who had been a prisoner and was paroled for exchange. He was in Richmond on the 29th and says peace was much talked of on the streets.

NOTE

1. Not identified.

McMichael's Plantation[1] Near Orangeburg, S. C.
East Bank, North Edisto Orangeburg Dist.,
February 11, 1865

We left Camp at 7 o'clock A. M. crossed the Edisto taking the main road to Poplar Springs. Our march of fifteen miles was easy and made early. The weather and roads are good. The XV A. C. crossed at Holman's Bridge and moved on the left to Poplar Springs, so as to support this if it should be necessary. It was scarcely expected the enemy would fight at Orangeburg, but it was quite possible, as troops can be thrown from every direction to this point with great facility by R. R. They could then strike our column as it crossed the river, or make an effort to prevent the crossing, or if they should have force enough to take the offensive. Any man of good military judgment would know that moving as we have done before, that the body of the troops now here, must be but a small portion of Sherman's whole force. At any previous period of the war, we should have had a desperate battle here.

The map can scarcely show a point where troops can be so readily concentrated. The R. R. lines of this point are perfect for the concentration of an army.

The swamps on the bank of this river are the same as we have found elsewhere. A battery on the opposite side commanding the road in the old style and, in fact, it appears to be the old game over again.

Both corps are now up and can co-operate in getting over the stream. We expect the enemy to resist more stubbornly than at any time before. General Corse is near enough to-night to report for duty. There are several indications this evening that the enemy will make a fair resistance, and perhaps fight. We hear the whistle of the locomotive every few minutes. A report comes in from the front that cheering has been heard over the river. The S. C. Militia was sent a couple of days since to the R. R. bridge over the Congaree River, but they could be easily returned. We know of no troops on the opposite side of the river but Stevenson's Division.

They prepared the ground where we now are last night for a battle, but left on our approach. Our Hd. Qrs. are well fortified.

The Charleston *Courier* says that Wade Hampton's Corps of Cavalry has been added to the operating force against us, while our information is that not more than one half of it is mounted and fit for service. The death of the Rebel General Winder[2] is announced. He was buried at Columbia a day or two since. Nothing from the left wing today.

I just hear that a space on the opposite side of the river has been found not picketed by the enemy. We hope to steal a march on them, and cross early tomorrow.

NOTES

1. This plantation was located just southward of the point at which state highway 74 crosses the North Edisto River at Shillings' Bridge.

2. Brig.-Gen. John Henry Winder. He was provost marshal at Richmond and in

November 1864 became commissary general for all prisoners east of the Mississippi. He died in Florence, S. C., 7 February 1865. He is now buried in Green Mount Cemetery, Baltimore.

Orangeburg,
Orangeburg Dist. S. C.
February 12, 1865

The main body of the command this morning was substantially the same as last evening. General Force had satisfied himself that two miles below, the east bank of the river was not picketed, and he could bridge the river there and cross. He moved his division down at daylight. To cross here he was obliged to cut a road through the bottom land for the infantry.

General Logan had found a road which crossed the North Edisto where the Caw Caw Swamp Creek empties into it. This made it necessary to cross two streams instead of the river alone. The bridge on this road is called Shillings' Bridge. General L moved his command to the bridge and demonstrated heavily against it, and then threw columns two miles each side of him, i.e. above and below. The main bridge was defended the same as the bridge immediately in front of Orangeburg. He pressed his work with his flanking columns very rapidly, and skirmished heavily on most of his line. With Generals Howard and Blair I visited most of the line of operations between 8 and 10 o'clock and then joined General Force, who was making his way over at the point mentioned.

The bridge was finished about noon, and the troops thrown over, and deployed as they reached the opposite bank.

The first intimation the enemy had of the crossing was just as the bridge was finished. A Rebel scout following the bank of the river ran into our men and fired his musket, but it was too late to make any resistance.

This swamp resembles the others very closely. While General Force was operating, Gen. G. A. Smith skirmished heavily with infantry and artillery. In a few minutes after General Force moved his division over, the enemy left their works, and our infantry followed in pursuit. General Howard and myself went around by the main road in hopes of getting over on horseback, but the bridge was burned, and we went to the town on foot. The town is a half mile from the river and by the time we could reach it, the two divisions of Force and Smith were occupying positions beyond the town. The enemy had fine open roads to retreat over, and they made the most of it. We took but few prisoners, but from them we learn that the enemy took the main road to Columbia. General Logan was making good headway and had secured a footing on this bank and would in a few moments have succeeded as General Blair did. When the enemy broke from his front, he charged them and captured about seventy men. In reality General Logan accomplished more than General Blair as he had by far the worst place to cross. Stevenson's division only was here.

As the troops crossed over, they went into position covering the R. R. east of the town, and set to tearing it up. Five or six miles are already destroyed.

Orangeburg contains about 800 people, and was, before we entered it, a fine little place with a fair proportion of churches, small cotton brokers' establishments, &c. &c. As our skirmishers entered town, one of the largest stores in the centre of town was on fire, and the fire just breaking through the roof. The building was occupied as a drug store and was filled mostly with liquors, resin &c. We took all the measures possible to stop the fire, but the day is dry and the wind blowing a gale. The fire spread rapidly, the buildings being close together and the yards filled with negro quarters and sheds helped to conduct the flames.

If the town had been built on purpose for a bonfire it could not have been bettered. All that could be done was to watch it on the windward side and the outskirts of the town. We occupied the town at 2 P. M. and at four one third or one half of the town was on fire and burning with the greatest rapidity. I think one half of the body of the town was destroyed. There were scarcely any male citizens at home, and many of the women were away, and most of the houses were burned without being molested.

We learned that the fire originated in this manner. Stevenson ordered that a large amount of cotton belonging to a Jew be burned, which was done when he left the town; when they fired the cotton he fired his own store, locked it up and went out with the Rebel army, and as we entered the town, both the cotton and store were burning. The Rebels burned the Jew's Cotton, and the Jew burned the Rebel town in retaliation. The man's name was Ezekial. There were several store-houses burned by the rebels, but the fire did not spread from any other. This fire was not so extensive as the one at Atlanta, but more grand and beautiful. Our soldiers assisted the inhabitants to save their property with the same good will as they would have stolen everything in town under other circumstances. The fire has been burning all the evening with great vigor. All the people say that our officers and men have treated them with great kindness and consideration.[1]

It takes some experience like this to dampen the people's spirit, and this has done it effectually for the present. Treat the people here kindly and they are impudent and disgusting, treat them as their own friends treat them, or without consideration and they become reasonable beings. Doubtless the Rebels will give us the credit for burning the town, but they will not be able to make the townspeople believe it.

I learn that our captures today amount to ninety-two prisoners, one hundred and fifty muskets; our loss is two killed, six wounded.

This is the last considerable stream before we cross the Congaree, and the one we had anticipated most trouble in crossing, but we have accomplished it with comparative ease. It rests now with the enemy to fall back or fight us.

General Sherman is with us tonight and has sent Slocum orders to move on Columbia two columns. He will probably have but little resistance as we have now turned all the streams which will cover the enemy's operations, for the present.

General Sherman also says S. D. Lee's Corps is at Augusta. Wade Hampton's Cavalry Corps is at Columbia, the militia at Fort Motte near Kingsville, this side of the Congaree. Wheeler is after Kilpatrick, and now the question is where and when these troops will concentrate? General Sherman tells me this evening that all the commanders, Grant, Schofield, Foster, and Thomas are pledged to keep the enemy busy in their respective fronts, while he is in here, and the General is much gratified by the news in the Rebel papers, that Grant is pressing Lee. Schofield is pushing Bragg,[2] Foster[3] is fighting Hardee about Charleston. The General says everything goes on well so far.

NOTES

1. "Unfortunately a portion of the city of Orangeburg has been burned, but not by our soldiers. The fire was first started by a Jew, from a feeling of revenge upon

the Rebels, who had destroyed fifty bales of cotton belonging to him. The high wind which prevailed spread the conflagration in spite of the efforts of our soldiers, who, under the orders of Generals Sherman and Howard, tried to extinguish the flames." Nichols, *Story of the Great March,* 149.

John G. Barrett, basing his version on Oscar L. Jackson's *The Colonel's Diary* (Sherron [Sharron, Pa.] 1922), tells it differently: "The first Federals to enter the town set fire to a large store standing at the head of the main street. High prevailing winds plus a general inclination on the part of the Federal soldiers to assist rather than extinguish the fires resulted in a general conflagration." *Sherman's March Through the Carolinas* (Chapel Hill, 1956), 58-59. At Orangeburg, Jackson was a major in the Sixty-Third Ohio, serving in Blair's XVII Corps.

2. Gen. Braxton Bragg.

3. On February 9 Foster turned his command over to Maj.-Gen. Quincy A. Gillmore.

Big [Beaver] Creek,
Pen Creek Church[1]
February 13, 1865

We have marched twelve miles today on an excellent road and over a good rolling country. The head quarters moved with two divisions of XV A. C. up the left bank of Caw Caw Swamp, the other two divisions of the Corps moved up the right bank. The XVII A. C. marched up the R. R. with instructions to destroy it to the crossing of the state road or as far as Lewisburg. General Blair sent the Mounted Infantry up the R. R. to burn the trestle and bridges, and if possible force the enemy to burn the bridge over the Congaree. General Blair reports his destruction of the R. R. complete. The two divisions of the XV A. C. with us made a detour of seven miles to cross Caw Caw Swamp, this morning, and lost so much on the distance march. The other two divisions of the Corps are six miles in advance of us at Sandy River P. O.

Today has been beautiful, clear and still. From the starting of the column this morning we could trace the tracks of each by the column of smoke from burning buildings, cotton, turpentine mills, pine woods &c. [Along] the line of the XVII A. C. on the R. R. the smoke lifted like a grand curtain here and there, tassled by a more dense column of smoke from a store house of cotton, or resin. The columns of smoke which marked Logan's line of march were more isolated, but in themselves were very dense. Many of these columns were really wonderful. The smoke rising from the pitch fields rolled up in volumes to the sky so impenetrable that not a ray of light could be seen through them. They looked like a dozen cities burning at the same time. I wish I had the power of describing the grandeur of this scene.

I think that during the half day I was riding from Orangeburg here, I scarcely took my eyes from it. I only wished for some one as company who appreciated it as keenly as I.[2]

The enemy have not molested, or even shown themselves today at all. It seems that they reached here at one o'clock last night, and left at daylight, taking the road toward Columbia.

Nothing from the left wing today.

NOTES

1. Pen Creek Church was located about eight miles northwest of the town of St. Matthews on U.S. highway 176.

2. "The magnificent spectacle of a fire in the woods was the striking episode of our march yesterday. The army moved through a tract of hilly country which was thickly clothed with pine forests. Many of the trees were dead, and all had been scraped in order to obtain the resinous substance which formed their fruit and life. Accidently or otherwise, the dry leaves and pine cones had caught fire, which ignited these trees, and for miles the woods were on fire. It was grand and sometimes awful to see the flames flying over the ground like a frightened steed. As we approached one of these forests, filled with flames and pitch black smoke, it appeared as if we were about to realize the imaginings of childhood, and see dragons and terrible beasts guarding the entrance to some forbidden ground. Wagons, horsemen, and foot-soldiers one by one disappeared into the gloom, to reappear here and there bathed in lurid light. Within, the fire singed our hair and clothes, while our maddened animals dashed hither and thither in an agony of fear. There was a terrible sublimity in this scene which I shall never forget; but it subsequently partook largely of the ridiculous when the column went into camp, each man so sooty and begrimed that it was almost impossible to distinguish African from Caucasian." Nichols, *Story of the Great March*, 153-54.

Sandy Run Post Office, S. C.[1]
Lexington Dist.,
February 14, 1865

The weather was good till 3 P. M. when it commenced raining, and the clouds now look like a settled storm. The roads have been good, and our troops and trains have moved easily. The country is hilly, not fertile, but few good plantations and those adapted to the raising of corn only. We have passed several large "Tar pitch and turpentine" mills. All the columns of the Army of the Tennessee had orders to concentrate here today. The first of our troops reached here at ten A. M. and are now closed up in supporting distance. The XV A. C. having the lead.

After the XV Corps had crossed the creek, the 29 Missouri Mounted Infantry were sent out to reconnoitre.

They had gone about four miles, when they overtook some Rebel cavalry guarding five Rebel gov't wagons.

They drove the cavalry off and captured the trains. They also found a ferry (Belts) over the Congaree. This we consider a valuable discovery, as we understood there was no crossing, and if the enemy resist us much at Columbia, we may use it to turn the city on the east. The farther bank of the river was guarded by five cavalry men. Our men fired upon them before they were seen. They left their horses and guns and took to the swamp, but as the river was not fordable they were left to come for their guns and get the equipments from the dead horses. This regiment also secured the bridge over Seven Hunting [Savany Hunt] Creek, and left a guard at it. General Woods' division has been sent to hold the ferry and bridge, and is now within eight miles of Columbia.

The XVII A. C. has done good work today.

The trains with one division moved here; the other two divisions reconnoitered to mystify the enemy, one division moving east to threaten an advance on the state road to Charleston.

They found the enemy's outposts, drove them in and then returned. The other division moved to Fort Motte and reached the R. R. Bridge at one P. M. The enemy set it on fire to prevent us from using it to cross the Army.

They could not possibly more fully carry out our intentions.

Junction Road is now sufficiently destroyed from Orangeburg to the Congaree River. Lt. McQueen[2] of the scouts found 200 negroes in a swamp where they had been secreted, and set them to burning the trestle work on the Rail Road, and then gave directions to have them all turned over to our Pioneer force. These Divisions of the XVII A. C. having returned, the Army of the Tennessee is all massed here, within fourteen miles of the City.

The roads for all our operations today have been good, but we fear they will be ruined by the rain tonight.

The incidents of the march were of no interest except the burning of the "tar pitch and turpentine" establishments, in some of which great quantities of material were stored. They make magnificent fires.

The enemy's line of works are reported to be this side of Columbia; the left resting at the mouth of Congaree Creek, on the Congaree River, following the left bank of the creek to the mouth of Six Mile Creek, up the left bank of it, and then across to the south fork of Twelve Mile Creek, down that till it strikes the Saluda River.

If this really proves to be the line, it is too long by one half for the enemy to hold, though with a large army it would be magnificent. From reports, Slocum appears to have outdone himself. He is said to be in the enemy's line of works, and not more than ten miles to our left. From what we can learn it seems the enemy have not more than one or two days expected us here. We constantly hear of small parties scattered all over the State, watching us, and apparently expecting us towards Charleston and Augusta.

They will probably be undeceived tomorrow as to our whereabouts. The negroes report all the male citizens of Columbia in the trenches.

A small party of Bummers today dug up seven thousand dollars in gold in the woods a half mile from any house. No notice will be taken of it by any officer.

NOTES

1. Located at the present junction of state highway 21 and U.S. highway 176.
2. Lieut. John A. McQueen.

IV Columbia

Near Congaree Creek,
Seven miles from Columbia, S. C.
February 15, 1865

We have had a hard day's work and have accomplished a fine amount of labor. Developments have been a little different from what we had expected. The morning was cold and rainy; the remainder of the day has been cloudy with a thick fog.

In the morning the 1st Division, XV A. C. moved on the state road supported by the 2nd and 4th divisions. The enemy skirmished back stubbornly about five miles, crossing Savany Hunt Creek, Thomas' Creek, and Dry Creek, which they reached by eleven A. M. We were unable to follow up till we drew the fire from the batteries but found a serious obstacle in the nature of the country. The place had once been a swamp then cleared and cultivated.

The rain had softened the surface so a man would sink to the ankle each step, horses deeper, and artillery could not be moved a step. The road is a causeway, ten or twelve feet high with deep ditches on either side.

This, under cover of the fog, and some blunder of a quarter master, was filled with wagons, ambulances &c, to within musket range of the enemy's works, and then no team could be gotten off or back—the fog only saved them.

The enemy directed their fire on the deployed troops, and did not fire on the road—the same silly blunder the enemy have made before, that of not opening with artillery on roads where troops must necessarily move. The salvation of this train was owing entirely to the fog. We had a few men injured by the Rebel fire, while lying in line of battle.

About 2 P. M. I went back to Sandy Run to conduct General Blair's column up to the front and was not present at the operations later in the P. M. But General Howard tells me that our skirmish line worked at the enemy without mercy, catching at every cover till they found the enemy's left, when they waded the creek waist deep. Sixty men crossed, turned the enemy's position and fired a volley into the back of the Rebel troops, before the enemy discovered them. The enemy abandoned the whole line at a stampede, and our troops followed directly over, saving the bridge. Two divisions were then thrown over, and advanced till they came to another position, a mile and a half distant, entrenched, where we went in position.

It was now night and very dark. After the first break the enemy showed no more infantry, but gave a magnificent display of cavalry, and in fact with a small force charged one flank of our skirmishers, but only succeeded in losing two of their own men killed. (Hampton's telegraphic report of this charge, to Davis, was so put and so much claimed to have been done, that Davis telegraphed back his appointment as Lieutenant General, C. S. A. This I learned from the telegraph operator. The facts as I state them of the charge are as I took them down from General Howard, Colonel Strong,[1] and others who were on the ground and saw it. The field is open and level, not a shrub on it. I have been thus definite in parenthesis to show on how small capital Hampton was made Lieutenant General. His telegraph to Davis was "I have repulsed Sherman's Army.")[2] This cavalry in line of battle was said to be magnificent. The front covered more than a mile, on the open field. It was evidently formed with the intention to make a grand charge on us if we showed the least weakness in our disposition, but fortunately our disposition was as perfect as General Hampton's, and General Howard describes the deploying of our troops as one of the most splendid manoeuvres of infantry he ever saw, in truth the best. General Woods' column was in advance, and moved over the bridge just beyond which the great field opened upon which he deployed his skirmish line, and line of battle and supports, so perfectly that no place could be discovered where Hampton could break it by a charge.

So much we have accomplished today.

The line we looked forward to as offering the most formidable resistance, is in our possession. This line so far as we have seen it is

strong, and in good condition. Whether they will concentrate tonight, or give us battle we cannot guess, or how strong the force
is, even. Our loss today is six killed and twelve wounded, so far as
I have learned, yet Slocum has done nothing. The feeling of disgust toward him in this Army is giving way to bitterness. We heard
the enemy's guns in his front at 3 P. M. yesterday, and while we
have been engaged all day, we hear nothing from him. General
Blair, who is a very prudent man, in speaking of officers, comments severely on him this P. M.

General Howard has word, while writing the last sentence, that
Slocum's troops have reached the Congaree tonight. His foragers
have been running into the head of our column for the last thirty-
six hours. This can be better appreciated when I say that one brigade of General Blair's Corps marched twenty-seven miles today
and the same brigade marched twenty yesterday and worked on
the R. R. all day. If General Blair's troops can march fifty miles in
two days, to assist in a fight, it appears that General Slocum ought
to move five miles, or at the most, ten to assist us. In fact it has
been our principal object for the past three days to reach this point
to assist General Slocum in his direct operations against Columbia,
but we have reached the ground first and he has not yet appeared
to help us.

NOTES

1. Lietu.-Col. William E. Strong, Howard's chief of staff.
2. Hampton was indeed promoted to lieutenant-general to take effect from February 14.

Saluda Factory on Saluda River
four miles from Columbia, S. C.
February 16, 1865

A little before midnight last night the enemy opened fire from a
battery in position on the north side of the river, firing into the
rear of our troops on this side. We had no artillery with which we
could silence it and they did considerable damage, killing an officer and several men, and wounding near twenty. The fire was very
annoying.[1] The enemy could see the position of the troops by the

camp fires. Our men at once built traverses and covered themselves in ditches for protection against the fire. The battery
opened again at daylight, but the fog prevented accurate firing. At
8 A. M. they opened again, but were soon silenced by DeGress'
battery. In fact he drove the men from the battery.

At 8 A. M. General Woods occupied the enemy's inner line of
works, and began to feel his way toward the bridge. General Howard ordered up the other columns, to be ready for an attack, and
then moved to the river. We arrived opposite the city at 9 A. M.
and found the bridge still burning. The Rebel sharpshooters on the
north bank of the river were very active. The streets of Columbia
were filled with cavalry. On the principal street, the one on which
the Episcopal Church and new State House stand, the enemy were
throwing up an earthwork. I ordered DeGress' battery in position
and shelled them out, and cleared the streets of cavalry in quick
time, but as the sharpshooters persisted in firing on our men, we
amused ourselves in shelling the town and seeing the people scat-
ter about the streets.[2] General Logan moved to the front of the
town. General Blair [moved] over the Congaree Bridge, which is
four miles above the bridge General Logan crossed, and reached
the river on our left at 10 A. M. At about 11 A. M. one of General
Slocum's staff came to General Sherman's Hd. Qrs. and reported
Slocum's column only a mile and a half out on the Lexington road.
This closed the Army up, and in the immediate vicinity of Columbia. The river at Columbia is too wide for our pontoons and General Howard moved the column up to Saluda Factory. The enemy
had burned a fine bridge here on their retreat. This stream was
bridged and the head of the XV A. C. passed over at 4 P. M. The
point of land between the two rivers is about a mile and a half
wide. We crossed a cavalry regiment first, which was followed by
infantry.

We knew there was also a bridge across Broad River and attempted to save it. The enemy had a brigade of cavalry on this side
of it, which had a fight of a few minutes with our advance, and
then retreated rapidly over the bridge and set fire to it. The enemy
had taken the precaution to cover the bridge with barrels of turpentine and resin; it burned like powder. The enemy then opened
with artillery directly on the bridge to prevent any attempt being
made to save it. It burned so rapidly that it fell in a half hour.

The column is moving over at the Factory, and will take till midnight to get the XV A. C. over and as much longer for the XVII. I have just come from General Slocum where I went to borrow some pontoons to assist in laying a bridge over the Broad River, as we have not sufficient to lay both bridges at once.

It appears that the left wing has been within twenty miles of this place for four days. General Slocum appears to account for the delay by saying his flanks were exposed, and he did not think us so near. By this I suppose he thought the enemy much stronger than they were. No one here feels satisfied with his explanation; as matters were, he might have taken the city, or by quick work when we came up here, cut off the Rebel force and captured a large proportion of it.

NOTE

1. "When Woods's division was in camp in the open fields at Little Congaree, it was shelled all night by a rebel battery from the other side of the river. This provoked me very much at the time, for it was wanton mischief, as Generals Beauregard and Hampton must have been convinced that they could not prevent our entrance into Columbia. I have always contended that I would have been justified in retaliating for this unnecessary act of war, but did not, though I always characterized it as it deserved." Sherman, II, 279.

"Captain DeGres [DeGress] had a section of his twenty-pound Parrott guns unlimbered, firing into the town. I asked him what he was firing for; he said he could see some rebel cavalry occasionally at the intersections of the streets, and he had an idea that there was a large force of infantry concealed on the opposite bank, lying low, in case we should attempt to cross over directly into the town. I instructed him not to fire any more into the town, but consented to his bursting a few shells near the depot, to scare away the negroes who were appropriating the bags of corn and meal which we wanted, also to fire three shots at the unoccupied State-House. Although this matter of firing into Columbia has been the subject of much abuse and investigation, I have yet to hear of any single person having been killed in Columbia by our cannon." Sherman, II, 278-79.

Columbia, S. C.
February 17, 1865

This day has been the most eventful one to us of the campaign, and one which the historian of South Carolina cannot forget. This morning Columbia was a beautiful little city, tonight it is a "Sea of fire."

The scene is both terrible and grand.

The skirmishing on Broad River commenced at day light. We

learned from prisoners captured during the operations that the cavalry had been relieved in the night by Clayton's[1] Division of S. D. Lee's Corps, of old troops. These were the best troops that could be put on to defend the river from a crossing. The sharp-shooting grew very warm as soon as it was light enough to see distinctly. The Rebel picket line was nearly as strong as a line of battle to oppose a crossing but the river must be crossed. General Woods first attempted to cross a few men in a pontoon boat, with a line to establish a ferry, but the current and fire of the enemy compelled them to fall back. The second attempt was made with a stronger force of men and boats, and a landing was effected under cover of artillery and infantry fire from our side, and the fire of the men from the boats. They then succeeded in keeping the enemy back until they were reinforced by other boat loads taken over. As soon as a rope could be gotten over, a ferry was established by boats being locked together and planked over. When enough men were over artillery opened, and the men advanced sufficiently strong to spring back the Rebel line, and finally drive it to the crest of hills to the north west of the city. In doing this we captured between thirty or forty men.

Even after our men reached the crest of the hill we noticed a great excitement among them which we supposed to be from an attack by the enemy. We made preparations to cross over men as rapidly as possible if they should be suddenly driven to the river. We were very soon disappointed by learning that the Mayor of the City[2] had [asked for] the commanding officer to surrender it, and the apparent excitement was the men gathering together to receive this dignitary. The city surrendered at 10 A. M. when the brigade which was over the river marched directly in.

At 11 A. M. General Sherman and staff and General Howard and staff rode to the city together and through nearly all the main streets. There were a few handkerchiefs waved by the families of "Teutonic extraction," one or two small flags seen, and the negroes went into demonstrations of delight, which I have never before seen equalled. They ran, shouted, yelled, danced, and cut up curlicues generally.

Thus far all went on well, but when the brigade occupied the town the citizens and negroes brought out whisky in buckets, bottles and in every conceivable manner treated the men to all they would drink. The men were very much worn and tired and drank freely of it, and the entire brigade became drunk. The enemy had taken the cotton out of the store houses and piled it in the main streets and set it on fire, which the citizens and soldiers, when we entered, were trying to subdue, and had nearly accomplished. But when they became thoroughly intoxicated, they began to break open the stores and plunder freely. The negroes, escaped prisoners, state convicts, and such other people as would all went into the work of pillaging with a will. The day was dry and the wind blowing a gale. The fire in the cotton sprang up, and set some of the buildings on fire. By this time all parties were willing to assist it on. The negroes piloted the men to the best places for plunder, and both men and negroes by evening were setting fires rapidly. These operations in the city occupied till night, and it was well in the evening before the fire gained its greatest height. The first Brigade was relieved, but it was not possible to get all the men out of the city. The second brigade was also relieved, as they had also soon become intoxicated. The third brigade, was put to work to stop the fire, and consequently were held in better control. They were not allowed to stop long enough to demoralize. Near the same time General Oliver's[3] Brigade was brought in to clear the city of the drunken men. They arrested all men on the street, and very frequently had to use force, and many men would not be arrested, and were shot. *Forty* of our men were killed in this way, many were wounded, and several dead drunk men were burned to death. The fire, pillaging and shooting men were at its greatest height from 10 o'clock till midnight.

I was unfortunately situated, as I had taken up my quarters with a "first family,"[4] to care for their safety. The family consisted of a clergyman, his wife, mother, and a lady who had just been confined;[5] they were all in a terrific state of excitement, and as my feelings were especially enlisted in behalf of the sick lady, I confined myself closely to the house to keep the family quiet. From the piazza of this house I had a splendid view of the fire, and as this house was the first one saved in this portion of the town, I could overlook the greater part of it. The saving of this house was the first real headway gained in stopping the fire. And even the negro quarters were burned within thirty feet of the dwelling.

One cannot conceive of anything which would or could make a grander fire than this one, excepting a larger city than Columbia. The city was built entirely of wood, and was in most excellent

Columbia on fire. *Harper's Pictorial History of the Civil War*, II.

condition to burn. The space on fire at midnight was not less than one mile square, and one week before, sheltered from 25,000 to 30,000 people. The flames rolled and heaved like the waves of the ocean; the road was like a cataract. The whole air was filled with burning cinders, and fragments of fire as thick as the flakes of snow in a storm. The scene was splendid—magnificently grand.

The scene of pillaging, the suffering and terror of the citizens, the arresting of and shooting negroes, and our frantic and drunken soldiers, is the other side of the picture, and this I will leave for the present for the imagination of those who choose to dwell upon it. It has for all these been sad indeed. I have in this war, seen too much suffering by far, and choose rather to remember the magnificent splendor of this burning city.

There were stored in the houses or cellars through the city quite large quantities of loaded arms and shells, which went off or exploded as the fire reached them.

In one or two localities, the explosion of loaded arms was like the firing of a line of battle, and compelled all in the vicinity to beat a retreat. The explosion of shells proved that some of the projectiles stored in private houses were very large, the report was like the firing of artillery. How or why these things were stored in private houses can only be guessed at.

This day's work has been one of marked success as a military achievement. We have the capital of the State, and the control of all rail roads up to this point. We have the city, too, without having to fight a great battle for it so far from a base of supplies and where our wounded could not be well cared for. The destruction of the city was against the wishes of our commanders, and was originally owing to the fires set by their own people, and doubtless with the expectation that the city would burn. How men can, or could be such fools as not to expect the city to burn up when a pile of cotton bales two hundred yards long was set on fire in the main street, with all the cords of the bales cut, as was the case, is more than I can tell. And on the other hand, why Johnson [Johnston],[6] Beauregard,[7] Hampton, and Wheeler should be such unmitigated fools as to wish to burn Columbia, is more strange. Yet I know the facts to be as I have stated, as I was one of the first to enter the city, and have been here since.

That all citizens have suffered here terribly no one can doubt, and that the fire was against the wishes of all our generals, I know.

Yet I believe the burning of the city is an advantage to the cause
and a just retribution to the state of South Carolina.

Yesterday while the enemy held the city, a magazine exploded
killing twenty rebel soldiers and one hundred women and children. The magazine was near the depot where these people were
plundering, and dropped a spark among the powder scattered
about.

I have written this record of the 17th on the morning of the
18th.[8]

NOTES

1. Maj.-Gen. Henry DeLamar Clayton.
2. Dr. T. J. Goodwyn.
3. Brig.-Gen. John Morrison Oliver.
4. The family of the Episcopal rector, the Rev. Mr. Peter J. Shand. The Rev. Mr.
Shand had been one of the signators of the letter from South Carolina citizens to
Confederate Secretary of War Seddon in December.
5. Mrs. Robert Wilson, the Rev. Mr. Shand's daughter.
6. Gen. Joseph Eggleston Johnston.
7. Gen. Pierre Gustave Toutant Beauregard.
8. The literature concerning the burning of Columbia comprises a full book-
shelf of its own. It is summarized, evaluated, and interpreted in Marion Brunson
Lucas's *Sherman and the Burning of Columbia* (College Station, Tex., 1976).
Lucas declares: "In sifting through the mass of testimony . . . few facts are self
evident. One conclusion that becomes evident, however, was that from beginning to end both sides held certain positions which never altered. South Carolinians were convinced that they had been invaded by barbarians who treated them
in an uncivilized manner and that 'Sherman was morally responsible for the
burning of Columbia.' Conversely, the Union officers and troops, for the most
part, accepted the invasion of South Carolina and the events which transpired in
Columbia as regrettable but little different from what had been happening in-
creasingly as the nature of the war steadily changed.
"Attempting to reconcile these diametrically opposed positions is, of course,
no easy matter. . . . Northern soldiers and generals, flushed with victory, often
grossly overstated their destructiveness. In the South the story of Sherman's
march was reported by elderly men and by women who were, as Clement Eaton
and Frank Vandiver have pointed out, probably the fiercest protagonists of the
Confederacy." Ibid., 134-35.
Allan Nevins, dean of American historians of the last two generations, wrote
that, under the circumstances, "a catastrophe was inevitable. . . . Scholars and angry or lurid Southern writers have chanted 'Who burned Columbia?' until it has
become a stale refrain. . . . No answer can be given that seems completely con-
vincing. . . . Three main theories have found support: first, that the fires spreading
from burning cotton were ignited by irresponsible vagabonds and some drunken,
retreating troopers; second, that Sherman willfully ordered the city burned, an
allegation that he strongly denied, and that seems incredible; third, that released
prisoners, emancipated slaves, and/or intoxicated Union soldiers or vagrant
Southerners were responsible. For each hypothesis some circumstances can be

found to offer partial support except the allegation that Sherman deliberately fired the city." *The War for the Union: Vol. IV, The Organized War to Victory. 1864-1865* (New York, 1971), 260-61.

Sherman's and Howard's reports of the fire are available in their autobiographies, in the official accounts, and in the proceedings of the Mixed Commission to settle the so-called Alabama Claims. Their words generally concur with Osborn's account. The most widely known of Southern accounts are James G. Gibbes's *Who Burnt Columbia* (Newberry, S. C., 1902), Emma LeConte's *When the World Ended,* ed. Earl Schenck Miers (New York, 1957), William Gilmore Simms's *Sack and Destruction of the City of Columbia, S. C.* (Columbia, 1865), and D. H. Trezevant's *The Burning of Columbia, S. C.* (Columbia, 1866). Included in the last of these is a record of the fire written into a letter to Trezevant by Osborn's host the Rev. Mr. Shand: "There was a row of cotton bales which *had been loosely packed,* and from almost all of which portions of the fabric were protruding. Along this line of bales there were numbers of Yankee soldiers, *and none but they*—the citizens who were present being confined to the pavements on each side of the street, and at a distance of thirty to forty feet or more from the cotton. The soldiers were passing to and fro, alongside of the bales, apparently in a state of high excitement, and almost frantic with joy; all, or most of them, with lighted segars in their mouths. I was standing nearly midway between the two corners, watching their movements, when on a sudden the bales at the market end took fire, and the wind being quite fresh, the flames increased and spread with fearful rapidity, and in a short time the whole, or at least the greater part, was in a blaze. The fire engines of the city were brought to the spot as expeditiously as possible and the fire was extinguished in the course of an hour. It was evident that it originated from the fire of the cigars, falling upon the loose cotton. Indeed there was no other way of accounting for it; and another is to be noted, that neither sparks nor flames were extended to the neighboring buildings and no damage was done except to the cotton." Trezevant, 15-16.

(Floyd C. Watkins asserts in his essay *"Gone With the Wind* as Vulgar Literature" that "loose cotton burns with a tiny flame, and baled cotton only smolders," giving as his authorities John Carter, a fire investigator for the city of Atlanta and J. W. McCarty of the Georgia Institute of Technology, a consultant for the Georgia Department of Agriculture. Richard Harwell, *Gone With the Wind as Book and Film* [Columbia, S. C., 1983], 204.) Trezevant comments (p.17) that the cotton on the street in Columbia "was so soaked and soddened, that it did not even burn from the heat of the conflagration of the night and remained for days on the ground, until it was incorporated with it 'by being constantly trodden under' foot."

The Rev. Mr. Shand's letter continues: "The fire was wholly put out by one o'clock P. M., and from that hour until between 7 and 8 o'clock P. M., there was no other fire in the city, and the burning of said cotton had nothing to do with the subsequent conflagration and destruction of the town. At the hour last mentioned, rockets were seen to ascend and immediately thereafter a fire broke out in a central portion of the city near the market, and the wind being still exceedingly high, it soon assumed alarming proportions. I stood in my front piazza watching it with much anxiety and though inclined at first to regard its origin as accidental, I was soon undeceived. The fire occurred, as I said, in a central part of the city and to the north of my residence, but I had been looking upon it but for a short time when I noticed fresh flames bursting out in the east, west and south, at points *very distant* from each other and not possibly caused by the communication of flames from one to the other. The revelry of soldiers in the streets and their shouts and exultation, as fresh rockets went up, and fresh buildings took fire, scenes which to some extent came under my own observation, added to the awful character of the occasion and gave rise to the painful impression that the city was doomed to desolation and ruin; a fact which was admitted and boasted of by some of the soldiers themselves. By midnight the whole city presented one vast sheet of flames, and in the midst, and during the progress of the appalling calamity, might be heard above all other noises, the demoniac and gladsome shouts of the soldiery." Trezevant, 16.

Columbia, S. C.
February 18, 1865

This morning we found the town settled down to comparative quiet. The fires had all gone out, or nearly so, and there was but little smoke rising. The people were scattered about the streets, stupefied by the terror of last night and their present destitution. The most of them had their sole worldly effects done up in a little bundle under their arms, which was as likely to be an old pair of boots as anything of more value. They had neither provisions nor clothing, nor did they know where to go to procure it. Their former record of wealth is of little account to them now. Our soldiers have settled down to obedience again.

This A. M. I rode through the ruins and was surprised to find the destruction so general. I judge three-fourths of the town is burned, i.e. so much of the capacity of the place. The outskirts south and east of the town are left, including the college[1] buildings, but not much besides this remains. All the densely built portion of the town is burned; the destruction by the fire is more complete than I ever saw before. There were very few brick or stone buildings, and very little besides wood used in the construction of the houses excepting the chimneys. Everything combustible has burned, and there remains on the site of the city only a forest of chimneys. The destruction and desolation is complete.

The bronze palmetto tree near the new State House stands after the fire, as beautiful as ever. This tree is a beautiful work of art and is the pride as well as the emblem of the state. The troops have in no way marred it, and as it is nearly the only thing which is uninjured, it will make even "Loyal South Carolina" a fine subject to expatiate upon in prose or poetry.[2] In the general conflagration very few of the buildings which were to have been destroyed were injured. The State Houses, depots, arsenals, magazines, government distilleries, &c. &c. were all on the outskirts of the town where the fire did not extend. There were a dozen or two locomotives, a large number of cars, machine shops, filled with machinery &c which we have been destroying today. General Sherman does not deem it best to leave anything the CSA can make use of because the main portion of the town is destroyed. I learn today that the battery on this side of the river which annoyed us so the night we crossed Congaree Creek, and from which DeGress drove the men, was not reoccupied by the Rebels. It was manned by the Cadets of the State Military School.[3] The "first families" stood a poor fight with the veteran mudsills.

The XV A. C. have been destroying RR today, towards Kingsville, XVII A. C. have been working toward Winnsboro. Slocum's column is not all across the Saluda River. He is moving toward Alston and the Broad River and Shelby R. R.

The entire force of troops which have been operating in front of us does not appear to be more than 10,000. We understand that Grant has swung up Lee's right a little and if this is the case, he must also be gaining a little.[4]

About eighty of our officers who have been prisoners here and were sent away the day before we came in town have escaped and joined us. The negroes throughout the whole country assist our men wherever they find them.

We find here a few citizens who have assisted our prisoners confined here among them, and most prominent are three Irish girls; they have been most faithful, and, indeed have done everything possible for the cause. They will go north with us.[5]

There were no fortifications about the city excepting the temporary ones thrown up as we approached.

NOTES

1. South Carolina College, now the University of South Carolina.

2. This metal palmetto tree stands on the grounds of the South Carolina State House. "Designed by Christopher Werner for an insurance company which rejected it, the iron Plametto tree was purchased for five thousand dollars by the South Carolina General Assembly in 1856 to honor the men of the South Carolina Regiment who had died in service during the Mexican War. The 'Palmetto Regiment,' commanded by Pierce M. Butler, had been the first to plant its flag atop the walls of Mexico City." Nell S. Graydon, *Tales of Columbia* (Columbia, S. C., 1964), 54-55.

Nichols admired this monument and noted: "The names of the fallen brave were inscribed in brass letters upon tablets appropriately arranged at the base.

One of our stragglers, while attempting to detach some of these letters, was at first warned, and, not desisting, was seized and severely handled by the soldiers for the commission of what they regarded as a sacrilegious crime." *Story of the Great March,* 171.

3. Cadets from the Arsenal. The Arsenal in Columbia and the Citadel in Charleston formed the South Carolina Military Academy, a legal entity created by the state legislature in 1861. The cadets from the two schools made up the Battalion of State Cadets. O. J. Bond, *The Story of the Citadel* (Richmond, 1936), 82.

4. In February the troops under Grant extended their line westward by thirty-seven miles, counting irregularities in the entrenchments. Nevins, *War for the Union,* 264.

5. "Three Irish girls" seems an unlikely phrase to use in describing Mrs. Amelia Feaster and two of her daughters, but they were probably to whom Osborn refers. The eldest of her daughters had been born when Mrs. Jacob Feaster was Mrs. Peter Burton and had taken the name of Mrs. Feaster's third husband, David Boozer of Newberry. She was named Mary Sarah A. Boozer and called Marie. "She was known as Miss Mary Boozer, and was considered one of the most beautiful girls ever seen in the state" (James G. Gibbes in the *Philadelphia Times,* Sept. 20, 1880). She was beautiful enough and bold enough to be noted by diarist Mary Boykin Chesnut who called her in December 1864 "the too famous Boozer." Chesnut, *Mary Chesnut's Civil War,* ed. C. Vann Woodward. (New Haven, 1981), 695. In a note (695n) Woodward remarks: "These two notorious women harbored an escaped Union prisoner during the war and ran off with Union forces after the burning of Columbia in 1865."

Mrs. Thomas Taylor wrote an article about wartime Columbia called "Two Equipages" saying: "The Boozer coach, with the glass windows partly folded back on hinges, 'exploited' a rare vision. A mother and daughter—Mrs. Feaster and Marie Boozer—the one rich, dark in coloring and costume, the other (occupying the whole front seat) a girl of golden hair, rose shades, blue orbs, healthy, poised, delicious, pressing into the soft cushions, wrapped in ciel blue and swansdown, leghorn hat, from which the white plumes fell, curling under upon the white and pink throat. It was an angel's *seeming*—and she, beautiful as Venus, the goddess of the chariot." In *South Carolina Women in the Confederacy* (Columbia, 1903), I, 251.

A Checkered Life, by "One Who Knows" (Columbia, 1878) is a brief biography of the famous beauty. It was written by Julian A. Selby. In 1915 it was republished in Columbia with an introduction called "A Study in Scarlet" by "Felix Old Boy," a *nom-de-plume* of the distinguished Professor Yates Snowden. The best account of the Boozer, however, is a novel, *La Belle,* by Elizabeth Boatwright Coker (New York, 1959). Although it is fiction, the facts of the hetaera's life were actually toned down to make the novel more believable.

Columbia, S. C.

February 19, 1865

The incidents of the day have not been so interesting as those of the two days previous. The weather continues fine. The city looks more dreary than before, and the destruction more complete. The smoke has cleared away, and the standing chimneys and dried trees look gloomy indeed.[1]

The day has been spent in the destruction of public property. We found about 4,000 small arms complete, 6,000 unfinished, 43 pieces of artillery, 10,000 rounds artillery ammunition, a half million rounds for small arms with a vast amount of cavalry and infantry equipments, &c. &c. The magazines were large, good, and thoroughly filled. The ammunition was destroyed by throwing it into the river. Unfortunately, in throwing it in, a percussion shell exploded a large amount of powder, by which we lost twenty men.

After removing the ammunition from the magazine, a sufficient quantity of powder was left in the magazines to explode them, and did no damage, otherwise. A very large amount of valuable property left by refugees in the depots was burned.[2]

The new State House, which was in the process of erection when the war broke out, is a magnificent work of art and was to have been the pride of the State. Two millions had already been expended on it and it is only finished to the top of the main walls. The walls are of brick, about five feet in thickness and overlaid, above the basement, by Tennessee marble, the basement by granite from the state quarries. The outside work of the pillars and capitals is exquisite. Each capital, I am told occupied the labor of six months, and I think from the examination I made of them, it would not be less. Heads of Calhoun and Hayne,[3] are carved in bas relief on the front, and admirably executed.

The whole work, so far as it is finished, is splendid, and is to be second as a house of legislation only to the capital at Washington. The walls are so strong that a 20 pds shot fired at a half mile range, made no impression except to mar the surface a little.[4] The interior frame work is all of iron, there was to be no wood about it. The building itself is uninjured, but the works and machine shops connected with it were burned and much valuable material and work destroyed. If the building had been finished, the state and country might well have been proud of it. It stands now alone, surrounded by the ruins of the city, and at its base the bronze Palmetto tree, uninjured, the emblem of the "Sovereign State of South Carolina."

The explosions of the magazines this evening caused the ground to tremble. I was a mile from them and felt it distinctly.

NOTES

1. In his Special Field Orders No. 42 of February 18, 1865, Gen. Howard wrote: "It having been brought to the attention of the commanding general that certain evil and evil-disposed soldiers of this command have threatened to destroy the remainder of this city with fire, it is ordered that all commanding officers and provost-marshals use the utmost vigilance by establishing sufficient guards and patrols to prevent at all cost, even to taking the life of any refractory soldier, a recurrence of the horrors of last night. . . . They will appoint provost-marshals, who will be authorized to call upon the corps commander for sufficient force to prevent burning, pillaging, and other acts subversive of good order and military discipline." *OR,* Ser. I, vol. 47, pt. 2, p. 475.

2. "The destruction of certain Confederate public property—that is, property made use of for furthering the interests of the war—was committed to me in Sherman's specific instructions. . . .

"The following are estimates of what were so destroyed: 1,000 bales of cotton, 19 locomotives, 20 box cars; many more had previously been destroyed by the great fire. Also, the buildings belonging to the railroad station—two large freight sheds, including 60 sets of six-mule-team harnesses, 1,000 pounds of trace chains, quantities of nails and spikes; about five tons of railroad machinery, with a large amount of articles of a military character; 650 car wheels; two buildings filled with Confederate stationery; 25 powder mills, the mills being destroyed by being blown up; an armory near the Congaree River, comprising warehouse, machine shops, foundries, and offices; beside the foregoing an immense amount of ordnance of every description. The smokestacks of six factories were ruined; a shed near the Common, containing ten tons of machinery belonging to the Confederate army, all packed in boxes, was consumed and the machinery broken up." Howard, *Autobiography,* II, 125-26.

3. John Caldwell Calhoun and Robert Young Hayne, who were earlier United States senators.

4. Osborn refers here to the shots fired by DeGress's battery.

V Across the Carolinas

Muddy Springs, S. C.[1]
February 20, 1865

We left Columbia early this morning and found a fair country
for about five miles, the remainder is the poorest country I have
ever seen. It is quite hilly, covered with small pines, and scrub
oaks. The soil is white, drifting sand and too barren for the meanest weeds to grow. We have collected no forage today. The enemy
appear to have moved out on this road but are making no resistance. This point is merely a cross road in a forest, with no houses
in reach, and only has value to us as furnishing water for the
troops. We have not found water enough within a dozen miles to
keep the men from suffering. The XVII A. C. is a little in advance
of us on the R. R. to our left. The XV A. C. destroyed the R. R. to
the Wateree, and burned the bridge.

The most interesting item of the day is the organizing of a large
refugee train, to follow the Army to the coast. There are several
hundred of these people, i.e. white people (there were about 800)
and nearly all the wagons of Columbia. Every cause imaginable has
induced these people to follow us. To escape starvation, to escape
the draft, those who have been kind to our men, to escape the
vengeance of the people, and to get what little traps they had where
it could be used or sold. This has been the case with a large number
of Jews, who have so loaded down the transportation with trunks,
that the General has given orders to expel them from the Army tomorrow. There are two gentlemen and three ladies with head quarters but the great majority are in an unpleasant condition and
troublesome today. They will be better organized and put under
army discipline tomorrow. Prisoners report that Charleston has
fallen into our hands, and that Grant has Petersburg.[2]

The first we think correct, the latter we do not believe, as we know Grant did not intend to take it, and if he has it, he has captured it accidentally.

Cheatham's[3] A. C. is on our left marching rapidly to pass us and Slocum is marching to keep ahead of him till we turn short to the right, and towards the coast where he may go ahead as far as he pleases.

The last of our troops left the city at 2 P. M. after having thoroughly cleared the city of all our men and attaches by skirmishing through it. The enemy entered it within a half hour after we left, with cavalry, coming in from the east along the bank of the river.

NOTES

1. Muddy Springs is approximately thirteen miles northeast of Columbia.
2. Charleston was occupied February 18. The rumor that Grant had taken Petersburg was just that, only a rumor.
3. Maj.-Gen. Benjamin Franklin Cheatham.

Harrison C[ross] Roads,
Fairfield Dist., S. C.
February 21, 1865

We left our camp this morning early and moved on the most direct road to this point. The first five miles were the same as the country we travelled over yesterday, but since has been growing rapidly better, and here it is quite productive, and well cultivated. The face of the country is rolling and seems well adapted to corn raising.

I was told today by the telegraph operator at Columbia, who is at these head quarters, a Mr. Soulé, that a telegram was received from Lee to Beauregard that a column of Federal troops, an army corps, was on its way from East Tennessee to Salisbury or Charleston, and that Beauregard must send his prisoners to Laurens, N. C. [i.e. S. C.] General Howard knew nothing of this column, but supposed it to be under Stoneman.[1]

The citizens still say the Yankees have Charleston. Cheatham's

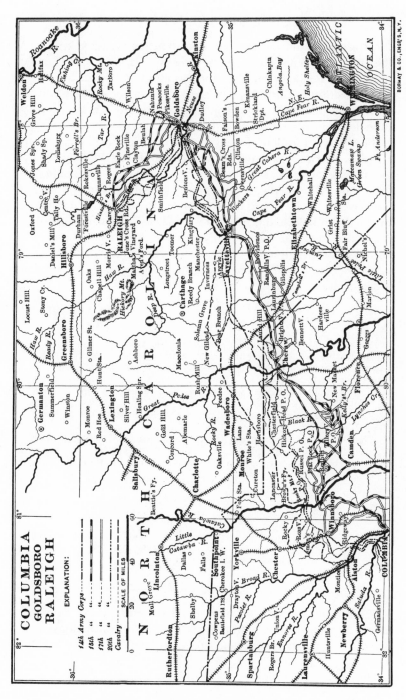

Map 4. Columbia to Raleigh, N.C. From *General Sherman*, by Manning Force. New York: D. Appleton and Company, 1899.

Corps is still on our left and reported to be six thousand strong.[2] The enemy are reported as having gone to Charlotte, but no one can tell which side of the river they went up. The position of our troops is, the XVII A. C. near Wynnsboro [Winnsboro], headed toward Poplar Springs.[3] The XV A. C. have three divisions here and one at Longtown.[4]

The rebels are still burning all the cotton, even small quantities at private houses. I saw a good deal on fire today. Wheeler, in a communication to General Sherman said that if he would not burn houses, he (Wheeler) would not burn the cotton. General Sherman replied that he hoped he would burn the cotton, as it would save us the trouble, and he did not burn houses, but where people abandoned their houses he should not take the trouble to protect them. The Rebel Army still talk and act as though they thought we were on a cotton expedition. Query, how do they imagine we are to take it out of the country?

NOTES

1. Stoneman did not begin his movement from Knoxville until his raid into western North Carolina and southwestern Virginia began March 20. On April 18 Sherman ordered Stoneman to join him near Raleigh via Durham's Station or Chapel Hill. This order was endorsed by Gen. Joseph E. Johnston so that Confederate troops would not interfere with the passage of Stoneman's command. *OR*, Ser. I, vol. 47, pt. 3, p. 249.

2. Actually Cheatham commanded about two thousand troops. *OR*, Ser. I. vol. 47, pt. 2, p. 1222.

3. The XVII Corps was headed eastward on the present South Carolina highway 41 toward its junction with S. C. 21.

4. Longtown was south of the present Wateree Lake in eastern Fairfield County.

Peay's Ferry, Wateree River,
Fairfield Dist., S. C.
February 22, 1865

We have moved but ten miles; are at the river where we will have to be bridged. The country is good, with fine plantations; the face of the country rolling, and the roads good.

We found the river picketed only by a half dozen men and they ran as soon as our advance showed itself but they had destroyed all means of crossing, and it was with considerable difficulty we finally floated over a squad of men on a raft made of limbs, fragments of boards, &c. to secure a line for a ferry so a bridge could be built. The stream is about three hundred feet wide, with a rapid current.

Two of our men were found today with their brains beat out, and from all appearances had been captured and then murdered.

We learn today from a negro, who left Charleston with the Rebel troops, that our forces have possession of the city, having taken the city, all the heavy artillery, some light batteries, and a great quantity of stores. The man says our troops turned the city by way of John's and James' Islands and that the Rebel troops came out by the way of Summerville and Florence. We flatter ourselves that we have done a good share of the capturing of Charleston. The Rebel papers say that Foster has been relieved, and Gilmore [Gillmore][1] placed in command of the Department of the South. Our substantial men of the old Army do not speak highly of Gillmore, in fact, rather contemptuously. They do not even give him credit of being by any means a first class engineer. There may be some truth in this, as the Senate, argued that matter some time whether or no to make him a major in the regular service, and Grant threw him overboard at the first opportunity. General Howard says that public opinion will be so much excited over the fall of Charleston, that whoever took it will be made Brigadier General in the regular service at once, while the city would have fallen if a gun had never been fired there. I do not think, however, that any such promotions will be made in Sherman's command without his approval, which he will not give to Gillmore.

General Howard told me today that the Mayor of Columbia told him that the whole number of men in the State, fit for military duty, and not in the Army was 1400. Pretty close scraping.

NOTE

1. Maj.-Gen. Quincy Adams Gillmore was ordered on 30 January to relieve Gen. Foster at Hilton Head. *OR,* Ser. I, vol. 47, pt. 2, p. 179.

Red Hill Post Office,[1]
Kershaw Dist., S. C.
February 23, 1865

This morning we turned fairly east and moved ten miles. The country over which we passed today is very fine, the best we have seen since we left the coast. It is very hilly, and the soil is the red clay of Virginia. The plantations are large and fine. The buildings are excellent.

The little town of Liberty Hill is the finest I have seen in the State. It is composed of the residences of wealthy planters of this country, in all about twenty houses, and all large and beautiful. The yards are beautifully laid out and finely cultivated. There are evidently no poor people in the place. We found the people very kind and highly cultivated. I have not been so much pleased with any town South.[2]

Two divisions of the XV A. C. moved on this road, two on the next feasible road south, and the XVII A. C. on the next road north, going through "Russell Place."[3] The XX A. C. is moving over the river about twelve miles above, while the XIV A. C. have not come up to the river yet.

The enemy have concentrated at Charlotte, and are expecting us that way. One thousand S. C. State troops passed through Liberty Hill on their way from Charleston to Charlotte yesterday. General Sherman sends us word again today that the enemy have murdered eleven of Kilpatrick's men, and the General has also ordered retaliation by killing the same number of rebels now in Kilpatrick's hands.[4]

NOTES

1. Red Hill Post Office is in northeast Kershaw County just west of Oak Creek bridge.
2. At Liberty Hill, Mrs. C. P. Poppenheim recorded on February 23: "Thousands of Yankees coming in; one command follows another in quick succession; all robbing and plundering. . . . What an awful feeling to come so close to hundreds of Yankees who are burning and destroying everything on the face of the land!. . . While waiting for the Yankees to pass, and looking on their fine horses and hundreds of stolen cattle, the refugees from Columbia began to pass; among them I recognized Mary Boozer and her mother in a carriage, she in a lively conversation with a gay looking officer riding by the carriage." "Personal Experience with Sherman's Army at Liberty Hill" in *South Carolina Women in the Confederacy* (Columbia, 1903), I, 259.

3. Russell Place was on a road connecting South Carolina highways 121 and 13, near the bridge over Beaver Creek.

4. Kilpatrick reported the incident: "An infantry lieutenant and seven men murdered yesterday by the Eighth Texas Cavalry after they had surrendered. We found their bodies all together and mutilated, with paper on their breasts, saying 'Death to foragers.' Eighteen of my men were killed yesterday and some had their throats cut. . . . I have sent Wheeler word that I intend to hang eighteen of his men, and if the cowardly act is repeated, will burn every house along my line of march. . . . I have a number of prisoners, and shall take a fearful revenge." *OR,* Ser. I, vol. 47, pt. 2, p. 533.

Sherman's order to Howard reads: "Now it is clearly our war right to subsist our army on the enemy. . . . I contend if the enemy fails to defend his country we may rightfully appropriate what we want. If our foragers act under mine, yours, or other proper orders they must be protected. I have ordered Kilpatrick to select of his prisoners man for man, shoot them, and leave them by the roadside labeled, so that our enemy will see that for every man he executes he takes the life of one of his own. I want the foragers, however, to be kept within reasonable bounds for the sake of discipline. I will not protect them when they enter dwellings and commit wanton waste. . . . If any of your foragers are murdered, take life for life, leaving a record in each case." *OR,* Ser. I, vol. 47, pt. 2, p. 537.

Williams Cross Roads,
Kershaw Dist., S. C.
February 24, 1865

We have moved eighteen miles today, the first seven miles being over a very bad road, the soil red clay; the remainder pine barrens and road good. It commenced raining last evening and rained till the middle of the A. M. Still we have done a good day's work. The command is scattered considerably, having all crossed at one bridge, and that with the long marches and bad roads, has scattered the column a good deal.

We have now reached the upland, or plateau, east of the Wateree river. The country is very sandy, and covered with pine forest, which is used for the manufacture of turpentine. There are some very large manufactories in this region.

The enemy has annoyed us a little today by hanging on our flanks with cavalry. It is reported they captured eleven of our men; we have captured about one hundred of them, the greater portion State Militia. Yesterday Lieutenant McQueen scouted toward Camden with seven men, and stampeded twenty-eight Rebels in one body, captured twenty-six of their muskets, and three prisoners. McQueen only went to the outskirts of the town, none of our

Treasure seekers starting out. *Harper's Pictorial History of the Civil War*, II.

troops have entered it yet. Prisoners captured today tell us a dispatch was received in Camden yesterday that Wilmington had fallen.[1] If this is true, we have the whole coast, but we have no idea of who captured it, or how it was done.

When McQueen went to the neighborhood of the town, the citizens stampeded and refugeed in every direction. A large number attempted to run the gauntlet in front of our column, and we have today captured about one hundred wagons, loaded with valuables, and a large number of good animals, some very valuable.[2]

Genl. J. E. Smith[3] captured today a pair of cattle,[4] imported from Cape of Good Hope. They are a real curiosity, known in this country by the people as the African Swamp ox. There is a bull and a cow. They bear still less resemblance to the common cattle than the American Buffalo though very different from either, but I have not time for a description. They are said to have been imported by Wade Hampton.

NOTES

1. Maj.-Gen. John M. Schofield wrote Gen. Grant from Wilmington on February 22 announcing the capture of that city. *OR,* Ser. I, vol. 47, pt. 2, p. 535.

2. Howard noted in a letter of February 25 to Sherman: "The advance yesterday captured some 50 or 60 refugee wagons and a large number of fine mules." Ibid., p. 565.

Harvey T. Cook in *Sherman's March Through South Carolina in 1865* (Greenville, S. C., 1938), quoted the *Fairfield Courier* of March 23, 1865: "Many persons were caught in the act of getting away. Among them were Messrs. Thomas Puryear and Cowley, who had with them valuable racing stock, including Caesar and Albion and others." p. 13.

3. Maj.-Gen. John Eugene Smith.

4. These were wildebeests.

Williams Cross Roads,
Kershaw Dist, S. C.
February 25, 1865

The head of column has not moved today, but the different detachments have been closing up and the Army is now more compact.

General Hazen passed within a few miles of Camden, and sent two regiments through to destroy the cotton and government stores there. He captured and brought away about 60,000 rations of commissary stores. Gen. John E. Smith's division had today quite a smart skirmish with a detachment of Rebel cavalry, supposed to be about 800 or 1,000 strong. As they were closing up to our column, the enemy captured some wagons and animals, and also captured a picket post of twenty men. They were then met by our skirmishers, and a little fight followed, during which two of our men who had been captured were brought out on the Rebel skirmish line, in an open field, and shot in cold blood. General Smith, who was on the ground, ordered two Rebels who he had just captured, out on our skirmish line, in plain view of the enemy and they were shot. In the skirmish we lost about twelve men wounded, and the enemy left twelve of their wounded on the ground.[1] Hampton's Cavalry is showing much more dash and better fighting qualities than Wheeler's ever did. I consider Wheeler and Kilpatrick officers of about the same calibre, neither of them large.[2] General Howard has recommended that if a Cavalry Corps is organized for this Army, that it be given to General Mower. I think this would be a great improvement on the present. Kilpatrick would command a division well enough under a superior, but he is barely fit to command himself.

Our foragers are getting reckless,[3] and by far too venturesome, and doubtless that within a few days past quite a number have been picked up by the Rebel cavalry.

The day has been very cloudy and cheerless. Wherever the roads are not sandy, they are very bad.

Later—I have just learned that about fifty prisoners have been captured today by troops in the rear. Several Rebel officers have been captured near the head of column, among whom were two captains with their seconds, going out to fight a duel. Their difference was in some way connected with a lady. Our officers tell them that as soon as we have time to look on we propose to have them fight it out, and they must keep at it till one is used up.[4] We have one colonel captured today. Captain Duncan has just returned from an expedition to Camden, where he finished the work of authorized destruction. He burned the bridge over the river, and captured some fine stock.[5] Among the stock captured is a white Arabian stallion which the citizens of Camden say belonged to Jeff Davis and is his pet saddle horse.[6] They also say he was sent here to avoid a possibility of capture by our forces.

NOTES

1. "February 25 at about 10 a. m. Young's command, of Butler's division, cavalry, 600 to 700 strong, captured 7 wagons, 7 enlisted men, and 4 contrabands while after corn at a plantation two miles in the rear of the camp. . . . I ordered one regiment to move out to drive them off. . . . The Forty-eighth Regiment Indiana Volunteer Infantry was selected, and deploying skirmishers, moved out, driving the enemy back, off the Camden road. Our wagons, however, had been driven rapidly over the bridge across Little Lynch's Creek, and having no mounted force I could not pursue them. In this skirmish we lost 2 enlisted men killed and 1 wounded. Two of our men were brutally murdered, in plain view of our skirmishers, after having surrendered, in retaliation for which I ordered two of their men, who were taken in our uniform, to be shot, which was done on the spot." Maj. Gen. John E. Smith in *OR,* Ser. I, vol. 47, pt. 1, pp. 318-19.

2. Wheeler and Kilpatrick were at West Point together, Wheeler in the class of 1859 and Kilpatrick in the May class of 1861.

Connolly wrote December 5, 1863: "Kilpatrick is the most vain, conceited, egotistical little popinjay I ever saw. . . . He is a very ungraceful rider, looking more like a monkey than a man on horseback." *Three Years in the Army of the Cumberland,* 348. Nichols, on the other hand, said of him: "His face is expressive of determination and daring. A firm chin, earnest mouth, prominent nose, clear gray eyes, and expansive forehead, make up a striking physiognomy. His beard is reduced to side-whiskers. He is an excellent, if not a graceful horseman. His officers and men . . . regard him with an enthusiastic affection." *Story of the Great March,* 249.

3. In his letter to Gen. Sherman on February 24 Kilpatrick wrote from Camp Creek in Kershaw County: "Stragglers and foraging parties of the Twentieth Corps were here yesterday, eight miles from their command, commiting acts most disgraceful. This house [Kilpatrick's headquarters] was pillaged at 10 A. M. yesterday by men of the Twentieth Army Corps. I have allowed foragers from the left wing to pass through my lines, and even assisted them. Yesterday, a detail sent out by Major Dunbar, my quartermaster, captured ten mules and four horses for his wagon train. An officer of the Twentieth Army Corps arrested them and took mules and horses away. I shall now allow no foraging parties to pass through or out of my lines, and I shall dismount and seize all horses ridden by infantrymen who enter my column. This I shall continue to do, unless otherwise ordered by you or until my people are treated with that respect and courtesy I feel their conduct and services demand. I also call your attention to the fact that foraging parties burned sufficient forage on this road to have fed my entire command." *OR,* Ser. I, vol. 47, pt. 2, p. 554.

4. "We captured," wrote Conyngham, "about ten refugee trains to-day. Among those captured were two officers, who were riding in a carriage when the Yanks pounced on them. They were well armed, but made no resistance. They said they were a principal and a second, going to fight a duel, and that the other parties had gone before them to the place of rendezvous. The officer captured was Captain W. F. De Pass, a celebrated duellist of South Carolina. His would-be antagonist was a Captain W. Courtney, a fighting quartermaster. Being chivalrous and obliging, we made every effort to catch the latter, in order to let them finish their little affair of honor in our presence, but failed." *Sherman's March Through the South,* 343.

5. "Major General Hazen's foragers approached Camden, and skirmished with some cavalry, driving them into the town, and, following them, soon took possession of it. They were supported by the 112th Illinois, Colonel Adams, of

Corse's division (4th). We found about fifty thousand rations of corn meal, and four thousand bales of cotton, which we destroyed. Major Generals Howard and Logan sent in detachments next morning, who destroyed all government property, public stores, the depot, and some public buildings. Captain John H. Devereux, of Charleston, post commissary at Camden, while retreating, rode into the head of General Hazen's column, and was captured.

"The mayor and city council had prepared a very pretty speech and address to General Sherman on surrendering the city. It was rather mortifying to them to have it unceremoniously occupied by some foragers." Conyngham, 343.

The damage to Camden was considerably more extensive than is easily discerned from *OR*. For a brief but incisive account see Barrett, *Sherman's March,* 101-102.

6. In 1862 Jefferson Davis wrote his agents in Charleston, "that a horse of mine—an Arabian of great value, has arrived . . . from Europe . . . and is now there awaiting transportation to this country [Richmond]. . . . I would not for many times the value of the horse that he should fall into the hands of the Yankees." Davis to Messrs, Fraser & Co., 22 July 1862, in Dunbar Rowland, ed. *Jefferson Davis Constitutionalist, His Letters, Papers and Speeches (Jackson, Miss., 1923), V, 297.*

In his excerpt from the *Fairfield Courier* of March 23, 1865 Cook quoted: "Below Camden the enemy did not trouble the inhabitants. Neither of Messrs. Boykin's and John de Saussure's places being visited. Gen. Chesnut lost horses, mules, and provisions, but the dwellings of his plantations were saved by one of his negroes. . . . Among the horses captured on Gen. Chesnut's place [was] the superb stallion presented President Davis by the Viceroy of Egypt. One of the Yankees after riding the animal through the streets, took off the saddle and patting him on the back, remarked, 'You're too fine to ride in these parts and we'll send you to "Ole Abe." ' " *Sherman's March Through South Carolina,* 13-14.

Tiller[']s Bridge,
Kershaw Dist., S. C.
February 26, 1865

The weather cleared up about 10 A. M. and since has been beautiful. We have moved twelve miles over a country of pine barrens, used only as a field for the manufacture of turpentine. The detachment which came out yesterday to take and hold the bridge till we should come up captured more than a hundred of the S. C. Militia, who said they were on their way home, having left the army when they reached the line of the foreign state of North Carolina. This story has been told by others whom we afterwards learned were on their way to protect Camden.

They have probably been instructed to make this explanation in case of capture. These men are the most contemptible crowd I have ever seen used as soldiers. Most of them old, gray headed

men, from fifty to sixty-five years of age, many of them have heads
as white as snow, and nearly all of them are infirm; there are a few
small boys among them. We shall be compelled to parole most of
them as they will be unable to march with the Army, and we have
not transportation for them. Humanity would demand that these
old cripples and little children be all carried in ambulances.
The late storm has made bad work here. This Creek, "Lynch's,"
has overflowed the swamp to the main bank, about a mile and a
quarter, and the water is all the way about two and a half feet deep,
and some of the way lifts a mule off his feet, and is still rising. We
deemed it necessary to cross a division at once, and threw a foot
bridge over the deepest portions, perhaps three hundred yards of
bridge, and marched a division over, the men either stripping and
carrying their clothes on their shoulders, or wading it, carrying
their cartridge boxes on their muskets. The men went over with
very little fault finding, but with a good many jokes fitted to the
occasion.

A party of foragers having started out in front of the troops after
they had crossed, were attacked by a cavalry detachment and had
a fine skirmish. The rebels left four men killed, and six horses on
the ground, and carried off their wounded. One of our men was
severely sabered about the head. This was all of our loss. This cavalry appears to be the same detachment we skirmished with yesterday, and day before, still trying to get around our front as is
represented by themselves.

Two Divisions of the XV A. C. are here, two at Kelley's Bridge,
five miles below, the XVII A. C. at Young's Bridge, nine miles
above. The left wing not heard from today.

We found today one of the Columbia police detectives on duty
with us in the Quarter Master's employ watching the refugees. He
is arrested.

We learn from both prisoners and scouts today that Hardee's
column [is] now at Cheraw. He is reported to have twenty thousand men, 23 light batteries, and an immense train. This is probably overestimated though comparatively correct.[1] Mr. Soulé, the
telegraph operator from Columbia, says Beauregard received the
official report of effective force through the officer of all detachments.

Hardee's in the District of Charleston reports 6,700 men; Dick
Taylor,[2] formerly Hood, 9,000; Wade Hampton's cavalry 5,500;

Wheeler about 6,000; Hoke's[3] Division before the capture of Fort Fisher, 8,000; a total of about 35,000 outside of Richmond, that we know of. With the captures at Wilmington, the prisoners we have, the killed, wounded and deserters, have reduced this sum eight or ten thousand.

Of course we do not know Sherman's intention for the next campaign, but it seems that our cavalry force should be so increased as to contend equally with the large cavalry force of the enemy, to be led by a better man than Kilpatrick. 20,000 cavalry, properly led, could drive all the cavalry in the Confederacy upon their main column, and hold it there in spite of all they could do. It is presumed Grant will have sent a force to cover his operations, but we need the same as much as he. Beauregard has a cavalry force now superior to Sherman. Lee has very little cavalry excepting the force in the Valley. Grant has considerable, and it is said to be in very fine condition.

NOTES

1. Hardee's corps numbered about eleven thousand.
2. Lieut.-Gen. Richard Taylor.
3. Maj.-Gen. Robert F. Hoke.

Tiller's Bridge,
Kershaw Dist., S. C.
February 27, 1865

The water continued to rise last evening till late, and this morning it would swim a horse over a long distance in the road. We commenced bridging today with pontoons, and trestle work, over such parts as would float the wagons or injure the ammunition and provisions. The work is well along this evening, and we hope to cross in the morning. This P. M. the water commenced falling and we learn that with a fall of two feet at Young's Bridge, we have eight inches here and two inches at Kelley's bridge. The column at Kelley's bridge has had the same experience that we have. At Young's bridge they have done better and are ready to cross. The left wing has been detained on the Wateree, or rather Catawba, river by this same freshet. The pontoons of the XIV A. C. have been carried away and cut their column in two. They expect though to repair it and save all their trains. The Rebel cavalry [show they are] still among us by fighting with the "Bummers," and driving in dispatch bearers and staff officers.

The supplies we brought from Beaufort are getting very low, notwithstanding the large supplies we have drawn from the country. General Mower says he has only hard bread for two days, though all the division commanders have from ten to twenty-five days supplies in their trains of meat, meal, and other supplies.

General Howard started two dispatches for Charleston today, one by a negro,[1] and the other by Lieutenant McQueen of the scouts. He belongs to Captain Duncan's company and is considered as a good man. He is to be escorted to the R. R. bridge below Florence by the General's escort company. We feel anxious for him, but hope the best.

The sufferings which the people will have to undergo will be most intense. We have left on the wide strip of country we have passed over no provisions which will go any distance in supporting the people. We have left no stock by means of which they can get more. All horses, mules and cattle, sheep and hogs have been taken. They cannot go outside of the country traversed for lack of transportation, and the Rebel commissary will not furnish it even if they could go for it. To refugee is their only hope, and many of them must go quick, as we scarcely ever leave provision enough to last three days and often not a meal of victuals for a single person where there are a dozen to feed and more than this not infrequently without a board or bed blanket to cover themselves with nor a shinplaster to buy with.

Even before we came into the State the privations were vastly greater than we had ever supposed. I had thought that away from the perils of active operations there was no great sufferings, but it was a mistake. Columbia was the farthest removed from the scene of active strife of any city South. It contained before the war 12,000 or 14,000 people. When we left Beaufort it contained 45,000. The most of this increase was by refugees, and government employees, by far the greater portion of them penniless. The support of most of these people was from ready money, silver ware, and jewelry, all of which, in many cases, had been a long time since expended.

While the real value of these depreciated, and price of the necessities of life continually rose. An instance or two will illustrate. A mechanic could live if very prudent, on a salary of $20,000 but could indulge in no luxuries. The rent of a small and comfortable cottage was $5,000 per month. Gold was, when we were operating between Beaufort and Columbia, $7.75 for one.

The Rev. Mr. Shan[Shand] tells me that previous to the war, his salary was $1,800.00. It has never been increased; his bill for firewood for his family last year was $5,000.00. One man whose name I have forgotten, but whom all acknowledge to be the most princely of Sea Island cotton planters[2] on the S. C. Coast, has lived for one whole year on corn meal mixed with water alone, and baked, and this because his poverty was absolutely so great he could get nothing else. The President of the College at Columbia,[3] told Major Whittlesey[4] he had lived for a year in the same manner. I learned that thousands were living in the same way. The family[5] with whom I stayed while in C[olumbia] consisted of four members, and they told me that before the war, each of them was worth more than half a million of dollars, and for one year past they had supported themselves by making drawers for the Confederate soldiery at one dollar per pair, equal in procuring a living, to *two* cents in gold, or four in greenbacks. These are by no means exceptions to the general rule, but illustrations of the rule. Mr. Halpin who is with us, a refugee from C[olumbia] has lived, until six months since in Richmond, and he presents matters there worse than in Columbia. He was present at the great bread riot in 1863,[6] and describes it as terrific. The military power in Richmond since then has kept the people under strict control but every day only increases the suffering. The people living away from the cities have fared better, as they have lived on just what the country afforded, and were not dependent upon purchase. Mr. Soulé tells me that from the day we cut the R. R. at Millen, in Ga. the Rebel army was placed on half rations, which has not been changed.

Unless the war closes within the year, the people of Georgia, South Carolina and North Carolina will do no producing this year, positively from an inability to do it, and partially from actual discouragement. People the world over raise crops for their support and making money, but if it yields them neither, they will not do much at it. This certainly has been the case in these three states, as well as in a considerable portion of Mississippi the last year.

There is not, nor has there been during the last military year, the large amount of supplies that newspaper men, and many intelligent officers, represent. When we left Atlanta, we had twenty days rations and 80,000 men to feed; we used up our twenty days rations and left nothing in a country covering 250 miles in length, and fifty in breadth, and were out a month and five days. The support of the animals comes entirely from the country. We have been out on this trip a little longer than before, and made the same distance, and covered the same or a greater breadth of territory, and have again left nothing. We started with fifteen days rations. Let any one make such calculations as they may see fit, from these facts, and then draw conclusions of how long they can support their people and army with even a show of humanity. The people will produce crops but a little while longer, and even if they should, there is now no communication by which they can take their produce to market, and a citizen population of one hundred thousand people are thrown out of the wasted districts into the producing districts, and probably two or three times a hundred thousand. We know already that the organized parties of deserters and tories to the rebel cause in West North Carolina are so strong that the rebel authorities cannot suppress or arrest them, and they too, are living off the country by foraging from it.

From these causes I do not think the Rebel armies will not fight, they will do so whenever an opportunity offers, which affords a hope of success. They still believe their government, their property, their honor, and their Southern pride is at stake, and they will fight for them.

In addition to what is said above of the people, there is one thing they invariably do, no matter how great the cost: they cling to *the niggers,* as the visible proof of their respectability and chivalry and no matter how great the sacrifices they are compelled to make to restore them, they willingly make the sacrifices.

NOTES

1. In his letter, written "In the Field" near Lancaster on February 24 Sherman told Howard: "If you possibly can employ a negro, make a cipher dispatch telling our general position and destination and an order of liberal payment." *OR,* Ser. I, vol. 47, pt. 2, p. 547.
2. Plowden C. J. Weston.
3. Maximillan LaBorde.
4. Maj. Eliphalet Whittlesey, Gen. Howard's judge advocate.

Treasure seekers returning to camp. *Harper's Pictorial History of the Civil War*, II.

5. The Shands.

6. April 2, 1863. John Beauchamp Jones gives a graphic description of the Bread Riots in his *A Rebel War Clerk's Diary* (Philadelphia, 1866), I, 284-86.

Tiller's Bridge,
Kershaw Dist., S. C.
February 28, 1865

The weather is again bad.

The dispatch of General Howard for Charleston did not leave here till daylight yesterday morning. Captain Duncan with his own company, Captain King[1] of the Escort with his company and a small detachment of men from the Signal Corps, in all about sixty, constituted the escort under Captain Duncan. This cavalry had reached the neighborhood of Mt. Elon, twenty-five miles from here where they were attacked by a superior body of Rebel cavalry.

Duncan fell back to a cross road two miles from Mt. Elon, and took position, covering the road to the best advantage his little force would admit of. By the time he had taken this position, it was dark, and as it was raining slowly, the night was extremely dark. The enemy were upon them the moment he was prepared, and demand made for a surrender, by Brigadier General Aiken, comd'g brigade.

Duncan made no reply but told the men to be ready to fire. The enemy came up within a few paces, and ordered a charge with the sabre, every word said could be distinctly heared. At the command—"charge," Duncan ordered—"fire," and a volley was given, and the enemy stopped. A little more firing was then done from both sides, the enemy firing high. The firing thus ceased, and the enemy began to feel for them, and closed up upon Duncan but he could only distinguish the men as they came close up. The men of each side began to mix together, the Rebels asking them as they rode up who they were. Fortunately all of Duncan's men knew each other's voices, while the Rebels, being in larger force, did not. Whenever a Rebel would ask of one of our men who he was, he generally received a shot in reply. General Aiken[2] rode up to one of Captain King's men, and caught him by the sabre belt, from behind, and attempted to jerk him from his saddle, the man instantly threw the muzzle of his carbine over his shoulder, and fired back. Aiken fell dead, from his horse. (We afterwards learned the shot struck him in the face, but killed him instantly.) The Rebels learning that Aiken had fallen, called for some one to pick him up and carry him off. This loss made the enemy fall back, and in a little while they all left. Lieutenant McQueen during the fight received a ball in the bowels, fired from sabre's length, but he set upon his horse long enough to ride a little way back. . . .

Some of the incidents of the fight show how close and desperate it was. One of the Signal Corps men borrowed a screw driver from his next man, to fix his pistol, and while he was working at it, one of his comrades came up and took the man who had lent the driver prisoner. He had borrowed the driver from a Rebel, who was waiting while he repaired his carbine. Another of our men was shot at, the ball passing through his coat collar and the flash burning both his neck and collar. Duncan heard the order given to carry off the [Confederate] Brigade Surgeon who was killed. (We have seen the battle ground since and there are seven graves of private soldiers. Aiken and the surgeon were buried at Mt. Elon. We found since, twenty-six men wounded in this skirmish at Cheraw Hospital, and they say the entire loss was sixty-nine men, nine more than Duncan had.) Duncan, after the enemy had fallen back, sent McQueen to a house nearby and then moved slowly back to the Creek (Lynch's). He had but fairly cleared the ground when the Rebel Brigade charged upon the Cross Roads with a great noise, and found nothing but empty air. Duncan impressed a citizen, and one of the men taking him on his horse, compelled him on the peril of his life to take him over the creek, which he did, and the squad was again safe.

Duncan's entire loss besides McQueen was two or three men. (All have been found or come in but one.) This little battle puts Duncan clear on the records as a fighting man, as well as a bold and venturesome one. The real key of his success was the coolness with which his own character inspired all his men. The superiority of arms—seven shooters and revolvers—and standing entirely on the defensive, and compelling the enemy to do most of the talking, and Duncan's men do most of the shooting. McQueen is indeed a sad loss. He is about twenty-two years of age, a polished gentleman, and [a] kind and genial spirit. He fired but one shot from his revolver before he was hit and with that killed his enemy. Duncan represents him cool and collected when he left him. [McQueen] said he was mortally wounded, but advised Duncan to keep his men well together and cool till he could cross Lynch's Creek, when he would be safe.[3]

General Blair crossed the creek this A. M. and went to within thirteen miles of Cheraw. He took ten couriers of Hardee's who report Hardee at Cheraw, with the garrison of Charleston, not very strong however. He asked to be allowed to go after him in the morning. I believe General Howard does not approve of it.

The XV A. C. still seem unfortunate at both bridges in getting over. The water in the swamp goes down slowly, both columns are bridging with trestle work, and laying sunken corduroy. The creek is now in fact a river, one and a quarter miles wide, with water from two to five feet deep, quick sand bottom, and swift current. The original creek is about two hundred feet wide.

NOTES

1. Capt. John L. King.
2. Col. Hugh W. Aiken, commanding the Sixth South Carolina Cavalry. Gen. Sherman wrote Gen. Howard March 3: "I met at Winnsborough Mrs. Aiken, wife of the very Colonel Aiken you report as killed in the fight with Duncan. . . . In her conversation with me she said she supposed her husband would have to 'submit or get killed,' and I answered that such was the case, but hardly thought so soon to be a prophet." *OR,* Ser. I, vol. 47, pt. 2, pp. 661-62.
3. This is a much more detailed account than is Capt. Duncan's report in *OR,* Ser. I, vol. 47, pt. 2, pp. 608-609.

Kellytown,[1]
Darlington Dist., S. C.
March 1, 1865

Today has been full of little accidents, though nothing serious has transpired. The day has been a little damp, not rainy.

The General becoming tired of waiting at Tiller's Bridge, came down this morning to Kelley's Bridge with head quarters where he hoped to cross by noon, but had to wait till four P. M. when we crossed with one brigade of infantry to come to this place. The bridge had cost a good deal of labor and was built of 600 yards of trestle work and the remainder of corduroy tied on sleepers sunk to the bottom of the water. The first heavily loaded team which attempted to cross, sunk the trestle into the quick sand, and broke the bridge. The team was the General's mess wagon, and it went under water but unfortunately top down and wheels up. However it was righted and is now here, but our mess is considerably reduced, especially such articles as the water would injure.

General Blair has not moved today; he reports that J. E. Johnston is in command[2] at Cheraw and has now the garrison of Charleston under Hardee and the garrison of Wilmington under Hoke. The same report yet of twenty-three light batteries and a large train. The General also reports that his foragers have met the foragers of the XX A. C. and that the Corps is crossing at Blackway's Bridge, above Young's. No more from the left wing or General Sherman, who is with the XIV Army Corps.

Kellytown consisted of one house.

NOTES

1. Now Hartsville.
2. By Gen. Lee's Special Orders No. 3 of February 22 Gen. Johnston was assigned to "command of the two military departments known as the Department of Tennessee and Georgia, and the Department of Georgia, South Carolina, and Florida, and the troops therein." Gen. Beauregard was, in this order, instructed to report for duty to Johnston. *OR,* Ser. I vol. 47, pt. 2, p. 1248.

"The important news is that Johnston has been restored to command. I do not imagine for a moment that this change of Rebel commanders will influence General Sherman in his purposes, yet it will alter the *modus operandi,* for Johnston cannot be treated with the contempt Sherman shows for Beauregard. The Rebel citizens are delighted with Johnston's restoration, for they profess to think him the greatest general in the country. I have never heard but one expression of opinion among the Southerners relative to the respective merits of Johnston and Lee. Johnston is regarded as much superior to Lee, especially in a genius for strategy.
. . .
"The restoration of Johnston to command is said by the Rebels to be a reflection on the management of Beauregard, which the haughty Gascon ought to resent. But he cannot help himself—nor, for that matter can Jeff. Davis, for the appointment of Johnston has been forced upon him by the people of the central Southern States. Davis is cursed by every one I see with the utmost bitterness. To him they attribute all their misfortune. Johnston's removal, and the insults heaped upon that General, was the work of the Rebel chief; and from that act followed a train of dire results. Had Johnston remained in command, Sherman would never have come to Savannah, and, of course, would not have been able to march through South Carolina.

"For our part, we should still have gone to Savannah, but might have been longer on the way. The only difference . . . is, while Davis's policy has scattered and broken up the Southwestern Rebel army, Johnston would have kept it nearly intact, and might have to-day reenforced Lee with twenty-five thousand men. The Rebels hope that Johnston will be able to recall and reorganize the army; but no man living has that power." Nichols, *Story of the Great March,* 197, 201.

Near New Market,
Chesterfield Dist, S. C.
March 2, 1865

The day has been cloudy and it has rained a little. The immediate neighborhood of our camp last night was a good country, but this side of it the country is the same as the pine barrens of Georgia, i.e. the pine forest with the ground covered with wire grass. This is the only section in the state where we have the pine timber and wire grass. The pine timber land is all barren of any undergrowth except scrub oak.

All the accounts we have received from Lynch's Creek show us that all our misfortunes have not deserted us yet. The quicksand has continued to give way and displace the trestle work of the bridge. The main bridge which is a substantial work of seven years standing has slid down stream three feet and one end settled about the same perpendicularly from the jar of the teams passing over it. We expect the whole command will be over tonight.

General Blair is in the same position as yesterday with two divisions of the XV A. C. closed upon him. The XX A. C. is at Chesterfield the XIV A. C. is moving on Woodsboro.

The Rebel forces were at Cheraw today making a threat of standing till we come up, more likely covering the removal of their materials. We are to move on them tomorrow. General Sherman does not think they will fight at Cheraw. General Howard thinks they will retreat tonight.

Captain Duncan went after McQueen today with an ambulance. He found him doing well, and apparently in excellent hands and well cared for. A surgeon accompanied him and pronounced his wound doing well, but thought it safer to leave him. The ball struck lower down and more on one side than the Captain thought. The doctor does not think the cavity of the abdomen is pierced at all.[1] An enlisted man who was supposed to be killed, was shot through the thigh and had been taken up by a family and well cared for. The Captain brought him away.

Two of our men today stampeded a company of Horse Guard Cavalry in the lower part of this district and captured several of their horses and shotguns.

The command is today running two grist mills, grinding meal for the troops. This, however, is always done where a mill can be found.

NOTE

1. "[McQueen] was finally placed in a household, where he was well cared for, but where, owing to the excitement then existing in the country, his life was believed to be in danger. [The Rev.] Dr. [A. Toomer] Porter [whose home and family had been protected by McQueen in Columbia] chanced to hear of the wounded officer and also of his weak condition and danger. The doctor immediately made his way to the house where he was confined by his wounds, stayed with him, and nursed him until he was able to move. Then he procured as easy a carriage as he could get and brought him through the intervening Confederate and Union lines, a distance of several hundred miles, to me at Raleigh, N. C.. . . .

"After many years of suffering from his wound and shortened leg, better medical attention and extraordinary skill on the part of a surgeon succeeded in restoring McQueen to complete health and robust condition." Howard, *Autobiography*, II, 123-24.

Cheraw,
Chesterfield Dist., S. C.
March 3, 1865

The day has given us one more town of the Confederacy and privilege of destroying a little more of their materials.

This morning General Blair moved his corps forward with Mower in advance, with the intention of going into town, or fighting for it.[1] The XV A. C. moved up to support. I have never seen troops moved with such energy as Mower moved his division. About six miles from town he passed the entrenched outworks of the enemy, but the moment they saw how rapidly he was moving, they retreated to the main work four miles from the town. He then made for their works, which the enemy left at his approach. The line of works was on Thompson's Creek, was well built and strong, but we discovered they had nothing but cavalry in it. General Mower pressed on so rapidly that they stampeded and though they set fire to the bridge, he reached it before it was injured, and started in pursuit of the enemy. He drove them at the same speed into town. They had attempted to skirmish wherever they could get a foot hold, and when they reached the town they began to fire from the houses. The streets were full of cavalry, so the General put in a section of artillery and cleared the street with wonderful rapidity. When our infantry skirmishers reached the town, they outdid the enemy in skirmishing from the houses. As they reached the houses they knocked out the windows on their end of the house, went through, and fired from the house and out at the windows on the other end. The enemy very soon, however, became stampeded and went over the river at full run, excepting one regiment which scattered and turned up the river on this side.

The bridge over the Pee Dee was covered as usual with barrels of turpentine and resin, and was fired. General Mower made an attempt to save it, but was of course unsuccessful. The depot and some of the store houses were also on fire. Among the plunder left was twenty-eight pieces of light artillery, two thousand muskets, and considerable other ordnance supplies, besides very large quantities of ammunition for the artillery and small arms. All this will be destroyed excepting enough ammunition to replace what we have used. This was done at Columbia, and we shall leave here with the same supplies we left Beaufort with.

There was a Rebel gunboat here last night. A letter taken with mail from one of the gunboat officers, says the boat is too large to manouver well in this stream, and speaks of it as "the remnant of the C. S. Navy." It is commanded by Capt. Johnston. This officer tells his mother in the letter, that [Gen.] Johnston has 30,000 men here. A letter from an army officer says they have 18,000. We entered the town at noon when General Howard sent an officer to the XX A. C. to let them know we held the place. He found them three miles this side of Chesterfield, feeling their way slowly down.

This town has been a pleasant one, and has the Southern aristocratic bearing, or rather outside show. The streets are wide and well shaded, the houses comparatively old and were once painted white. None but the "first families" paint their houses white in South Carolina. The town also shows considerable age, and I am told dates back beyond the Revolution. The regular population would be about two thousand people.

The newspapers captured here give us a good deal of information, which we were anxious to get, concerning the fall of Charleston and Wilmington &c. They put on a grave countenance, over it all, and in spirit are evidently glaring, they solicit the people to look ahead till the tide of war shall turn in their favor. They expect us at Raleigh but will probably feel better about that bye and bye.

The announcement is made of the action of the Rebel Congress to put in the army all between the ages of seventeen and fifty.[2] [It] is in the papers and the action of the Rebel House to put in the negroes. If they had not waited so long before taking this step, it would have been a serious one for us but I think they are too late, and the proposed organization is not good. The only way the Rebels can fight negroes, is to place them in old regiments on the same active footing as the white soldiers, but still hold him as a slave. They then could fight him, as well as they could any of their troops, and that is, too, the best way for us to fight them, excepting we should give them their freedom.[3]

In neither case should they have any promotion. This would throw overboard on each side the question of inequality and at the same time would maintain it. The Southron would have his slave to do the work he assigned him, which would be to fight for his master's independence. On the other hand, we would acknowledge his freedom, and his right and duty to fight for it. Promotion could well be forbidden, and of necessity must be forbidden, on the ground that the negroes are an uneducated class, and an officer must have intellectual cultivation. The prejudices of the Army should be but very little consulted. An army is supposed to do the will of the state, and the state governs the armies according to the best interests of the state and the army. This may be an original view of this matter, and out of place here, but that it would be the best, i.e. the most effective organization of mixed armies, I believe all will concede it after thinking seriously of it. The maintenance of nationality among our troops, for instance German organizations into regiments, brigades, & divisions at the breaking out of the war, was a failure, and certain of the organizations would not fight, but when this plan was abandoned, and the troops mingled, all of the troops partook of the spirit and will of the American, and so it would be in the other case. We shall be compelled to acknowledge the negro, sooner or later, as a citizen, and if Jeff. Davis, Robt Toombs, Ben Wood or Vallandigham, cast a vote ten years from now in the Untied States, he must put [it] in the same box with the ballot of his black coachman. This war has cost too much blood, and the negro, has been too true to our Army, for the country ever to leave another opening to depopulate the country on the question of slavery or inferiority of race.

NOTES

1. "General Blair entered here about 11:30 a. m., skirmishing with the enemy's cavalry." Howard to Sherman, Cheraw, March 3, 1865—1.40 P. M. *OR,* Ser. I, Vol. 47, pt. 2, p. 661.
2. The Confederate Congress on March 13 passed a bill approving the enrollment of Negroes in the army. Nevins, *War for the Union,* 278.
"Upon the question of slavery there is but one opinion. The secessionists gave up the principle that they were originally fighting for, when they made soldiers of their negroes. . . . As for those who have always been inimical to slavery, they seem to recognize in the President's proclamation a binding obligation to do away with slavery. Whether or not that grandest deed of all time was effective, except as a war measure, is sometimes questioned; but the people of the South have accepted it as a fixed and irrevocable fact that the slaves are no longer property, but FREE." Nichols, *Story of the Great March,* 300.
3. In both the Confederate and Federal armies Negroes served in separately organized black regiments under white officers.

Cheraw,
Chesterfield Dist., S. C.
March 4, 1865

The enemy left the opposite bank of the Pee Dee last night, and this morning the pontooniers are laying a bridge.

One brigade (Fuller's) was thrown over by a temporized ferry to hold the bank while the bridge was laid, but the enemy did not develop. There is a large plantation on the opposite bank of the river, a mile wide, and at the further edge of it we can see the Rebel outpost, or a picket line. A train of cars was burned about ten miles below by our cavalry. One [car] loaded with ammunition made a heavy explosion. A detachment of cavalry has been sent by the General towards Florence to see what can be found there.

This Army will cross here, and the left wing at Sneedsboro. General Sherman has again joined this Army with his head quarters. He is with us three fourths of the time.

Citizens tell us that Schofield is at Fayett[e]ville with a portion,

Refugee train. G. W. Nichols, *The Story of the Great March.*

or all, of his command. One report is he is there with 6,000 men, others say he has a large army. He was to meet us at Goldsboro and Sherman knows of no change, but intimates if he is at Fayetteville he will turn on Raleigh before stopping.

Today the President "veteranizes" for four years or "during the war," and the soldiers are going into ecstasies over it, and are having through all the camps a Gunpowder Jollification, from powder taken here. The General has been trying to stop it all the evening, but has been unable to do so yet. I think the Army has far more confidence in the President than the country at large. At all events, the confidence is implicit. This probably arises in part from the fact that he is Commander-in-Chief of the Armies and in that capacity bears a strictly military relation to them.[1]

NOTE

1. "March 4 was made a day of jubilee. The last news received from the outer world was that of the re-election of President Lincoln; and this was the day upon which he was to be inaugurated. The event was celebrated in as grand form as the surroundings would permit. At noon, when it was supposed the ceremonies were transpiring at Washington, a national salute was fired from the captured artillery, large sea-coast pieces. In order to make as much noise as possible, and at the same time destroy the guns, which could not be carried away, they were charged to the bursting point, and when the salute was ended, the work of destruction was found to be complete. In the meantime, the lusty lungs of thousands of wildly exultant men added to the din." Hedley, *Marching Through Georgia*, p. 398.

"One of the wealthiest citizens in [Cheraw] is a Mr. McFarland, whose interest in blockade running has, it is said, been very profitable to him. I hear that a liberal use has been made of his choice wines. Many a bumper was filled there yesterday to the health of Mr. Lincoln, and confusion to South Carolina." Nichols, *Story of the Great March*, p. 202.

Cheraw,
Chesterfield Dist., S. C.
March 5, 1865

The enemy have left our front, and the scouts report the front clear, the enemy having taken the direction of, and probably passed through Rockingham.

The XVII A. C. has crossed the river and turned south toward Bennettsville, the head of column in this evening on Naked Creek. A portion of the XV A. C. have crossed and moved out five miles.

The XX A. C. will cross here on our bridge, the XIV A. C. and Kilpatrick will cross at Sneedsboro. All the Artillery, small arms and ammunition, captured here with a large store house full of cavalry equipments and other stores have been destroyed today.

We have had some fires in town today which spread from the cotton burning.

This town stands on a bluff on the west side of the Great Pee Dee River and has a fine site. The river is about five hundred feet wide here and the current deep and swift.

The country in the immediate neighborhood is good and well cultivated.

We still have rumors that Schofield is at Fayetteville.

The rumors do not seem to come with any great force. The people say Schofield captured a train of cars with prisoners at Whitesville [Whiteville], west of Wilmington.[1]

NOTE

1. Gen. Schofield did not leave Wilmington until March 6.

Easterling's Mill,
Marlborough Dist, S. C.
March 6, 1865

The XVII A. C. moved on the road next the river to Bennettsville. The XV A. C. moved in two columns, directly south east from Cheraw, about twelve miles.

The expedition sent to Florence has returned and report the enemy there too strong to venture an attack. The force which opposed them was cavalry and they saw trains loaded with troops coming in. They brought back twenty-five prisoners. General Howard is not satisfied with the result, and thinks if more vim had been used, the troops would have accomplished more, [and] at all events, known better what was at Florence than they appear to now.

A severe accident occurred this morning at Cheraw. The large amount of ammunition found in town was thrown into a ravine, with the intention of destroying it there, or leaving it. I do not know which. At any rate, it was a bad place to put it. Considerable powder had been scattered over the ground. As the trains were passing over the pontoon bridge, some of the powder scattered, took fire, and acted as a train to the ravine. The whole mass, several tons, exploded. There were a large number of teams, and some troops near by.

For a moment it is said the men and animals were all stupefied, then the animals stampeded, and it was with great difficulty they were quieted again. We lost by this explosion three men killed and perhaps a dozen wounded.[1]

The weather is beautiful, the roads good, and the country fine, with plenty of supplies. On the plantation where we are now in camp more than a hundred bales of cotton are now burning, marked C. S. A.

NOTE

1. Gen. W. B. Woods wrote Capt. Fred H. Wilson, A. A. A. G., First Division, Fifteenth Army Corps, from Phill's Creek, S. C., March 6: "The explosion was caused by ignition of a large quantity of rebel ammunition which had been found in the town of Cheraw and hauled out and thrown in a deep ravine lying between the town and the pontoon bridge. The ammunition consisted of loaded shells and loose powder. The bottom of the ravine to the depth of four or five feet was filled with it, and powder was scattered up the banks of the ravine, and for several rods from the edge of the ravine. While the brigade was halting, having stacked arms to await the passage of the train, of which it was the rear guard, some of the men at a distance of several rods from the edge of the ravine are reported to have applied fire to some small cakes of powder found on the ground. The fire immediately ran to the edge of the ravine, down the bank, and exploded the immense piles of ammunition in the bottom of the ravine. One man of this brigade was killed and 1 officer and 4 men wounded. After diligent inquiry I am unable to ascertain the names of the men who set fire to the powder, but I have no doubt they were ignorant, as I was myself, that any explosive material was in the ravine." *OR,* Ser. I, vol. 47, pt. 2, p. 701.

Brightsville,
Marlborough Dist., S. C.
March 7, 1865

We have only moved eight miles today, roads fine, the country is a fine corn producing one, and the inhabitants are more thrifty than usual. The Army is lying still to supply themselves with provisions and are now using all mills to grind corn. There are plenty of mills and large quantities of corn. We are also partly waiting for the left wing. The XX A. C. is over the river, but that portion which crosses at Sneedsboro is still behind.

The enemy does not develop today. Colonel Williams[1] who commands the expedition to Florence is here, says there were two bridges of cavalry, one regiment of infantry, and two pieces of artillery there. The prisoners had all been removed. The General does not think he knew anything about it.[2]

Our Army is becoming greatly burthened by negroes and refugees. The comments in the Rebel papers on Governor Brown's[3] message are very severe and of that tone that looks like a final rupture even providing we do not accomplish our work before such rupture can take place.

NOTES

1. Col. Reuben Williams.

2. Col. Williams reported: "On the morning of the 5th of March the command proceeded to Darlington, destroying all the trestle work between Dove's Station and that place, burning the depot building and 250 bales of cotton, and destroying the printing office at Darlington. The command immediately proceeded to carry out the instructions received from department headquarters to go to Florence and destroy the depot, rolling stock, &c. . . . About this time the enemy reenforced his left with infantry and drove back our right in some disorder. . . . Finding that I was outflanked and outnumbered by the enemy, and with a force of 400 moving in my rear, I concluded to withdraw the command and at once proceeded to do so." *OR*, Ser. I, vol. 47, pt. 1, p. 255.

3. Gov. Joseph E. Brown, of Georgia, carried on a series of disputes with President Davis throughout the war. By this time he was threatening secession from the Confederacy and asking that its constitution he amended to abolish the President's control over the army. In his *Message . . . to the Legislature of the State of Georgia, Convened in Extra Session, Macon, Georgia, February 15th, 1865* (Macon, Ga., [1865]), Brown raved about Davis: "The night is dark, the tempest howls, the ship is lashed with turbulent waves, the helmsman is steering to the whirlpool, our remonstrances are unheeded, and we must restrain him, or the crew must sink together submerged in irretrievable ruin."

Laurel Hill,
Richmond Co., N. C.,
March 8, 1865

There is little of interest today, we have moved fifteen miles though a fine country, well cultivated, and affording plenty of forage. It has rained all day, the roads would have been good but for the rain; they became very bad before night.

We crossed the South Carolina and North Carolina line at 8 o'clock this A. M. and we felt relieved in getting out of the most contemptible state in the Union, as regards the face of the country, and in fact everything in it. There is nothing in it or its people to place it on an equality with the meanest state of the Union, much less to place it in the van in all great movements, political and military. It has but one element of which it can boast, and that is *Treason.*

We have travelled about 350 miles in the state and have seen all the characteristic portions of it, and I insist that it is the meanest patch of country in America. The people are a cringing sycophantic race, who have always been led and gulled by a dozen ambitious blockheads.

The XV A. C.is here, the XVII a little in advance. The left wing further north, and about even with us.

Laurel Hill is a village consisting of a fine church, an old church not so fine, no other houses in town.

General Sherman today desired that General Howard would not reach Fayetteville before the left wing, and directed him to move slow till it passed. General Howard suggested that it was a fair race and the stake open for either to take. General Sherman said General Slocum and his command were feeling sore about his taking all the towns, and said the right wing must hold up. But General Sherman said hold easy and let Slocum occupy the place. I should not be surprised if the city surrendered to some of our troops notwithstanding. We will see.

Randallsville,
Richmond Co., N. C.
March 9, 1865

We have moved today nineteen miles through a fine country, having the general characteristics of the southern country. The roads, considering the storm of yesterday were fair. The bridge over Lumber River had been destroyed, and occupied [us] till one o'clock to repair it.

Gen. Sherman sent Sergeant Emmick of Duncan's Co. to Wilmington with dispatches. He is well versed in the mysteries of scouting. He goes dressed as a Rebel lieutenant.[2]

United States Arsenal at Fayetteville. *Harper's Pictorial History of the Civil War,* II.

NOTES

1. Sgt. Myron J. Amick. "Sherman very much wished to get communications to Wilmington. . . . After consulting with Captain Duncan, I selected Sergeant Myron J. Amick, Fifteenth Illinois Cavalry, and Private Geo. W. Quimby, Thirty-second Wisconsin, the two enlisted men that had made with Duncan the perilous and successful expedition down the Ogeechee and communicated with the fleet." Howard, *Autobigraphy,* II, 139.

2. Sherman's *Memoirs* say: "I traveled with the Fifteenth Corps and on the 8th of March reached Laurel Hill, North Carolina. Satisfied that our troops were at Wilmington, I determined to send a message there; I called for my man, Corporal [James] Pike, whom I had rescued [from the prison] at Columbia, and instructed him in disguise to work his way to Cape Fear River, secure a boat, and float down to Wilmington to convey a letter, and to report our approach. I also called on General Howard for another volunteer, and he brought me a very clever young sergeant, who is now [1875] a commissioned officer in the regular army. Each of these got off during the night by separate routes. . . ." II, 293.

Davis Bridge,
Robeson Co., N. C.
March 10, 1865

We have moved thirteen miles. The forenoon was cloudy and rained a little; the P. M. is fine. The rain yesterday and last night made horrible roads for us today. This country is a partial quick sand district, and it is impossible to pass a train over the native soil. A great part of the country will not bear a horse to be ridden over it, unless the horse has great muscle and keeps moving. The trains have moved but a little distance, and that distance has every foot been corduroyed, and in many places the first layer of timbers has sunk below the surface and the corduroy been relaid.[1]

The XVII A. C. is on this creek, the XV A. C. about eight miles back. The left wing is a little ahead of us.

I saw General Sherman today. He thinks the enemy will fight at Fayetteville. General Howard does not think so, unless we crowd them so fast they cannot get off. The entire Army is moving on the town on roads centering there, and will be able to assist each other if the enemy choose to bring on a battle.

General Sherman still says General Howard must let Slocum in the town, a sorry compliment, and one that calls out a great many remarks here.

NOTE

1. Gen. Howard regarded the weather at this time as such a hindrance that he commented on it in his official, over-all report on the campaign in the Carolinas: "March 9, excepting the three days at Lynch's Creek, this and the day following were two of the most tedious of the campaign. The rain continued and the roads grew worse and worse. The soil seemed to be sandy, and the roads would have answered for light wagons, but after a few wagons had passed over the whole bottom seemed to give out, and in places, the wagons left the roadway, they sank to the wagon body in the quicksand; and what was particularly discouraging, our corduroy of rails or poles would itself sink down and necessitate a reconstruction." *OR,* Ser. I, vol. 47, pt. 1, p. 203.

Fayetteville,
Cumberland Co., N. C.
March 11, 1865

This morning Gen. Giles A. Smith's Div. XVII A. C. moved up to assist in taking the town. Capt. Duncan was sent ahead with his company of a dozen men to see what was in front. He stampeded the Rebel pickets and dashed in town after them, and went to the centre of the town where he found Butler's division of cavalry, not expecting us so soon. He [Duncan] was very soon attacked, and seeing serious difficulty ahead, he sent all his men out of town, expecting himself to get out by the speed of his horse, when they began to crowd him. He tried to escape, and failed. They captured him and he is now a prisoner. The sergeant with the men fell back to the creek at the edge of the town and skirmished so well that the enemy did not venture to attack them, besides the chance would have been against them if they had attempted a retreat. They were reinforced as soon as possible by mounted men and at 10½ o'clock they made another effort to enter the town and succeeded in taking it and holding it. The main force of the Rebel cavalry division was doing the best it could to get over the bridge. Smith was hurried up and was on hand in a few minutes, and making an effort to secure the bridge and to save it. The XIV A. C. was on hand. About the time we fairly got in the city General Smith sent his men to put up a flag on the market place, and had just succeeded in getting three of them up when the XIV A. C. men came up for the same purpose. [Archibald] Mowhill [McLean], the Mayor was looking for some official to whom he could turn over the city. Some wag of an officer knowing the feeling about the capture of the city directed him to Colonel Strong, Chief of Staff for General

Howard. He put the written article of surrender which was placed in his hands in his pocket, and then looked up General Slocum's chief of staff, to turn it over to him. As soon as General Howard found General Slocum, he gave directions for his, i.e. General Howard's, troops to be removed from the city and the town patrolled for any of the Army of the Tennessee that might be in it. So this question of who should occupy the town first closed up in a very amusing manner, and in a way which no one could take exception to. It is reported that two or three of our men were killed today in cold blood after they were captured, but the truth of it is not known. We have since learned that Wade Hampton, Lieutenant General, killed one of them with his sabre after the man was wounded. He ordered the man to surrender, and he making no reply Hampton killed him with his sabre. It is not known whether he could or would not surrender, but Hampton was seen to kill him.[1]

There is a fine old U. S. Arsenal here and one for which the old officers seem to have a warm attachment. It is in good repair. It is built on the same general plan as the one at Washington, but smaller, and with more taste. General Sherman says he "will not leave two bricks of it together." The military store-keeper at the arsenal formerly belonged to General Sherman's regiment in the old Army, and appealed to the General for assistance or protection.[2] The General gave him the most severe reproof I have ever heard one man give another, and sent him out of his sight, after telling him that a "man who had turned traitor to the flag he had served under was too vile a thing to be in his presence."

Kilpatrick has been unfortunate. Hampton attacked him a couple of days since, at four o'clock in the morning and completely surprised him charging in among his men, and capturing his artillery, head quarters, clothing, and in fact everything. He escaped on a mule, and the brigade was temporarily stampeded. Kilpatrick went after another brigade, and returned, and soon defeated the enemy and recaptured nearly everything, excepting prisoners taken. He says he lost 150 men. The enemy claim over 400.[3] The brigade was commanded by Colonel Spencer,[4] son of Dr. Spencer of Champion, Ill.

NOTES

1. "Two of the three casualties were reported as having been inflicted by General Hampton himself but this failed to impress the Confederate General Lafayette

McLaws, who was by this time fed up with tales of South Carolina heroism. In his order book [in the Southern Historical Collection, University of North Carolina, Chapel Hill] he wrote: 'Report says he killed two with his own hand, but the chivalry have fallen so deep into the pit of "want of chivalry" that they are constantly inventing Munchausen as to the prowess of those from that state, or defaming others in order that they appear elevated by the contrast.' " Barrett, *Sherman's March,* 132.
    2. Barrett identifies this man as Edward Monagan.
    3. In his reserved fashion Sherman reported this incident: "A day or two before [on March 10], General Kilpatrick, to our left rear, had divided his force . . . interposing between our infantry columns and Wade Hampton's cavalry. The latter . . . broke across this line, captured the house in which General Kilpatrick and General Spencer [the Colonel], were, and for a time held possession of the camp and artillery of the brigade. However, General Kilpatrick and most of his men escaped into a swamp with their arms and returned, catching Hampton's men in turn, scattered and drove them away, recovering most of his camp and artillery; but Hampton got off with Kilpatrick's private horse and a couple of hundred prisoners, of which he boasted much in passing through Fayetteville." Sherman, II, 294.
    Trezevant says that Kilpatrick was "surprised by Hampton, and in *dishabille* [sic], he ran for the woods, leaving his mulatto doxy to follow as she could." *Burning of Columbia,* 25. In an appendix (p. 29) to Trezevant's account Felix G. DeFontaine, editor of the *Daily South Carolinian* (his office had been destroyed in the sack of Columbia) wrote: "Gen. Kilpatrick does not figure very boldly in the closing scenes of the war . . . . After his famous race to the swamp, when he took his precipitate departure in his shirt and draws, leaving his fair and frail school marm behind, the great Yankee cavalryman kept well under the wing of the infantry." In reality Kilpatrick's guest was Marie Boozer.
    E. L. Wells of Hampton's cavalry wrote a vividly detailed eye-witness account published in 1884 as "A Morning Call on General Kilpatrick." It describes the skirmishing around the house which proved to be the general's headquarters and continues: "Just then there bolted from the door a sorry-looking figure in his shirt and drawers. The fugitive made no fight, but cutting loose and springing astride a horse 'tarried not on the order of his going,' but sped for safety through the fog and powder-smoke as fast as a militia-man . . . .
    "And now in wild alarm there emerged from the house, whose weather-boards were fast being perforated by chance bullets, a strange apparition, one quite out of place in such wild scenes—a forlorn, forsaken damsel—one who was 'neither maid, wife, or widow,' and who was 'attached' to headquarters. She looked for a moment disconsolately at her carriage, which was close at hand, as if with the vague idea in her dazed head that it was high time for her to be leaving, and then stood in mute despair as it broke upon her that it could not move without horses. Seeing that she was in imminent danger from stray shots that were flying about, a cavalryman dismounted and conducted the poor thing, in all courtesy, to a drainage-ditch, within which she crouched in safety, as if it had been a rifle pit." *Southern Historical Society Papers,* XII (1884), 127-28.
    4. Col. George E. Spencer.

Fayetteville, N. C.
March 12, 1865

[To A. C. O.] A steamer has just arrived here from Wilmington and will return at once.[1] I have enjoyed this campaign so far and it has been in every way a success. General Sherman says he will send the President a summary of what has been done in such form that it can be given to the public.[2]

/South of this parallel we have left the enemy no communications by which General Lee's army or the city of Richmond can be supplied. We have left the country through which we have passed in no condition to supply another army which may need to pass over it, if indeed it can supply the necessaries of life for the people living in it. The arsenals at Columbia, Cheraw and this place have been destroyed. Those still left to the Confederacy are at Richmond, Lynchburg and Salisbury.

/ Most of Orangeburg and Columbia are burned. The fire at Orangeburg being set by a citizen and that at Columbia by the enemy's cavalry. Probably a large portion of Cheraw was burned and the people here say a large part of Charleston.

So far every thing appears to be going on well, but we are driving all of the enemy's forces together and they will soon be bunched. We may then expect they will make at least one grand effort to partially restore their fortunes. General Johnston is reported to have 30,000 men and General Hardee brings from Charleston and the coast cities 20,000 more, so the citizens report. If these people are correct in this statement, their combined forces will add 50,000 men to the Army of Northern Virginia. I do not believe they have so many.

General Kilpatrick made a blunder a couple of days ago by which he lost 150 prisoners which he had captured and fifty of his own men. Captain Duncan, our chief of scouts, was taken prisoner in this town yesterday. He charged into the town with a few men to see how many men General Hampton had and what they were but could not get out quick enough to save himself. His recklessness did not carry him clear through the war without mishap.

NOTES

1. The tugboat *Davidson.*
2. Sherman's chief official communications from Fayetteville were to Secretary of War Stanton and Gen. Grant. To Stanton he wrote: "I know you will be pleased to hear that my army has reached this point, and has opened communications with Wilmington. A tug-boat came up this morning and will start back at 7 P. M.

"I have . . . done all that I proposed, and the fruits seem to me ample for the time employed. Charleston, Georgetown, and Wilmington, are incidents, while the utter demolition of the railroad system of South Carolina and the utter destruction of the enemy's arsenals at Columbia, Cheraw, and Fayetteville, are the principals of the movement. These points were regarded as inaccessible to us, and now no place in the Confederacy is safe against the army of the West. Let Lee hold on to Richmond, and we will destroy his country; and then what use is Richmond? He must come out and fight us on open ground, and for that we must ever be ready. Let him stick behind his parapets, and he will perish." Sherman, II, 296.

Fayetteville, N. C.
March 12, 1865

[To S. C. O.] A little river steamer from Wilmington arrived here this morning and will return at noon.

This campaign so far has been a very pleasant one and very effective in accomplishing the work General Sherman set out to do. We occupied this city yesterday after a little fight and the enemy went out of one side of it as we came in at the other.

So far this campaign has been a great success and will prove to be of great value in the final closing of the war. We have marched about 400 miles, destroyed about 200 miles of railroad and all the factories of three large manufacturing cities, Columbia, Cheraw and Fayetteville, where supplies were produced for the southern armies. The enemy's cavalry fired the cotton in Columbia as they retired and we entered and the burning of nearly the entire city resulted. Pretty much the same thing occurred at the little city of Orangeburg, but a citizen there fired his own store and from the burning of that building nearly the entire city was burned.

You can readily trace our line of march on the map by the following places through which we passed commencing with Beaufort, then to Pocotaligo, Hickory Hill, Midway, Orangeburg, Columbia, Winnsboro, Cheraw to Fayetteville.

The army has done a great deal of skirmishing and the artillery has been a good deal used, still there have been no heavy battles. We have had only one real mishap. That was in the cavalry, where we lost 150 men we had taken prisoners and about fifty of our own killed and wounded. I especially regret this as the cavalry was commanded by Colonel Spencer, the son of Dr. Spencer of Champion. The Colonel is a good man and a good officer.

Charleston and Wilmington have fallen into our hands as a result of the campaign in rear of them. Their garrisons have passed north by our front and are beyond our bill of operations. We have now crowded all the armies of the Confederacy near together and it is reasonable to expect that they will fight when they get together. That will be pretty soon, but I hardly think we shall have a general battle with General Lee's and Johnston's armies united until after this campaign is over. We are to leave this place in a day or two and it is hardly probable you will hear from me again until this campaign is finished. General Sherman says he is headed for Goldsboro.

The enemy has been miserably commanded since we have been on this campaign or we should not have gotten through so easily. General Beauregard commanded until after we took Columbia since which Gen. J. E. Johnston has been in command. General Sherman says he is one of the ablest, if not the ablest, general in the Confederacy and he does not think he will leave us long without a battle. But as he has not a large or very effective army with him, it is not to be presumed that he can hinder us long.

Fayetteville, N. C.
March 12, 1865

The citizens here tell us that Hardee reached this place Friday night with 20,000 men, and left on Saturday night with this force and the small garrison of the town, going toward Raleigh.

The principal item of news today is in the arrival of a tug boat from Wilmington. Sergeant Amick reached Wilmington in about forty-eight hours after he left Laurel Hill, having ridden nearly a hundred miles.

The boat left Wilmington at 2 P. M. yesterday, and ran the gauntlet of rebel musketry from both sides of the river, for several miles. The officer in charge is deserving of great credit for coming up so promptly. A naval boat is below a few miles, some of the officers having landed and come through on foot. They are considerably chagrined that the tug beat them in coming through. The tug returned this evening, taking down Colonel Conklin, Chief Quarter Master of this Army, to procure and meet us with supplies when we reach communications. Our Army is greatly in need of supplies, especially clothing.[1] Very many of the men are barefooted, and have been so for a long time. I judge one fifth of them are wearing clothing picked up in the country, many dressed entirely in gray. The men however appear to find no fault.

Yesterday we captured a moderate steamer, which will be sent down, loaded with refugees, who came from Columbia, with us.[2] We have two pontoon bridges over the river which is at this place 300 yards wide. The arsenal is being battered down and thoroughly destroyed.[3]

I have seen since we came in town twelve guns captured here. The town is fortified on the river against gun boats, and the arsenal is surrounded by a line of works, apparently intended to resist cavalry raid or detachment of marines from destroying the arsenal.

The town contains perhaps three thousand people, is old and timeworn. It has probably been a fashionable town, but now looks old and rusty. A portion of the town is built on a series of little hills, perhaps one third of it on a plain. The country surrounding the town is as poor as the Lord could well make it.

A rumor reaches us today that the enemy have evacuated Richmond and Petersburg. It was brought by the naval officers. It is not credited and more than this, we hope it is not so. We are too much cumbered with wagons, negroes &c. and the men are too poorly clothed to covet a ground engagement with the combined Rebel Army. We could, however, sacrifice the encumbrances and do as well as ever, which, of course, we would do if necessary. I do not, however, believe the rumors.

I will refer here to the manner in which Sergeant Amick carried his dispatches to Wilmington. General Sherman wrote the dispatch on tissue paper, Amick then made an incision in a plug of tobacco and shoved the dispatch into the center with his knife after which he bit off the portion where the incision had been made which obliterated all appearances of the incision and then returned the tobacco to his pocket. I asked him that in case some Rebel asked for a chew of tobacco, how he could furnish it without risk.

He replied he had another plug for contingencies. He rode the seventy miles from Laurel Hill to Wilmington in about twenty-four hours and beat one of General Sherman's scouts who had gone down the day before, one day in reaching his destination.[4]

NOTES

1. In a message to Gen. Alfred Terry at Wilmington, Sherman said on March 12: "I want you to send me all the shoes, stockings, drawers, sugar, coffee, and flour

you can spare; finish the loads with oats or corn. Have the boats escorted and let them run at night at any risk." *OR,* Ser. I, vol. 47, pt. 2, p. 803.

2. "I also authorized General Howard to send back by this opportunity some of the fugitives who had traveled with his army all the way from Columbia, among whom were Mrs. Feaster and her two beautiful daughters." Sherman, II, 295.

To Terry, General Sherman said: "General Howard just reports that he has secured one of the enemy's steam-boats below the city, and General Slocum will try to secure two known to be above, and we will load them with refugees, white and black, that have clung to our skirts, impeded our movements, and consumed our food. . . . I must rid my army of from 20,000 to 30,000 useless mouths, as many to go to Cape Fear as possible, and balance will go in vehicles, and captured horses via Clinton to Wilmington." *OR,* Ser. I, vol. 47, pt. 2, p. 803.

Gen. Howard, as did they all, hurried to get a letter for his wife into the mail. His letter is undated but left Fayetteville March 12 on the *Davidson.* "I am," it says, "so impatient to see you that I hardly have the heart to write you a letter. A little tug Str. [commanded by Ens. Charles Ainsworth] made its way up the river (the Cape Fear) and has thus connected us by a slender thread with the world again, for it seems as if we have been out of it for some time. It is no small work we have done to accomplish a march of four hundred miles through the heart of the enemy's country without base of supply . . . .

"This time we have not been altogether deprived of ladies' society. We brought from Columbia quite a number of men, women & children, who have tagged along in wagons, ambulances or on mules, horses or on foot. We have had two families [the Halpins and the Soulés] at these Headquarters, who have completely mastered all the discomforts of military life and enjoyed the novelty . . . .

"Miss Boozer with her mother Mrs. Feaster were entertained by Colonel Conklin[,] Chf Qmr. I mention them because we have seen so much of them the last three weeks and I have learned that ladies can campaign. Mrs. F. & daughter were burnt out by that terrible fire at Columbia and though rich were suddenly reduced to poverty. She went from Phila[delphi]a and returns thither." Howard to Mrs. Howard, ALS, Fayetteville, N. C., [March 12, 1865]. Howard Collection.

3. In his letter of March 12 to Gen. Grant, Sherman noted: "We cannot afford to leave detachments, and I shall therefore destroy this valuable arsenal, so the enemy shall not have its use; and the United States should never again confide such valuable property to a people who have betrayed its trust." Sherman, II, 297.

4. Cpl. James Pike became lost shortly after leaving Laurel Hill but did reach Wilmington after Amick and Quimby. Pike, *Scout and Ranger* (Cincinnati and New York, 1865), 383.

Cade's Plantation,
Cumberland Co., N. C.,
March 13, 1865

We moved head quarters over the river today. The XVII A. C. crossed, the XV A. C. remaining on the opposite side.

The left wing, excepting one division, is over the river. The XX A. C. moved through the town in review before General Sherman.

I saw a portion of the troops; they were looking well with exception of clothing.

One steamer and two gunboats have arrived from Wilmington today, and the captured steamer has gone down with refugees. The people we had at head quarters have left us. They were pleasant people, and seemed to enjoy the camp much, and appeared to regret leaving us. The steamer which came up this evening brought a staff officer from General Terry. He knows nothing of Schofield having been defeated by Bragg, as Bragg reports officially. Said staff officer appears to think General Sherman is not sound in his military plans, and says he will overturn all the rules and regulations of civilized warfare.

He will be more surprised than he is now when he has campaigned with him a little while.

There is of late a strong tendency to believe Johnston will fight us between here and Goldsboro, covering his own flanks by the Cape Fear and Neuse Rivers. Since Johnston has been in command, he has been very active in moving from place to place rapidly and concentrating all his forces. This looks as if he wished to get his army together and discipline it by hard work for some special purpose. There are rumors that the forces left at Charlotte, Salisbury, and Raleigh are concentrated at Raleigh.[1]

Bragg in his reports says S. D. Hills [Gen. Daniel H. Hill] and his troops behaved gallantly at Kinston.[2] This shows reinforcements from Virginia. Lee says Sherman must and will be defeated; from such items we draw our conclusions. It is directly against Lee and Johnston's interest to allow us to unite with Schofield. The Rebels have all through given us credit for having from 30,000 to 35,000 men. When they get everything together, they will have about the same number. If they attack us, it will probably be about ten miles from this place marked on the map "Dead Fields" "battle ground", or at the "Battle ground" probably this side.

This, by the map, appears to be the strategical point for a battle field. I think now is the best time they will have, and they better take advantage of it.

NOTES

1. "We must not give time for Jos. Johnston to concentrate at Goldsboro'. We cannot prevent his concentrating at Raleigh, but he shall have no rest. . . . If we can get the roads to and secure Goldsboro' by April 10th, it will be soon enough;

but every day now is worth a million of dollars. I can whip Jos. Johnston provided he does not catch one of my corps in flank, and I will see that the army marches hence to Goldsboro' in compact form." Sherman to Terry, March 12, 1865. *Sherman,* II, 298.

2. Bragg claimed a victory over Gen. Jacob D. Cox of Schofield's command at Kinston, N. C., on 8 March. On March 10 Bragg decided he could not move successfully against the Yankees and moved to join Johnston. *OR,* Ser. I, vol. 47, pt. 1, pp. 1078-79. Schofield claimed a victory for Cox. *OR,* Ser. I, vol. 47, pt. 2, p. 803.

Cade's Plantation,
Cumberland Co., N. C.
March 14, 1865

The command is nearly all across the river. I think Kilpatrick is still on the opposite side. There has been in our Army today a general cleaning out of surplus animals, picked up in the country, the best selected and the remainder shot. The steamers now here are lying loaded with sick and wounded to be sent to Wilmington; this will lighten our column much.

We are also collecting the refugees and negroes from the entire Army to be sent to Wilmington by land, under escort. Our column will again be free and in fighting condition. Supplies have reached us to some extent by river, mostly coffee and sugar, and a few shoes, some thousands of them. One vessel loaded with forage for animals has come up, much to the disgust of all concerned, when hard bread and clothing could just as well have been sent up. Sending this steamer with forage shows a great lack of appreciation by the commander at Wilmington of the real necessities of this Army.

Cade's Plantation,
Cumberland Co., N. C.
March 15, 1865

The Army has moved out today though our head quarters has not moved. The left wing has four divisions, at the head waters of South River, without trains. The remaining two divisions are on the road parallel next south, with the trains of the Army, the other four divisions being light and unencumbered. We have the same general disposition, nearly all of the XV A. C. is on the left road of the Army and in light order. The XVII A. C. passes through Clinton, on the southern road, with two divisions free. This disposition leaves four divisions of the left wing to receive the first shock of the enemy, three divisions of the XV A. C. in supporting distance, and two divisions of the XVII A. C. light and ready to turn wherever they may be required. In this way Sherman has nine divisions which can, in a little while, be brought into a pitched battle, and by parking the trains and having a guard, we can turn two more divisions wherever they may be required, making eleven divisions in all.

These dispositions show that Sherman apprehends that Johnston will make an effort to strike his column, and it also shows that Sherman knows he is in the presence of a man far superior to Beauregard. Our forces are better commanded than Johnston's by the subordinate officers. The Rebels have, for the number of troops, by far too many officers. With the full grade of General they have Johnston, Beauregard, and Bragg; Lieutenant Generals Hardee, D. H. Hill, Hampton, S. D. Lee, Stewart, Cheatham, &c.; Major Generals Hoke, Butler,[1] Young,[2] Jackson,[3] McLaws, Humes[4] &c. &c. &c. and a whole regiment of Brigadier Generals. We are short of a full complement of officers, either General officers, field or line officers but we have sufficient to command our men well.

We have had a new and strange sight today. As the Army crossed the river, the refugees were separated from the column, and camped near the river, to the number of 7,000 negroes, and several hundred refugees. They are to be sent to Wilmington by land, crossing South River at Clinton, and then taking the road south to Wilmington. This afternoon they were moved out three miles to get them in moving shape.

They moved past our head quarters like a flock of black sheep, and were certainly the greatest curiosity I ever saw. A majority of them were women and children though there were a good many able bodied men. A few house servants were well dressed, the great majority of them were very scantily clad, if clad at all. The field hands were in the field dress which, by the way, most of them had worn since the breaking out of the war, and patched and

The tug-boat Donaldson moving up the Cape Fear. *Harper's Pictorial History of the Civil War,* II.

mended till the present time. The cloth had once been the ever-lasting butternut or gray, but is now the color of the ditch they wallowed in last. This troop of negroes is of all ages, sexes and colors, the black however, predominating. The dress ranged from good to nothing, but mostly very ragged and filthy. It took three hours for them to pass a given point. The escort for them is rather weak, though I do not think they will require a stronger one, as the enemy can have no possible advantage in attacking them, except in wanton cruelty, as they now would be a detriment to the South.[5]

Another boat came up in the river tonight, with supplies.

In a dispatch from General Terry we learn he will be at Faison's Depot on Sunday, also that the reported victory by Bragg was a farce, and that he was thoroughly whipped. It is a query whether Bragg lies to Davis officially, or whether these dispatches are only intended for the people, "to fire the Southern heart." Sheridan,[6] Terry says, is expected down in this country before long, and as the last place we heard of him, he was at Charlottesville. Va., we expect to hear from him next on the west of Richmond. It is to be hoped he will join us. With his own brains and cavalry, he could soon use up Hampton, who since we left Columbia is the only person who has annoyed us.

NOTES

1. Maj.-Gen. Matthew Calbraith Butler.
2. Maj.-Gen. Pierce Manning Butler Young.
3. Maj.-Gen. John King Jackson.
4. Maj.-Gen. William Young Cown Humes.
5. Howard wrote his wife on March 16 from "Near Fayetteville" that he had seen the refugee column on its way to "Wilmington & freedom." He commented: "Bundles on their heads, children in arms, men on mules, women in old wagons, all poorly clad & many with little to eat. They will do anything[,] suffer anything for freedom. They go they know not where. I can only think and say to myself God will care for them." ALS, Howard Collection.

"As I look back upon the extraordinary march we have made," declared Nichols, "and reflect upon the stupendous difficulties which have been in the way of a successful transit of even so large an army as this, the fact of its accomplishment with twenty-five thousand useless, helpless human beings, devouring food and clogging every step onward, will remain one of the marvels of military operations." *Story of the Great March,* 252.

6. Maj.-Gen. Philip Henry Sheridan. Howard told Mrs. Howard in his letter of March 16: "We have just got that Sheridan is expected through to join us in a few days." Sheridan remained in Virginia, blocking Lee's possible routes south and cutting off his communications.

East of Fayetteville, N. C.
March 15, 1865

[To S. C. O.] I see by the papers that a Major Osborn has been wounded and captured on the North Carolina coast. I am not that man and I do not know who he is.

We leave this locality tomorrow to move on towards the coast and will again be out of reach of mail facilities for several days. It is more than probable that the enemy will fight somewhere between here and Goldsboro. So far as I can see every thing on the military program is now working well. The territory which can now be made available by the enemy for supplies is very small, only about one half each of Virginia and North Carolina. I do not believe, however, that Mr. Davis intends to abandon the contest until his army is actually whipped and practically destroyed on the field. You must remember the Confederacy, its government, its territory, its every thing is concentrated in these two armies, now between General Grant and General Sherman and when these two armies are destroyed then the Confederacy is a thing of the past and as absolutely nothing as if it had never been thought of. This the enemy knows as well as me. Therefore I expect a good deal more fighting before this result is fully accomplished. But this fighting now must come soon and I think you will see the last of the war in June.

East of Fayetteville, N. C.
March 15, 1865

[To A. C. O.] Since I wrote last we have crossed the Cape Fear River and now move forward at once. We have cause to believe the enemy will fight again in three or four days. I have no misgivings as to the result.

Near Jackson's Farm,
Sampson Co., N. C.
March 16, 1865

Last night the main body of the troops were at South River, about twelve miles in advance of our head quarters. This morning we started at three o'clock and were up with the Army at six. I never saw much worse roads than we came over a greater portion of the way. There really seemed to be no bottom within reach of a horse's feet that would bear him. There had been a good deal of rain within a couple of days and the Army passing over the roads had ruined them. There is a large train back yet, which will have a sorry time in getting through.

The South River is the same as most of the streams we have passed. It is overflowed about half a mile and is about two feet deep on the flats, in places deeper. The enemy made the usual stand on the bank of the river, and were turned out in the usual manner, by fording the swamp and striking the flank. General Corse had the bridge rebuilt when we reached the stream. We found the enemy again on the bank of a creek six miles this side of the river near a fork in the road. They were however, on the main road, while we wished to move on the road to the left; so we pitched into them with skirmishers and kept them busy until the head of column passed on the other road and then left them to their own enjoyment.

The roads are poor and the country flat this side of the river, most of it being covered with water. We have had occasional showers all day. Tonight we have had a very heavy shower during which a gust of wind blew down all our tents but two, leaving all hands sitting outdoors in the most severe shower we have experienced on this campaign. The General's tent did not go over.

We learn tonight from a staff officer of General Sherman's that Slocum has had a severe fight with Hardee.[1] He found him in position between the Cape Fear River and the head waters of the South River, covering the road where Slocum wished to turn to the right. Slocum was compelled either to dislodge him or turn back. He chose the former. In the main part he was very successful. He captured quite a large number of prisoners and drove the enemy from two positions and uncovered his passage. Hardee retreated at dark. I do not think General Slocum or Sherman made calculations for this skirmish. In fact, it appears to have been a smart little fight, but we took more prisoners than we lost, all told. I think some five or six hundred, while Slocum reports his own loss at three hundred in killed and wounded. The General calls the fight "Kyle's Landing." If Hardee's dispositions of troops had been a little better, he would have been more successful. The few captured appear to have been an out post which was cut off from retreat. Hardee has gained nothing by fighting or [in] morale by this move-ment.

We found three of our wounded men today who had been left at houses by the enemy. They appeared to be well cared for so far. They were too badly wounded to be moved and were left to the mercy of the citizens who promised to care well for them.

NOTE

1. Slocum's troops fought Hardee's at Averasboro.

Jackson's Cross Roads,
Sampson Co., N. C.
March 17, 1865

We have marched but six miles today, but have closed up well. The XV A. C. here, and the XVII A. C. at Beaumans [Beaman's] Cross roads. The train is not quite up but is closed up well together and the guard is sufficiently strong to protect it. The roads con-tinue the same as yesterday and have all to be covered before the train can pass over them.

The word we have from the left wing amounts to the same as we had last night. Johnston left in the night, and Slocum made his usual day's march today. Kilpatrick captured Colonel Rhett[1] a day or two since. He is the man who had command at Fort Sumter for a long time. He was commanding a brigade, and had just put out a picket line, when one of Kilpatrick's staff rode round his line and took him prisoner and bought him out on the same track the aide went in.

Captain Duncan returned today, having made his escape night before last. He was in rebel hands three days. He was captured in Fayetteville by Wade Hampton and staff, after he had passed through his troops.

In running, passing through Hampton's Command, he had fired all the loads in his revolver when Hampton and his staff charged in and caught him. As soon as he gave his name they knew him, and his record, and gave directions not to let him escape if every other man got away.

The third night he was put in a log house with other prisoners with the guard on the outside. He made a hole through the floor in tearing off fuel for the fire, and got through it and off without being discovered. He was dressed in a fine uniform and had it stripped from him in Hampton's and Butler's presence. His watch, pocket book, and finger rings were taken from him while Butler was examining him about the location of our troops. This is a specimen of "Southern Chivalry," "first families," ["] Gentlemen born," "Aristocracy of America," the "born to rule" people of which so much has been said. My association and knowledge of the Southern people is that they are an inferior race compared with the North, made so by their peculiar institution and its attendant habits and teachings.

The clothing which replaced that taken from Duncan was mean and ragged, and through its appearance [he] was able to pass himself off for a private soldier and so found an opportunity to escape. He had been twice transferred to other rebel provost marshalls since his capture, and the one from whom he escaped did not know of his value but thought him a private soldier and worthy of no especial attention.[2]

NOTES

1. Col. Alfred Rhett. Nichols reported: "Kilpatrick, who has the advance, ran into a strong body of Rebel infantry this afternoon, and skirmished with them until night came on. He captured several prisoners, among them Colonel Rhett, son of the noted Robert Barnwell Rhett, one of the 'first family' names of which South Carolina is so proud. From the conversation of this Rebel colonel, I judge him to be quite as impracticable person as any of his class. He seemed most troubled about the way in which he was captured. Some of Kilpatrick's fast riders got inside his skirmish line, and one of them, without any sort of regard for the feelings of a South Carolina aristocrat, put a pistol to the colonel's head and informed him in a quiet but very decided manner, that 'if he didn't come along he'd make a hole through him!' The colonel came; but he is a disgusted man. From what I know of the sentiments of Kilpatrick's men, I make no doubt that they would have had but little scruple in cutting off one branch of the family tree of the Rhetts if the surrender had not been prompt." *Story of the Great March*, 254.

Sherman wrote of this prisoner of war, a "former commandant of Fort Sumter," that "he was a tall, slender and handsome young man dressed in the most approved Rebel uniform, with high jack-boots beautifully stitched, and was dreadfully mortified to find himself in our hands. . . . [I] heard afterward that Kilpatrick had applied to General Slocum for his prisoner, whom he made march on foot the rest of the way to Goldsboro', in retaliation. There was a story afloat that Kilpatrick made him 'get out' of those fine boots, but restored them because none of his own officers had feet delicate enough to wear them." II, 300-301, 302-303.

Hitchcock wrote that Rhett dined at Sherman's mess "and was treated with entire courtesy by Gen. Sherman, as also by Slocum and Jeff. C. Davis, who were old acquaintances of his. He . . . expressed his opinions about military matters and everything else with a frankness quite refreshing. He denounced Jeff Davis (who beat his father Barnwell Rhett for the presidency of the C. S. A., though Colonel R. did not remind us of this)—as a 'fool.' " *Marching with Sherman,* 288.

2. "While the battle of Averysboro [sic] was in progress, and I was sitting on my horse, I was approached by a man on foot, without shoes or coat, and his head bandaged by a handerchief. He announced himself as the Captain Duncan who had been captured by Wade Hampton in Fayetteville, but had escaped; and, on my inquiring how he happened to be in that plight, he explained that when he was a prisoner Wade Hampton's men had made him 'get out of his coat, hat, and shoes,' which they appropriated to themselves. He said Wade Hampton had seen them do it, and he had appealed to him personally for protection, as an officer, but Hampton answered him with a curse." Sherman, II, 302.

Lee's Store,[1]
Sampson Co., N. C.
March 18, 1865

We have moved fourteen miles, have had a fine day and good roads. We had a skirmish of about twenty minutes at this place. The troops are well closed up, and so are the trains but they are not quite up to the main body.

General Blair reports the same state of things, but says his roads were bad. The left wing is moving abreast of us on the road leading to Cox's Bridge. The XIV A. C. had a brisk skirmish today about four miles from the head of our column. We turned the head of our column towards Slocum to see what there was of it, when the enemy left.

The Army is about twenty-four or twenty-five miles from Fayetteville. This immediate neighborhood appears to be a productive country and quite well cultivated, but most of the country is flat, and in a state of nature.

The report of the late fight of the left wing[2] that we got today makes a more serious thing of it. It sums up in this way. Our total loss between five and six hundred. Captured 300 sound prisoners, fifty wounded ones, and thirty of the enemy dead left on the field, and three pieces of artillery captured. Doubtless the enemy lost the usual ratio of wounded, which would make their wounded amount to 200. So the visible results of the engagement make an even thing of it.

General Sherman still thinks Johnston will fight, either tomorrow or at Goldsboro, but we have a rumor that Schofield is at Goldsboro, though it is only a report from sick soldiers who were sent from them here as, they say, the town was being evacuated. Prisoners report Pickett's[3] and Gordon's[4] division here from Richmond and that heavy ordnance and ordnance stores are being sent from Richmond to Greensboro.

General Blair reports that the refugees and negroes had reached Clinton in good condition. The General had captured there a large supply of Confederate stores and provisions and had increased the train of the refugee column and sent them forward with plenty of supplies.

NOTES

1. Twenty-six miles from Goldsboro.
2. At Averasboro.
3. Brig.-Gen. George Edward Pickett.
4. Maj.-Gen. John Brown Gordon.

Falling Creek Church, or Dead Fields,
Sampson Co., N. C.
March 19, 1865

We have marched fourteen miles over a very treacherous road. The day has been pleasant.

Quite early this morning we heard on the left,[1] heavy and rapid firing, but as General Sherman brought his head quarters over from the left wing today, and was with us, we took it for granted it was a cavalry fight and kept on our march. The firing kept on until afternoon when General Howard, becoming uneasy, sent me to General Slocum with instructions that General Slocum should call on the XV Corps for all the troops he might wish. I had only gone back about two miles when I met General Sherman, and he told me he had just heard from General Slocum, and he had a fight with Debrill's [Dibrell's][2] division of cavalry, whipped them, that all was right now, and that I should leave the troops as they were and make no changes in the present disposition. He said also that he was going direct to General Howard and that I might as well return. I concluded, however, to go on and see how the column was getting over the road. I had gone but a little way, when I met a staff officer of General Slocum's, and he said they had driven the enemy, and they were then retreating towards Cox's Bridge and asked that the right wing should push down and cut them off. As General Howard had made my movement discretionary with myself to a great extent, I thought the best thing to be done was to hurry up the whole Corps to the front, as the head of column was only three or four miles from Cox's Bridge. I did this, but later in the P. M. the firing was again very heavy, and had the peculiar sound of a pitched battle, and near evening I understood this was the case and reports were by no means satisfactory, but it had become too late to turn back. I had informed General Howard of the change in orders, and General Sherman was with him. I felt no uneasiness about it, thinking if the troops yet required to be sent to the left, another order would be sent down. When I joined General Howard in the evening, I found General Sherman had said nothing to him about countermanding his order, and he was a good deal disappointed in my not having gone to General Slocum. I explained the matter to which General Sherman replied very emphatically "Yes, I told him so," upon which I felt a good deal relieved.

Later in the evening some of General Slocum's staff came over and reported the fight as having been very severe, with the varying favorable and unfavorable character which always attends a pitched engagement. The Rebel position was completely covered by the fighting of the cavalry, so General Slocum could not get at the real condition of affairs in front. The cavalry fell back suddenly, and by that means induced General Slocum to detach two or three of the leading brigades to turn the enemy out of position. General Carlin's[3] division XIV A. C., moving on the main road, when within a mile and a half of Bentonville Cross Roads, or rather forks, he was struck by the Rebel forces *en masse*. They gave no notion whatever of their intended attack. The Rebel cavalry had succeeded in keeping all detachments and stragglers back upon Slocum's column. The Rebels had out no skirmishers, and appeared to move from a line of works which was the case. The

Rebel line was at an angle of about forty-five degrees to the road, and when they appeared they struck the head of his column and threw it back to the right, and coming in on this angle they also had a flank and front fire on the column. The movement was admirable and one which no moving column could withstand. This division was sprung back, and reformed on a line across the road and half a mile in rear of where the head of column was struck. The loss was considerable, the division losing perhaps 400 prisoners and quite a number of killed and wounded. The enemy miscalculated in not following up this first assault with new troops, and more vigor. As soon as the new line was formed, the men threw up entrenchments, and from this Johnston could not dislodge them. The column was hurried up as fast as possible, and the line lengthened and connected wherever there were any breaks in it. By the time our men were ready, the enemy moved on to assault them. The assault was repulsed. They fell back, reformed, and charged again, making in all five distinct and separate charges. The last one, just at sunset, was desperate in the extreme. The assaulting column seemed determined not to yield and turn back. Our men standing up to the work with great gallantry. Many of the Rebel dead and wounded are reported to be lying within twenty-five yards of our works and covered by the musket fire of both lines.

Night has put an end to the fight for today. Our loss is estimated at two thousand, the enemy's loss, is, of necessity, very heavy. Long experience has taught us that an assaulting party is always very much the greatest sufferers, and the ratio of losses depends mostly on the strength of the defensive works. Our line was but a medium one as the rapidity of the enemy's movements gave but little time to build works.

We are now about ten miles from Slocum on the same road, with Johnston between us, consequently about eight miles from Johnston.

We learn from prisoners that Johnston said, in an address to his troops, this morning, that Sherman was marching on four roads, that he (Johnston) had 40,000 men, and intended to whip Sherman in detail before he could make a junction with his different columns. From this, it is possible he may turn on us tonight, and try this column. He certainly would have done so, had he been more successful in repulsing Slocum, and he may still think he has paralyzed Slocum, so that he can safely attack us. The XV A. C. have gone into position and are entrenching thoroughly. The XVII A. C. have received orders to reach here by day break.

They have eight miles to come. Should we not be attacked at daylight we will look for Johnston ourselves.

NOTES

1. This was the beginning of the battle of Bentonville, another Federal victory but, though a larger fight, a no more clearly defined one than the battle of Averasboro.

In his report of the campaign through the Carolinas Gen. Howard wrote of this action of March 19: "I heard heavy firing in the direction of Bentonville and sent Major Osborn, my chief of artillery, to go back to the rear division (General Hazen's) and direct him to go to the assistance of General Slocum in case of need, and also to see General Slocum and explain the situation of things and call for force if he needed it from the rear of General Logan's column. Major Osborn met the general-in-chief en route. The general had just received a message that he had then only a division of cavalry in his front and was driving them." *OR*, Ser. I, vol. 47, pt. 1, pp. 205-206.

2. Brig.-Gen. George Gibbs Dibrell.
3. Brig.-Gen. William Passmore Carlin.

> Camp near Mill Creek,
> 2 miles from Bentonville,
> Johnson Co., N. C.
> March 20, 1865

The day has been fine and the roads excellent. We moved at daylight to Cox's Bridge, where we found the enemy in small force of artillery and infantry, but as the road leading to Johnston's Army turned off a mile before we reached the bridge, and was uncovered, we turned down it, leaving one brigade and a battery to watch the enemy at the bridge. The enemy burned the bridge within an hour after we turned toward Johnston. We had moved about a mile, on the direct road towards Johnston, when we ran upon the Rebel cavalry outpost and the skirmishing commenced.

It proved to be Young's Cavalry of Hampton's command. We drove them as fast as the infantry could march. At noon we struck a brigade of infantry covered by a rail barricade, and received a volley from them, which did a little damage, perhaps cost six or eight men.

We stopped long enough to close the column up and get the men well in hand, when we dislodged this force and pushed on to develop the enemy. We came to the immediate vicinity of the main line and went into position as the troops came up and commenced operations to find the right of Slocum's line. We could guess where that was only by the geography of the country, its topography, and what we could draw out of the citizens, and the occasional sound of artillery [in] the neighborhood of Slocum's right. The enemy knew we would make this effort at once and took all the precautions they could against it. They had strong skirmish lines out and skirmished very stubbornly to prevent the junction, but we gained it by three o'clock, and passed the remainder of the P. M. in getting the command up. At night we succeeded in getting, as we think, in the immediate neighborhood of the army.

As soon as the lines were connected, I went over to General Slocum. I found them doing nothing but holding the line and awaiting our arrival. The enemy are in strong force in his front. The enemy has abandoned the left of their line and swung that flank back, so as to cover all the roads centering here, the Rebel right now resting on Mill Creek, and the left near or on the river, the center covering the roads leading into Bentonville. Consequently their line is the convex formation. As a general rule the best junction possible.

I asked General Slocum how he thought the battle stood, when they ceased fighting, as both parties held the line confronting each other. He replied "we whipped them." The country where the battle was fought is a dense swamp, or more properly, a quicksand flat. There is but little water standing on the surface, but it is a water level, and holds up infantry in manoeuvre well but will not bear to draw artillery over without great difficulty. Horses travel over most of the ground with difficulty, and have to be kept moving to keep above ground. The ground being so level, assisted very much the effectiveness of the musketry. The ground offered no cover for the assaulting party. The battle field is a dense wood, with a great deal of swamp brush in places. There was but one small open field on the battle ground. The enemy must have lost not less than 5,000 men in killed, wounded and prisoners, to have an even ratio with our loss and the manner in which the battle was fought.

Near Mill Creek,
Johnson Co., N. C.
March 21, 1865

The A. M. was occupied in throwing the entire line forward and entrenching much nearer the line of the enemy, and by this means connecting our main line from the left of the Army of Georgia to our right. The Corps were in position from the left to the right XX A. C., XIV A. C., XV [and] XVII having reserves on each flank. Kilpatrick was on the extreme left with his left well reversed. About now General Mower was ordered to move forward beyond our extreme right and feel for the enemy.[1] He did so, and by some mistake, or being misled by the topography of the country, his left became detached from the right of the main line while he was crossing a swamp. He came upon the enemy in position and dislodged them, and still pushed on until he was directly in the Rebel rear. The enemy here turned upon him, and attacked him with great impetuosity, striking his front and both flanks at the same time. His flanks were thrown into a little confusion, but the General held his command up well, and fell back over the swamp. When he was attacked he sent word to General Blair, and reinforcements were ordered in to his support, but they did not get up [in] time enough to assist him any. I think there was some blunder in this movement. I understood General Sherman ordered Mower in person to make the advance and neither General Blair, or General Howard knew of it, and were not responsible for failing to support him. The moment General Howard heard of Mower's condition, he ordered the Corps into his assistance, but he had returned before the Corps could move. Had General Sherman given General Howard the order instead of doing the unsoldierly thing of giving a division commander orders direct, we should have gained a splendid victory, instead of a repulse. Mower had gained all the preliminaries of a victory. He had turned the whole Rebel position, and broken over their works, and opened a field engagement in their rear, where we could have whipped them in an hour.

Mower's whole loss was perhaps 200.

When General Howard knew of Mower's condition he ordered the XV A. C. to commence operations on their front. We commenced to throw forward the skirmish line, and captured the enemy's skirmish line on a front of a mile and a half, within a hundred yards of the enemy's main line. This we held, though the enemy made attempt after attempt to recapture it. The enemy lost quite heavily in this skirmish during the P. M., and in truth the skirmishing amounted to almost a battle. From the nature of the ground, and the position of the troops, we could only get two batteries in, but their position was most excellent.

These operations appear to me to have settled down to a question of who can stay here the longest, and so claim the record of a victory. The enemy's line of retreat toward Smithfield is open and General Sherman thinks it so covered by Mill Creek that he cannot cut it. The position is so covered with earth works that we must lose too many men to care to break it, and we have no fears of Johnston making another attack on us. The point is *morale,* and who shall have it. If we back first to go for supplies, Johnston gets the *morale,* and if we make Johnston leave first, we keep our record good.

The removal of Beauregard and placing Johnston in command of the Rebel forces here was a good stroke of policy for Davis. From Atlanta to Columbia, we have never found over 3,000 men to oppose our advance, but once, and that was at Savannah. To be sure they had men at Columbia, but they were so poorly handled that they amounted to nothing.

NOTE

1. "General Mower, ever rash, broke through the rebel line on his extreme left flank, and was pushing straight for Bentonville and the bridge across Mill Creek. I ordered him back to connect with his own corps; and, lest the enemy should concentrate on him, ordered the whole rebel line to be engaged with a strong skirmish-fire.

"I think I made a mistake there, and should rapidly have followed Mower's lead with the whole of the right wing [Howard's], which would have brought on a general battle, and it could not have resulted otherwise than successfully to us." Sherman, II, 304.

Near Mill Creek,
Johnson Co., N. C.
March 22, 1865

At daylight this morning, General Logan reported the enemy's works evacuated, and no sign of their presence in his front. At six o'clock General Mower was at the crossing of Mill Creek below Bentonville. General Sherman gave orders to halt at the creek and only picket it to cover operations in the rear. The order, however, did not reach the front till a portion of Woods'[1] division was over the creek, and fighting with the Rebel rear guard.

Woods was withdrawn as rapidly as possible.

We looked over the field of operations a little and found them much as I have described. We also visited the field of General Slocum's fight which has the characteristic of a battle field where a desperate battle has been fought. The graves of the enemy's dead, the dead horses, broken material, the lines of earth works, trees cut down with artillery, and the whole forest scarred and cut with musketry &c. &c.

As soon as the abandonment of the enemy's position was known, General Sherman ordered the left wing to move for Goldsboro today and the right wing tomorrow. The roads are bad and the troops moving slowly.

In General Sherman's congratulatory address he says: "We beat the enemy yesterday." I was really unaware that any one was beat or whipped *yesterday.*[2] The general operations of the four days terminated in our favor, and we have the *morale* and record. Doubtless Johnston was whipped here and all his plans disarranged, but I can't see that it was done *yesterday.* If any one day's work whipped Johnston, it was by General Slocum on the 19 and he, and not us, should have the burthen of glory for it.

This battle has placed Slocum firm on the record and has now all to his support. It was his first great battle, and he fought it well. Since leaving Columbia he has more than ever shown a spirit of cordial co-operation and support. He acknowledges to General Blair, his chagrin at not having himself taken Columbia, and said he owed his failure to do so to his inability to bring the XIV A. C. up in time.

I have always since Gettysburg had a strong prejudice against him. His peculiarities are unpleasant, and one is not apt to reform his prejudices in favor of an unpleasant man. He did well here, and I am glad of it.[3]

General Sherman announces today that Schofield is at Goldsboro. General Terry[4] [is] at Cox's Bridge, and we hear that we are to have a little rest and then try it again.

Last summer we had a fighting campaign. Those since have

been directed against lines of communications and supplies, the general destruction of property, impoverishing the enemy's country, taking cities and military depots, without the loss of a great amount of life. The winter has been occupied in manoeuvre, more than in fighting. The enemy's forces are driven together and so concentrated that they will be able to compel one more campaign, at least, of severe fighting. Lee's forces are of sufficient strength to carry on a campaign for a good portion of the summer against Grant. Johnston is very careful of his men and will make the most of them, and we may expect this summer's campaign to be much the same as that of last summer. I hardly expect so long and continuous a campaign as that of last summer, though it is a question of men, and who can endure the draught of blood the longest.

When, and even before, the war had fairly begun the South frankly said they would be independent or exterminated. The country took them at their word, and slowly and surely the work of extermination has been going on, yet it is by no means slowly. The people of the North can form no conception of the barrenness of the South in able bodied men; they have all been absorbed. An able bodied white man of military age is a curiosity in the South. Governor Brown of Georgia says there are only 1,400 men in the state fit for military duty, not now in the Army. The mayor of Columbia told General Howard there were 1,450 in South Carolina. Thus, the largest state and the most treasonable state in the South together cannot furnish 3,000 men, not enough to stand a morning skirmish without being annihilated. Lee's Army, said to be 65,000 men, and Johnston's of less than 40,000 will be pretty much exhausted before the summer is out. There are no large armies from which to draw reinforcements, as was the case last summer, from large garrisons and strong reserves, scattered all through the South.

It is by no means the men alone that are passing away in the South. Great numbers of families are leaving the country, or at least did so until we acquired all the coast. This is especially true of the "first families." The military operations directly and indirectly have destroyed great numbers of their population. The recklessness of the enemy in fighting where the citizens are exposed, the shelling of cities, the explosions of magazines and store houses, R. R. and steamboat accidents, the burning of towns, all tend to a destruction of the population.

Thousands have gone to the northern states and have become incorporated in the population of that section, and will never be known again as of the southern population.

Our Army has travelled over thousands of miles of territory which will be abandoned by the inhabitants who will never return, and these sections will grow up to a wilderness. The population, by all these means, becomes unsettled and loses its adhesiveness. The constituency of the South which has always governed the people, and given it its peculiar tone, is already in poverty. The wealth acquired during the war has no stability about it and will do the holders but little good. There is not now, nor has there been for some time, any civil government in the South. There is an indirect military control of women and children, and a direct military control of all able bodied men, from head quarters at Richmond, but when this is gone, all government is gone. They may fight, and I think will, with a moving army after Richmond is taken, but it will be in their last agony, and subject them to the contempt of the whole world. Richmond is now the strongest city on earth, and if this cannot be held by their combined armies, there is only murder in any future fighting.

NOTES

1. Maj.-Gen. Charles R. Woods

2. "With the knowledge now possessed of his small force, of course I committed an error in not overwhelming Johnston's army on March 21st, 1865. But I was content to let him go." Sherman, II, 306.

3. "The battle of Bentonville was General Slocum's fight. While his name is honorably associated with almost every great battle of this war . . . the bloody combat at Bentonville was peculiarly his own affair, out of which he has come with fresh laurels. The unexpected attack, the fierce assaults, several times repeated, called for all the resources of a brave, cool, experienced soldier; but Slocum was more than equal to the necessities of the hour, for he was victorious, and his success justified General Sherman's selection of him as the commander of the left wing of the army." Nichols, *Story of the Great March,* 271.

4. Maj.-Gen. Alfred H. Terry.

VI Peace and the Grand Review

Falling Creek Church, or "Dead Fields,"
Sampson Co., N. C.
March 23, 1965

We moved this morning from our camp near the battle field, and are now on the same camp we occupied on the night of the 19, now on our way to Goldsboro. The roads have been good, and the weather fine.

The left wing has crossed Cox's Bridge this morning, and will be in town this evening. General Terry is here with two Divisions, making nine thousand men. Ames's[1] division [of] white troops, and Paine's[2] division of colored.

I called on General Ames this morning. He tells me General Howard is a Brigadier General in the Regular Army.[3] We knew nothing of it before. It is a promotion well deserved.

NOTES

1. Maj.-Gen. Adelbert Ames.
2. Brig.-Gen. Charles Jackson Paine.
3. Howard's promotion dated from December 21, 1864.

Goldsboro, N. C.
March 24, 1865

We moved up here today, and placed the troops in defensive position about town, with instructions to entrench, so they may rest as much as possible without anxiety about their position. As the troops passed through town, they passed in informal review before General Sherman at his head quarters. They are certainly the most ragged and tattered looking soldiers I have ever seen belonging to our Army. It is almost difficult to tell what was the original intention of the uniform. All are very dirty and ragged, and nearly one quarter are in clothes picked up in the country, of all kinds of gray and mud color imaginable.

Physically, they are in excellent condition, and only need new uniforms and rest and regular food for two weeks, when they will be equal to any labor that may be imposed upon them. The *morale* is perfect.

Goldsboro is a little town of 6 or 800 people built about the Junction of the R. Roads and is two miles from the [Neuse] River. There are a few fine houses, and the remainder are small cottages. I don't think many of the "first families" lived here. The country around is high and moderately cultivated—but, like nearly all of rebeldom, is sandy.

I heard General Sherman remark today that the march of this Army from Savannah to this place, the consequent capture of Charleston, without going within a hundred miles of it, and the junction of this Army with a column moving from Kinston, and another from Wilmington, would be considered by able military men as one of the most perfect military movements in history.

The results of this campaign are very great, and yet the loss of life is comparatively small as compared with other campaigns followed by great results. The State of South Carolina in this campaign has been the greatest sufferer, and is ruined for a quarter of a century to come. And for any military purpose, it is lost to the Confederacy and can now only be made to cover the Rebel armies in falling back of the Savannah River, and so leave its ruined territory between us and themselves. There is no R. R. communication through it. On the route we travelled all wagon bridges are burned and an army without a pontoon train will be put to great strength in getting over it, while the citizens must depend on small ferries &c. for local use. The district east of our line of march was exhausted by Hardee's garrison at Charleston. The only rich portion west of our march is the Abbeville District and this Dick Taylor's army must have greatly impoverished. The entire state is now but little better than the Sahara.

In all the South there is no affection for the old government of the United States. All the people are sick of the war, and many, counting the cost, would rather stop now. While the greater portion of the people expect to gain their independence yet, they base their faith, as they say, on the fact that Grant has been unable to drive Lee out of Richmond. But they are most like Micawber, "waiting for something to turn up," but what that something is, no one can tell. The females say that "something tells them that they will yet be free." As a people, they are more easily deceived than any other people I have ever seen.

They believe anything that a "first family" may tell them without for a moment considering how absurd it is, or whether it is in the range of probabilities, or even possibilities. Their military leaders are the most unmitigated liars on earth, and appear to have no more scruple in falsifying to their superiors than to the people. Much of their military reputation is based upon this system of lying about their military operations. We find ourselves more firmly convinced of this on finishing this campaign, than ever before.

We now have an Army together with which General Sherman may feel perfectly safe to cope with the consolidated armies of Rebeldom. Sherman, as our immediate leader, has conducted us through the different campaigns from Chattanooga with great ability, and in this one he has shown no less of the bold and daring spirit than in the one for Atlanta. But I feel willing and proud to give the great burthen of honor to the man [to] whom I believe the whole world and history will accede it, Grant.

Goldsboro, N. C.
March 25, 1865

[To S. C. O.] We have finished the campaign through South and part of North Carolina and are now resting here where we shall probably remain for a fortnight.[1] We have accomplished a great deal since we left Savannah. Our trip lasted fifty-five days and in that time we have marched 500 miles. We have captured and destroyed, in a miliary sense, all the large cities in the interior of South Carolina, excepting Camden; destroyed about 200 miles of railroad and thoroughly impoverished a strip of country fifty miles wide the entire distance.

In North Carolina we fought one battle at Averasboro, one at Bentonville and a small one near there two days later, in all of which we were successful. We have also destroyed a vast amount of military stores of all kinds and especially of ordnance, together with the means of manufacturing them. We destroyed large arsenals in Columbia, Cheraw and Fayetteville. The railroads are so completely ruined that practically the southern limit of the Confederacy is at Charlotte, North Carolina. On our line of march we have captured eighty pieces of artillery, besides all that which has fallen into our hands by the evacuation of Charleston on account of this raid behind it. We left Beaufort with very few supplies and have lived off the country for fifty-five days.

The state of South Carolina, is today substantially ruined and for the next six months cannot [do] any more than feed the women and children in it. The best bridges are destroyed. They were nearly all burned by the enemy to impede our march. As a result of this policy of burning bridges, the facilities for travel by wagon in the state are much lessened and, in a large portion of the state, nearly ruined. No state except Virginia has suffered as much as South Carolina and yet only three months ago the enemy thought it could not be injured or its cities taken.

But our work is not all done yet. General Lee's army is at Richmond and General Johnston's army is in front of us. A few other detachments are in the south and west. These are all now. I think the next campaign will bring the armies of Generals Lee and Johnston together between here and Richmond where a general battle will be fought.

NOTE

1. "We reached Goldsboro," reported Howard, "by two easy marches. . . . As the corps passed before the general in chief the men presented a strong, hearty appearance, but they were actually in rags and almost shoeless; but in less than ten days they have been refitted with everything a soldier needs." *OR,* Ser. I, vol. 47, pt. 1, p. 207.

Goldsboro, N. C.
March 30, 1865

[To A. C. O.] General Sherman has gone on a visit to General Grant but will be here again soon.[1] The enemy appears to be working hard to get ready for a success in the final struggle which cannot be much longer postponed.

NOTE

1. It is generally assumed that Sherman and Grant would work out plans for future moves and that Sherman hoped Grant would restrain his operations against Lee until the two Federal generals were operating together. When Sherman stopped for an evening meal in New Bern, a crowd demanded a speech. The *New York Herald* for March 31 quoted him: "I'm going up to see Grant for five minutes and have it all chalked out for me and then come back and pitch in. I only want to see him for five minutes and won't be gone but two or three days." He went by the steamer *Russia* from Morehead City to City Point. There he me with Grant and President Lincoln on board the *River Queen* March 27 and 28 and on at least one day with Vice-Admiral David D. Porter. Sherman returned to North Carolina on the navy's steamer *Bat*.

Goldsboro, N. C.
March 31, 1865

[To A. C. O] General Sherman returned today from his visit to General Grant.[1] We are to move about the 10 of April. The General thinks General Grant will compel General Lee to fight today or tomorrow and in so far as possible he will force him to take the offensive.[2] General Sherman has always adopted this method whenever he could.

I will as soon as possible bring up my detailed journal of this campaign. It is more full than any I have before written.

NOTES

1. "After I had been with [Grant] about an hour or so, he remarked that the President, Mr. Lincoln, was then on board the steamer River Queen, and he proposed that we should call and see him. [Mr. Lincoln] remembered me perfectly, and at once engaged in a most interesting conversation. He was full of curiosity about the many incidents of our great march, which had reached him officially and through the newspapers and seemed to enjoy very much the more ludicrous parts—about the 'bummers' and their devices to collect food and forage when the outside world supposed us to be starving." Sherman II, 324.

2. "Both General Grant and myself supposed that one or the other of us would have to fight one more bloody battle, and that it would be the *last*. Mr. Lincoln exclaimed more than once, that there had been enough blood shed, and asked if another battle could not be avoided. I remember well to have said that we could not control that event; and I inferred that both Jeff. Davis and General Lee would be forced to fight one more desperate and bloody battle. I rather supposed it would fall on me somewhere near Raleigh; and General Grant added that, if Lee would only wait a few more days, he would have his army so disposed that if the enemy should abandon Richmond, and attempt to make junction with General Jos. Johnston in North Carolina he (General Grant) would be on his heels." Sherman, II, 326.

Goldsboro, N. C.
April 4, 1865

[To A. C. O] In writing this detailed account ordinary of the campaign from Savannah to Goldsboro, it has been my intention, so far as possible, to give you an idea of the campaign as it looked to me during the operations.

I made it a practice each evening before retiring, to minute down the incidents of the day, what information we had received, the substance of our speculations, the enemy's doings, and what his movements indicated. In fact I attempted to transfer the items of the head-quarters to paper, without at any time intimating what we intended to do in the future, for the notes might, by some mishap, fall into the enemy's hands. In transcribing them, I have endeavored to adhere closely to the notes, and only when it was necessary to modify the phraseology, have I departed from them. There will be quite a number of miscalculations noticed, of the enemy's intentions and his whereabouts; yet I have transcribed them, that you may judge how accurately we calculated on all of Beauregard's and Johnston's movements.

I have also had copies made of the Special Field Orders, of General Sherman's letters to General Howard, and General Howard to General Sherman, with a few letters written by Generals Blair and Logan to General Howard on current events. These will give you an impression of the manner in which correspondence is carried on between general officers while conducting a campaign, and that while Army and Corps commanders maintain their official dignity with credit to themselves, they sometimes fall from their lofty position, and their letters amount to no more than the letters of other people.

The official report of General Howard and other official papers will make a good standard by which to measure the other matter.

Hoping the perusal of this paper, will give you and perhaps other members of the family, as great pleasure as it has given me to prepare it for your gratification.[1]

NOTE

1. With this letter to A. C. Osborn was transmitted "the detailed journal" referred to in T.W. Osborn's letter of March 31, the entries on pages 80-146 of this volume. The official papers mentioned are not reprinted here.

Goldsboro, N. C.
April 7, 1865

[To S. C. O.] I have been very busy since we arrived here in getting the artillery ready for the next campaign.

Of course you know more about the result of General Grant's work than I do. The last word we have was a telegram from the President saying Richmond is in our possession.[1] General Sherman also has dispatches from General Grant to the same effect. These dispatches indicate that General Lee is being severely pressed and all is now progressing well. I have no doubt much more has been accomplished than has been reported to us and results now are much more positive.

I have long believed that General Grant is the best general this country has produced and one of the greatest any country has produced. The Army of the Tennessee was the first Army he commanded and all the old members of it believe in his ability most sincerely. We hope that next news from him will be that still more positive results have been secured in these final acts of this desperate war.

The Confederate government has now gone down. I have long known and often said there was nothing of it except Lee's Army. This is now on the move and the capital in our possession. I do not believe the fighting is over. I think there must be a good deal yet, but from this time forward the enemy is only an organized army but with no located organized government to which that army owes allegiance.

This army is still lying about Goldsboro making good progress preparatory for an immediate advance. General Sherman has a splendid army, increased one third by the addition of Schofield's Army of the Ohio and it is in most admirable condition. The late changes at Richmond may cause some changes in his plans but if so I do not know of it.

NOTE

1. In his letter to his wife on April 7 Gen. Howard said: "Our time for moving was set for next Monday [April 10], but the news from Richmond may modify the General's plans materially." ALS, Howard Collection.

Goldsboro, N. C.

April 8, 1865

[To A. C. O.] The news from the Army of the Potomac is very gratifying. Of course you have later information than we. The hard pounding of last summer has had its effect on General Lee's Army. It was by no means lost. The activity of General Sherman this winter has been very fruitful of good results in the final breaking down of that Army. We have General Grant's dispatch to General Sherman in which he says he estimates General Lee's Army at 20,000 men. Our information indicates that General Johnston has 23,000 infantry and 10,000 cavalry, or a total in both armies of not far from 45,000 effective men.

In a couple of days we shall move toward Raleigh with 90,000 effective men. The organization of General Sherman's camp is much the same it was last summer. At that time, however, there was a greater difference in numbers between the three armies. We then had the Armies of the Cumberland, Tennessee and Ohio, now we have the Armies of the Tennessee, Georgia and Ohio, 30,000 each. On the coming campaign General Howard has the right with the Army of the Tennessee, comprising the XV and XVII Corps; General Schofield the center with the Army of the Ohio, comprising the X and XXIII Corps; and General Slocum has the left with the Army of Georgia, comprising the XIV and XX Corps. General Kilpatrick has the cavalry numbering about 8,000 men. The several Corps are commanded in the order above named by Generals Logan, Blair, Terry, Cox, Davis and Mower. Every one of these Generals is capable of handling his Corps in defending or of fighting the battle successfully, no matter how severe.

General Grant is believed to have with him 125,000 men of all arms. General Thomas is reported to have 50,000 in his Army. His Headquarters are at Nashville. The Army of the Gulf commanded by General Canby,[1] comprising the XIII and XVI Corps, is placed at 35,000 and General Wilson's cavalry, said to be now raiding in Mississippi and Alabama, is placed at 20,000. If the above figures are correct or approximately so, we have in the active armies 350,000 men. It appears by these figures, that the north after four years of war is just getting ready to fight. I think the above figures are approximately correct. General Sherman says we still have plenty of troops in reserve.

The only ordnance depots now left to the enemy are those at Raleigh, Salisbury and Lynchburg. We will have Raleigh by the 20 and we are in hopes General Stoneman will be able to strike Salisbury from the west.

When this campaign now in progress is over, General Grant will occupy the place in the esteem of the nation I think him entitled to, that of the first General this country has produced and this war developed.

NOTE

1. Maj.-Gen. Edward R. S. Canby.

Goldsboro, N. C.
April 9, 1865

[To S. C. O.] General Sherman leaves again tomorrow morning to the interior in search of General Johnston's Army which now lies about 30 miles west of us. I do not think Johnston will fight.

I do not know whether our lines of communication are to be kept open or not. If so I will write, but if not I cannot do it. I doubt very much whether General Sherman has any clear idea of just what he has to do beyond the one thing of searching General Johnston's Army. So far as we know, the success of General Grant over General Lee is complete and that Army is substantially gone.

Goldsboro, N. C.
April 9, 1865

[To A. C. O.] We leave tomorrow morning to look after General Johnston and his Army. It is reported lying at Smithfield, half way between here and Raleigh. I do not think he will fight, but this is uncertain. We shall be in Raleigh Wednesday or Thursday whether Johnston fights or not. As his Army and the fragments of Lee's Army are now the only objective points our future movements are uncertain.[1]

NOTE

1. Hitchcock stated in his letter to his wife written at Goldsboro April 10: "The late victories have changed our programme somewhat. Grant telegraphed Sherman from Parksville on the 6th that 'the rebel armies are now the only strategic points'; and while he is looking after Lee,—perhaps has found him by this time,— we start to hunt up 'Jo Johnston.'" Hitchcock, *Marching with Sherman*, 293.

Raleigh, N. C.
April 19, 1865

[To S. C. O.] Last evening General Johnston with the approval of General Breckinridge,[1] the Confederate Secretary of War, surrendered all the Confederate Armies. This makes a clean sweep no matter how many men are still under arms. The articles of capitulation are now on their way to Washington for approval by the President.[2] At General Howard's headquarters this evening General Slocum said to General Stoneman that he did not think the President would accept the terms as they were too liberal. General Logan agreed with General Slocum. General Sherman said he had given the terms he understood President Lincoln wished given but if they were not satisfactory he would demand such as the President might desire. I can hardly think he had made terms which leaves the surrender of all the Confederate Armies nominally an open question. We shall see.

This last week's work eclipsed any thing we have accomplished before. It is the winding up, the summing up, of all that has been done for four years. But a fearful cloud is drawn over it all. The assassination of the President has filled the Army with sadness. We have the joy of our success and the sorrow for the President's death. Here the sorrow is greater than the joy.[3]

We are given to understand this army will be mustered out of service soon after we arrive in Washington which will probably be in about thirty days.

NOTES

1. Maj.-Gen. John Cabell Breckinridge had been Confederate Secretary of War since February 4.
2. Maj. Henry Hitchcock carried the papers to Washington. President Andrew Johnson rejected the terms Sherman proposed. Gen. Howard wrote to his wife from Raleigh on April 18: "Gens. Sherman and Johnston met yesterday between

Conference between General Sherman and General Johnston. G. W. Nichols, *The Story of the Great March.*

the lines to arrange terms of settlement. They did not quite agree and I am afraid that Johnston cannot sufficiently control his subordinates to effect the terms most likely to lead to peace, but I believe his disposition is good and that he will do the best he can." ALS, Howard Collection.

3. Gen. Sherman was last with President Lincoln on March 28. "Of all the men I ever met," he wrote, "he seemed to possess more of the elements of greatness, combined with goodness, than any other." II, 328.

Gen. Howard said in his letter of April 18: "Yesterday the dreadful news came to us of the death of our beloved president. He thus seals his great work with his life. The grief is almost universal and completely depressing amongst the officers. I have seen more than one general officer shed tears in speaking of Mr. Lincoln. But he has gone to his reward. Would God he might have lived to enjoy in this life the fruits of his faithful labor."

Raleigh, N. C.
April 19, 1865

[To A. C. O.] The war is over. General Johnston, approved by General Breckinridge, Confederate Secretary of War, last evening surrendered all the enemy's forces. A draft of the terms were sent to Washington for ratification by the President. An officer left with them last evening. Generals Slocum and Logan think they will not be ratified by the President and General Sherman thinks they will.

Could we have imagined, a few weeks ago, that it was possible for the Confederacy to have collapsed so suddenly and effectually. Twenty days ago, to all outside appearance, it was in a sufficiently good and substantial condition to last at least several months longer. Today there is absolutely nothing of it.

General Johnston yesterday told General Sherman that this Army was the best and most perfectly organized Army that ever existed, that history speaks of nothing like it since the days of Julius Caesar.

But all we have done and all we have won is nearly counterbalanced by the assassination of the President and Secretary Seward.[1] I presume the whole country is oppressed by the same sorrow and to the same extent that exists in the Army. Indeed I know it must be so. Here ninety-nine out of every hundred officers and men believe this to be the act of the Confederate government. And it has been with considerable difficulty that the Army has been restrained from acts of revenge. It was necessary to guard the city two days to prevent its destruction, but all is quiet now and there will be no trouble. The discipline of this Army has certainly come to the aid of the people of Raleigh just at this time.[2]

This is a beautiful little city of 6,000 or 7,000 people. No damage has been done it.

NOTES

1. At the time of President Lincoln's assassination an attempt on the life of Secretary of State William H. Seward was also made, but he survived.

Gen. Joseph E. Johnston's *Narrative of Military Operations* (New York, 1874), p. 402, says that on April 18 "General Sherman met me at the time and place appointed—the house being that of a Mr. Bennett. As soon as we were without witnesses in the room assigned to us, General Sherman showed me a telegram from Mr. Stanton, announcing the assassination of the President of the United States. A courier, he told me, had overtaken him with it, after he left the railroad-station from which he had ridden. After reading the dispatch, I told General Sherman that, in my opinion, the event was the greatest possible calamity to the South."

2. Hitcncock wrote home April 24: "I was told that when we returned to Raleigh that night, that the soldiers stood silent around in the camps, in little squads, silent or talking in subdued but bitter tones, and many of them weeping like children, after they heard it. I heard officers who, I knew, always denounced and strove against the outrages in our marches through Georgia and South Carolina swear in bitter terms that if our army ever moved again they would never spare nor protect another house or family. The Commanding officer at Raleigh instantly doubled all his guards (protecting the citizens) that night. Still, I am glad to say no violence occurred, nor will any. Our men are too well disciplined, and even those officers who feel most acknowledge that indiscriminate vengeance is not to be thought of." *Marching with Sherman,* 307.

Raleigh, N. C.
April 24, 1865

[To S. C. O.] The President has rejected the terms of the capitulation sent to Washington. . . . Of course General Johnston has the privilege of accepting the terms presented by the Secretary of War. It is not unlikely he will do so, but this is by no means certain. From what I learn, I do not believe he can again get so liberal terms as those now offered, if he should determine to make any further resistance.

The murder of the President, appears to have outraged the feelings of every one in the Army and out of it. Why such a thing should have been done just now is beyond all comprehension.

General Grant arrived here this morning and has called on General Howard. His countenance is still as fresh as when I saw him at Chattanooga. He shows the wear of his heavy service very little.

Raleigh, N. C.
April 24, 1865

[To A. C. O.] President Johnson refused to accept the terms of the surrender of the Confederate Armies as agreed upon by General Sherman and the Confederate Secretary. In brief these terms were that General Johnston for Davis and through General Breckinridge agreed to surrender every thing, all officers military and civil to be paroled; the state legislatures to convene and take the oath of allegiance to the United States, a copy of the oath to be filed at Washington and then proceed with the government of the states, but in all things subject to the government at Washington. This plan may or may not have been acceptable to President Lincoln, but General Sherman understood it was what he desired. Probably he knew this to be the case as he had both seen and corresponded with him shortly before his death. I am disposed to believe this identical plan was blocked out by Mr. Lincoln. In substance Sherman said this was as he understood the President.[1] However, President Johnson rejected it and General Grant came with the officers who had taken the memoranda to Washington when they returned. They arrived last night.

Information was at once sent to General Johnston, that the terms of surrender were rejected and the armistice was at an end. Also, that this army will move against him as soon as the terms of the negotiations will permit, but as he commands an Army his surrender will be accepted on the same conditions as those granted to General Lee. The orders are issued for the Army to move in the morning and so the matter rests tonight. I am inclined to think General Johnston will surrender.

About the time General Johnston asked for terms, General Wilson with his cavalry force was at Columbus, Ga., capturing every thing he came to. General Johnston asked General Sherman to stop him. General Wilson had just then demanded the surrender of Columbus and the officers and citizens informed him an armistice was in force and asked him to stop hostilities. To this General Wilson paid no attention and compelled the surrender, after which he gave permission to correspond with General Johnston by telegraph for orders from General Sherman. The General telegraphed him to hold all he had and wait for further orders. Since the rejection of the terms of the surrender General Johnston has been put to the unpleasant service of sending a cipher dispatch to General Wilson, to go on and that the enemy has no force to stop him and no ordnance stores except those at Augusta and Athens. These General Wilson can reach sooner than General Johnston can.

General Grant is the same quiet appearing man he was when I saw him at Chattanooga and appears to have no greater fondness for being seen now than he had then. His appearance does not indicate that he is much worn by labor or anxiety.[2]

NOTES

1. In Sherman's *Memoirs* the General left a record of his conversations with President Lincoln aboard the *River Queen* on March 27 and 28: "I inquired of the President if he was all ready for the end of the war. What was to be done with the rebel armies when defeated? And what should be done with the political leaders, such as Jeff. Davis, etc? Should we allow them to escape, etc.? He said he was all ready; all he wanted of us was to defeat the opposing armies, and to get the men composing the Confederate armies back to their homes, at work on their farms or in their shops. As to Jeff. Davis, he was hardly at liberty to speak his mind fully, but intimated that he ought to clear out, 'escape the country,' only it would not do for him to say so openly. As usual, he illustrated his meaning by a story: 'A man once had taken the total-abstinence pledge. When visiting a friend, he was invited to take a drink, but declined, on the score of the pledge; when his friend suggested lemonade, which was accepted. In preparing the lemonade, the friend pointed to the brandy-bottle and said the lemonade would be more palatable if he were to pour in a little brandy; when his guest said, if he could do so "unbeknown" to him, he would not object.' From which illustration I inferred that Mr. Lincoln wanted Davis to escape, 'unbeknown' to him. . . .

"Mr. Lincoln was full and frank in his conversation, assuring me that in his mind he was all ready for the civil reorganization of affairs at the South as soon as the war was over; and he distinctly authorized me to assure Governor Vance and the people of North Carolina that, as soon as the rebel armies laid down their arms, and resumed their civil pursuits, they would at once be guaranteed all their rights as citizens of a common country; and that to avoid anarchy the State governments then in existence, with their civil functionaries, would be recognized by him as the government *de facto* till Congress could provide others.

"I know when I left him, that I was more than ever impressed by his kindly nature, his deep and earnest sympathy with the afflictions of the whole people, resulting from the war, and by the march of hostile armies through the South; and that his earnest desire seemed to be to end the war speedily, without more bloodshed or devastation, and to restore all the men of both sections to their homes. . . . When at rest or listening, his legs and arms seemed to hang almost lifeless, and his face was care-worn and haggard; but the moment he began to talk, his face lighted up, his tall form, as it were, unfolded, and he was the very impersonation of good-humor and fellowship." II, 326-28.

2. From Raleigh, Gen. Howard wrote his wife early on April 26: "Gen. Grant came back with Maj. Hitchcock (Sherman's messenger to Washington) was present at the review of the 11th Corps day before yesterday and yesterday he visited and rode amongst the camps of the 15th. The men received him with great enthusiasm." ALS, Howard Collection.

"Gen. Grant," Hitchcock wrote home from aboard Gen. Grant's dispatch boat M. Martin in the Chesapeake Bay on April 22, "is in almost every respect a very unlike man to Gen. Sherman, in demeanor as well as appearance. I have had some conversation with him, partly to deliver some verbal messages Gen. S. sent by me in addition to the written dispatches, partly also informing him of details of our march from Goldsboro to Raleigh not included in those. He is very quiet and taciturn, with none of Sherman's vivacity of appearance or manner and none of his off-hand, ready, entertaining conversation. . . . I find him a younger looking man than I expected, also better dressed, thanks to a new or nearly new uniform, and his expression is also somewhat sterner than I imagined." *Marching with Sherman,* 305.

Raleigh, N. C.
April 27, 1865

[To S. C. O.] Yesterday General Johnston surrendered his Army to General Sherman, accepting the conditions sent from Washington.[1] This time the surrender includes all the forces east of the Mississippi River. Most of those in the south had already surrendered to General Wilson. I believe there are a few troops yet in Texas who have not surrendered, but we have men enough there to take care of them. So this time I think I can safely say the war is over.

The greater portion of General Sherman's Army will, in a few days, start for Washington to there be mustered out of the service. We shall probably arrive in Washington about the first of June. This is the way it all looks now. Mishaps are possible which will change the plans a little and upon which we cannot now calculate. All the arrangements for the surrender have been completed, but many details are to be looked after yet. With these, however, General Howard's Army has nothing to do. We are through with our work.

NOTE

1. Howard's letter of April 26 says: "I go with the Gen. to meet Johnston today and expect other terms will be arranged." Hitchcock wrote at 10:30 that evening: "I did not go out today; Gens. Howard, Slocum, and Blair each with one aid,

went with Sherman, and only his two 'personal aides' went with him. They have all just got back, and the general fact is all that is yet made public here—but you will have learned the details by telegraph." *Marching with Sherman,* 315.

Raleigh, N. C.
April 27, 1865

[To A. C. O.] General Sherman yesterday received the surrender of General Johnston and there is no force any where else able to keep up active hostilities. So now the war is finished. Hard and continued pounding has finally accomplished the end we sought. The great American insurrection is now a matter for history to deal with. Our work is over and the reestablishment of civil government in these states belongs to another branch of the government.

The formal surrender of the Army in front of us will take place at Greensboro several days hence.[1] General Schofield will be left with his Army, the Army of the Ohio, in command of this department.[2] The Armies of the Tennessee and of Georgia will leave here on Saturday the twenty-ninth for Washington to be mustered out of service. By the first of July we shall be home as private citizens.

I think I have been very fortunate in living through this war. I have by no means been careful to protect myself.

NOTES

1. Such a formal surrender did not come about. Gen. Sherman's field order No. 66 of April 27 announced the agreement with Gen. Johnston to the soldiers, and the several governors of the states immediately concerned were informed of it by telegraph. It was published by Johnston in his general order no. 18 of April 27. "Preparation and signature of the necessary papers occupied the officers of the two armies until the 2d of May." Johnston, *Narrative of Military Operations,* 414-18. The parole of Johnston and his staff was signed by Gen. Schofield at Greensboro on May 2. *OR,* Ser. I, vol. 47, pt. 3, pp. 379-80.

2. "*I understand,*" wrote Hitchcock April 26, "that Sherman now intends to turn this army over to Schofield who will march it . . . to Richmond." *Marching with Sherman,* 316.

Rogers' Cross Roads, N. C.
April 30, 1865

[To A. C. O.] We are now twelve miles on our way to Washington where we are to be on the first of June. We expect to rest several days at Petersburg.

I see by the papers, that the administration and the country at large are very bitter against General Sherman on account of the terms of surrender he gave General Johnston. I knew at the time they were liberal, still he gave the terms he had learned from Mr. Lincoln were desired. General Sherman did what he believed to be for the best interests of the country and was honest in doing what he did. Much said in the papers about it is pure hash. He is as true to the country and as earnest for its welfare as is either President Johnson or Secretary Stanton and, judging from all I see in the papers, vastly more of a gentleman.[1]

NOTE

1. M. A. DeWolfe Howe wrote with admirable restraint in a note to Hitchcock's letters of April 22: "Sherman's indignation with Stanton over his public comments on the terms of Johnston's surrender led to a quarrel holding a large place in the annals of the time." *Marching with Sherman,* 318.

Oliver L. Spaulding, Jr., summarized the situation succinctly and admirably in his sketch of Sherman in the *Dictionary of American Biography,* (New York, 1935), XVII, 96: "In his eagerness to put an end to the war he inserted in his draft terms which were political in nature and beyond his province. This fact, however, was explicitly recognized in the agreement signed, which, in effect, was merely an engagement by the generals to do their utmost to secure approval by their respective governments. But the feeling at Washington was bitter by reason of the assassination of Lincoln, and the agreement was repudiated with a vigor and discourtesy which deeply offended Sherman. At the final grand review in Washington, he publicly refused to shake hands with Stanton, although he became reconciled later."

Petersburg, Va.
May 8, 1865

[To S. C. O.] We arrived here Saturday evening after a march of 160 miles in six days. The march was too rapid, while there is no cause for haste. The troops were tired, but were rested by a day or two in camp. We start again this morning for Richmond and from there we understand we go to Alexandria. The Armies of the Potomac, of the James, of the Tennessee, of Georgia and General Sheridan's Cavalry are all moving to the vicinity of Washington and will be there together. We expect to reach Alexandria about the 20. Soon after that I presume we will be mustered out of service.

Petersburg, Va.
May 8, 1865

[To A. C. O.] We arrived here Saturday, after a six days trip from Raleigh. The army is in excellent condition. I understand there is to be a grand review of all the armies at Washington. If this proves to be correct can you not come and see it? It will be a sight certainly not to be seen again while we live.

Near Washington, D. C.
[ca. May 17, 1865]

[To A. C. O.] The troops are gathering rapidly about Washington. But of all matters appertaining to the Army now you will learn from the papers. The report has reached here that Jeff Davis has been captured somewhere in Georgia.[1]

NOTE

1. Davis was captured May 10 at Irwinville, Irwin County, Ga.

Washington, D. C.
May 23, 1865

[To A. C. O.] On the 18 I was assigned by the War Department with my present rank as Assistant Commissioner for the Bureau of Refugees, Freedmen and Abandoned Lands for the state of Alabama. I am retained in service by a special order of the Secretary of War. The order suspends the muster out of Major and Brevet Colonel T. W. Osborn, of the First New York Artillery.[1]

This will be new work for me and will partake for more of civil services than any in which I have yet had experience. I will now go north and visit the family and after a few days return and go south.

The grand review of the Armies commenced to-day. The cavalry, the IX, V and II Corps were reviewed, in all 110,000 men. The Armies of the Tennessee and of Georgia will be reviewed to-morrow. The weather is very fine and a vast number of people are here to witness the review.[2]

I had a seat on the grand stand today and met many prominent men I had not before seen. Among them were President Johnson,[3] Secretaries Stanton, Dennison,[4] Speed[5] and others together with many of the foreign representatives.

I have had more or less acquaintance with nearly all the prominent generals and a very agreeable acquaintance with several of them.[6]

NOTES

1. In a letter from Goldsboro March 30 Gen. Howard wrote to Maj.-Gen. W. F. Barry, chief of artillery, Military Division of the Mississippi: "I have the honor to request that you recommend Maj. T. W. Osborn, chief of artillery of this army, for two brevets. First, for gallantry and remarkable efficiency at Gettysburg, to be brevetted lieutenant colonel. Second, for faithfulness and efficiency in the performance of his duties during the Atlanta, the Savannah, and the Carolina campaigns. I have constantly pressed his claim and think that some accident must have caused his case to be overlooked. Interested as you are in your own department I doubt not you will aid me in procuring Major Osborn's promotion." *OR,* Ser, I, vol. 49, pt. 3, p.61.

2. "By invitation," wrote Sherman, "I was on the reviewing-stand, and witnessed the review of the Army of the Potomac (on the 23d), commanded by General George Meade in person. The day was beautiful and the pageant was superb. Washington was full of strangers, who filled the streets in holiday-dress, and every house was decorated with flags." II, 376.

3. President Andrew Johnson.

4. William Dennison, Lincoln's Postmaster-General.

5. James Speed, Lincoln's Attorney General.

6. Who but Gen. Sherman deserves the last word? He wrote: "The morning of the 24th was extremely beautiful, and the ground was in splendid order for our review. . . . Punctually at 9 A. M. the signal gun was fired, when in person, attended by General Howard and all my staff, I rode slowly down Pennsylvania Avenue, the crowds of men, women, and children densely lining the sidewalks, and almost obstructing the way. . . . When I reached the Treasury-building and looked back, the sight was simply magnificent. The column was compact, and the glittering muskets looked like a solid mass of steel, moving with the regularity of a pendulum. . . . We rode on steadily past the President, saluting with our swords. All on his stand arose and acknowledged the salute. . . . I then took my post on the left of the President, and for six hours and a half stood, while the army passed in the order of the Fifteenth, Seventeenth, Twentieth, and Four-teenth Corps. It was, in my judgment, the most magnificent army in existence—sixty-five thousand men, in splendid *physique,* who had just completed a march of nearly two thousand miles in a hostile country, in good drill, and who realized that they were being closely scrutinized. . . . The steadiness and firmness of the

tread, the careful dress on the guides, the uniform intervals between the companies, all eyes directly to the front, and the tattered and bullet-riven flags, festooned
with flowers, all attracted universal notice. Many good people, up to that time,
had looked upon our Western army as a sort of mob; but the world then saw, and
recognized the fact, that it was no wonder that it had swept through the South
like a tornado." II, 377-78.

References

PRIMARY MATERIALS

Unpublished Letters and Papers

Oliver Otis Howard. Letters. Howard Collection. Bowdoin College Library, Brunswick, Maine.

Thomas Ward Osborn. "Autobiographical Sketch." Florida State University, Tallahassee.

Thomas Ward Osborn. Papers. Colgate University, Hamilton, New York.

Documents

Brown, Joseph E. *Message. . . to the Legislature of the State of Georgia, Convened in Extra Session, Macon, Georgia, February 15th, 1865.* Macon, 1865.

Sherman, William Tecumseh. "Report of Major General William T. Sherman to the Hon. Committee on the Conduct of the War," U. S. 38th Congress, 2d Session. Joint Committee on the Conduct of the War, *Supplemental Report. . .*, 2 vols. Washington, D. C.: Government Printing Office, 1866.

U. S. War Department. *The War of the Rebellion: A Compilation of the Official Records of the Union and Confederate Armies. . .*, 128 vols. Washington, D. C.: Government Printing Office, 1880-1900.

Newspapers and Articles

Gibbes, James E. *Philadephia Times* (Sept. 20, 1880).

Hesseltine, William B., and Larry Gara, eds. "Sherman Burns the Libraries," *South Carolina Historical Magazine,* LV, no. 3 (July 1954).

Osborn, Thomas Ward. "The Artillery at Gettysburg." *Philadelphia Weekly Times* (May 31, 1879).

Poppenheim, Mrs. C. P. "Personal Experiences with Sherman's Army at Liberty Hill" in *South Carolina Women in the Confederacy,* vol. I. Columbia: The State Co., 1903.

Spaulding, Oliver L., Jr. "Sherman, William Tecumseh" in *Dictionary of American Biography,* vol. XVII. New York: Scribner's, 1935.

Taylor, Mrs. Thomas. "Two Equipages" in *South Carolina Women in the Confederacy,* vol. I. Columbia: The State Co., 1903.
Wells, E. L. "A Morning Call on General Kilpatrick", *Southern Historical Society Papers,* vol. XII (1884).

Books

Bowman, S. M., and Lt.-Col. R. V. Irwin. *Sherman and His Campaigns.* New York: C. B. Richardson; London: Stevens Brothers, 1865.
Bradley, G. S. *The Star Corps or, Notes of an Army Chaplain, During Sherman's Famous "March to the Sea."* Milwaukee: Jermain & Brightman, 1865.
Chesnut, Mary Boykin. *Mary Chesnut's Civil War,* ed. C. Vann Woodward. New Haven: Yale Univ. Press, 1981.
Connolly, James A. *Three Years in the Army of the Cumberland. . . ,* ed. Paul M. Angle. Bloomington: Indiana Univ. Press, 1959.
Conyngham, David P. *Sherman's March Through the South.* New York: Sheldon and Co., 1865.
Harwell, Richard, ed. *A Confederate Marine.* Tuscaloosa, Ala.: Confederate Publishing Co., 1963.
Hedley, F. Y. *Marching Through Georgia.* Chicago: Donohue, Henneberry & Co., 1890 (c. 1884).
Hitchcock, Henry. *Marching with Sherman. . . ,* ed. M. A. DeWolfe Howe. New Haven: Yale Univ. Press, 1927.
Howard, Oliver Otis. *Autobiography.* 2 vols. New York: Baker & Taylor, 1907.
Howard, Oliver Otis. "Deposition," Mixed Commission on British and American Claims. . . , *Who Burnt Columbia?* Charleston, S. C., Walker, Evans & Cogswell, 1873.
Jackson, Oscar L. *The Colonel's Diary.* Sherron [Sharron] Pa., 1922.
Johnston, Joseph E. *Narrative of Military Operations.* New York: D. Appleton and Co., 1874.
Jones, John Beauchamp. *A Rebel War Clerk's Diary.* 2 vols. Philadelphia: J. B. Lippincott, 1866.
LeConte, Emma. *When the World Ended,* ed. Earl Schenck Miers. New York: Oxford Univ. Press, 1957.
Nichols, George Ward. *The Story of the Great March. . . .* New York: Harper & Brothers, 1865.
Pepper, George W. *Personal Recollections of Sherman's Campaigns in Georgia and the Carolinas.* Zanesville, Ohio: H. Dunne, 1866.
Pike, James. *Scout and Ranger.* Cincinnati and New York: J. R. Hawley & Co., 1865.
Rowland, Dunbar, ed. *Jefferson Davis Constitutionalist; His Letters, Papers and Speeches.* 10 vols. Jackson: Mississippi Department of Archives and History, 1923.
Sherman, William Tecumseh. *From Atlanta to the Sea,* ed. B. H. Liddell Hart. London: Folio Society, 1961.
Sherman, William Tecumseh. *Memoirs.,* New York: D. Appleton, 1875; 2 vols. (4th ed.) C. L. Webster & Co., 1892.

Simms, William Gilmore. *Sack and Destruction of the City of Columbia, S. C.* Columbia, 1865; rpt. Oglethorpe Univ. Press, 1937.

Taylor, Richard. *Destruction and Reconstruction...*, ed. Richard B. Harwell. New York: Longmans, Green, 1955.

Thorndike, Rachel Sherman, ed. *The Sherman Letters, Correspondence Between General and Senator Sherman from 1837 to 1891.* New York: Scribner's, 1894.

Trezevant, D. H. *The Burning of Columbia, S. C.* Columbia: South Carolinian Power Press, 1866.

Wainwright, Charles S. *A Diary of Battle: The Personal Journals of Colonel Charles S. Wainwright, 1861-1865,* ed. Allan Nevins. New York: Harcourt, Brace & World, 1962.

SECONDARY MATERIALS

Barrett, John G. *Sherman's March Through the Carolinas.* Chapel Hill: Univ. of North Carolina Press, 1956.

Bond, O. J. *The Story of the Citadel.* Richmond: Garrett and Massie, 1936.

Coker, Elizabeth Boatwright. *La Belle.* New York: Dutton, 1959.

Connelly, Thomas L. *Autumn of Glory, The Army of Tennessee, 1862-1865.* Baton Rouge: Louisiana State Univ. Press, 1971.

Cook, Harvey T. *Sherman's March Through South Carolina in 1865.* Greenville, S. C.: 1938.

Davis, William Watson. *The Civil War and Reconstruction in Florida.* New York: Columbia Univ. Press, 1913.

Foote, Shelby. *The Civil War: A Narrative from Fredericksburg to Meridian.* New York: Random House, 1963.

Gibbes, James G. *Who Burnt Columbia.* Newberry, S. C.: 1902.

Graydon, Nell S. *Tales of Columbia.* Columbia, S. C.: R. L. Bryan Co., 1964.

Harwell, Richard B. *Gone With the Wind as Book and Film.* Columbia: Univ. of South Carolina Press, 1983.

Kilpatrick, Judson, and J. Owen Moore. *The Blue and the Gray: or War Is Hell,* rev. and ed. Christopher Morley. Garden City, N. Y.: Doubleday, Doran & Company, 1930.

Lewis, Lloyd. *Sherman, Fighting Prophet.* New York: Harcourt, Brace, 1932.

Liddell Hart, B. H. *Sherman, the Genius of the Civil War.* London: E. Benn, 1930.

Lucas, Marion Brunson. *Sherman and the Burning of Columbia.* College Station: Texas A&M Univ. Press, 1976.

McFeely, William S. *Grant.* New York: Norton, 1981.

———*Yankee Stepfather.* New Haven: Yale Univ. Press, 1968.

The National Cyclopedia of American Biography.... New York: J. T. White & Company, 1904.

Nevins, Allan. *The War for the Union: Vol. IV, The Organized War to Victory. 1864-1865.* New York: Scribner's, 1971.

Selby, Julian A. *A Checkered Life.* Columbia, S. C., Daily Phoenix, 1878.

Wallace, John. *Carpetbag Rule in Florida.* Jacksonville, Fla.: Da Costa Printing and Publishing House, 1888.

Index

The Fiery Trail: A Union Officer's Account of Sherman's Last Campaigns was composed into type on a Compugraphic digital phototypesetter in ten point Garamond with two points of spacing between the lines. The book was designed by Sheila Hart, typeset by Point West, Inc., printed offset by Thomson-Shore, Inc., and bound by John H. Dekker & Sons. The paper on which the book is printed is designed for an effective life of at least three hundred years.

THE UNIVERSITY OF TENNESSEE PRESS: KNOXVILLE